T0301358

Technological Systems and Intersectoral Innovation Flows

NEW HORIZONS IN THE ECONOMICS OF INNOVATION

Series Editor: Christopher Freeman, *Emeritus Professor of Science Policy, SPRU – Science and Technology Policy Research, University of Sussex, UK*

Technological innovation is vital to the competitive performance of firms and of nations and for the sustained growth of the world economy. The economics of innovation is an area that has expanded dramatically in recent years and this major series, edited by one of the most distinguished scholars in the field, contributes to the debate and advances in research in this most important area.

The main emphasis is on the development and application of new ideas. The series provides a forum for original research in technology, innovation systems and management, industrial organization, technological collaboration, knowledge and innovation, research and development, evolutionary theory and industrial strategy. International in its approach, the series includes some of the best theoretical and empirical work from both well-established researchers and the new generation of scholars.

Titles in the series include:

Technological Systems and Intersectoral Innovation Flows

Riccardo Leoncini

University of Bologna, Italy and
CERIS-CNR, Milan Research Section, Italy

Sandro Montresor

University of Bologna, Italy

NEW HORIZONS IN THE ECONOMICS OF INNOVATION

Edward Elgar
Cheltenham, UK • Northampton, MA, USA

Published by
Edward Elgar Publishing Limited
Glensanda House
Montpellier Parade
Cheltenham
Glos GL50 1UA
UK

Edward Elgar Publishing, Inc.
136 West Street
Suite 202
Northampton
Massachusetts 01060
USA

A catalogue record for this book
is available from the British Library

Library of Congress Cataloguing in Publication Data

Leoncini, Riccardo, 1959–
    Technological systems and intersectoral innovation flows/
Riccardo Leoncini, Sandro Montresor.
        p. cm. (New horizons in the economics of innovation)
    Includes bibliographical references and index.
    1. Technological innovations. I. Montresor, Sandro, 1968–
II. Title. III. Series.

    T173.8.L46   2003
    658.4'06—dc22

                                                    2003057278

ISBN 1 84064 682 9

Printed and bound in Great Britain by MPG Books Ltd, Bodmin, Cornwall

Contents

Figures

Tables

Preface

The development of a systems perspective on the innovation process is perhaps the most important development in relation to innovation economics and policy of the past two decades. Building on the insights of leading scholars including Freeman, Nelson, Lundvall and Edquist, among many others, we now have new conceptual tools to understand the diversity of innovation performance across economies and industries and over time.

This book is a significant addition to the literature in terms of its conceptual and empirical contribution. In particular, the systems perspective allows a close connection with the idea of complexity and the networked nature of knowledge generation processes and it also opens up new perspectives on innovation policy by proposing the idea of innovation system failure as an alternative to the traditional market failure approach. We learn from this perspective that firms never innovate in isolation, that the sources of innovation knowledge are distributed across organisations in an economy and between economies, and that the firm is the unique locus for combining together different kinds of knowledge for an innovative purpose.

All of these themes are reflected in this work through its two-fold approach of focusing on technological systems and analysing their content in terms of innovation flows. This enables the authors to develop rich empirical analysis of differences in innovation systems across the OECD nations and to engage in detailed case studies in the automotive and chemical industries in four European countries.

Their imaginative use of statistical measures and their results certainly provide material to stimulate other scholars to work in this still developing area and indeed to confront the major problem of revising our national statistical categories to reflect more accurately the nature of innovation in and between economic sectors.

Stan Metcalfe

Acknowledgements

This book gathers some of the work on technological systems that we have been developing in several years of close collaboration at the Research Institute on the Dynamics of Economic Systems of the National Research Council (IDSE-CNR) of Italy (now CERIS-CNR, Milan Research Section), and, more recently, at the University of Bologna (Faculty of Law and Department of Economics).

The list of people and organisations to whom we are thankful would be very long and impossible to articulate in a few lines. However, we are, first of all, very grateful to Gilberto Antonelli, who offered us the opportunity to engage in the research activity of which this book is one of the most visible results and provided us with scientific guidance and continuous support.

We also wish to thank Giulio Cainelli, Chris DeBresson, Nicola De Liso, Alain Decker, Edward Lorenz, Giandemetrio Marangoni, Stan Metcalfe, Anna Montini, Bart Nooteboom, Renzo Orsi, Paolo Pini, Alessandro Romagnoli, Paolo Saviotti and Roberto Zoboli for useful comments and suggestions on previous versions of some of the papers that make up this book.

We had several opportunities to present the material of this book in various seminars and conferences. In particular, we want to thank the participants at the Tenth Annual Meeting of AIEL (Bologna, 1995), the EAEPE 1997 Conference (Athens), the Twelfth AISSEC Conference (Siena, 1999), the European Meeting on Applied Evolutionary Economics (Grenoble, 1999), the Third Annual EUNIP Conference (Dublin, 1999), the EAEPE 2001 Conference (Siena) and the Workshops of the MURST Project 40% 'Infrastrutture, competitività, livelli di governo: dall'economia italiana all'economia europea'.

We also gratefully acknowledge financial support from the Special Project of the National Research Council (CNR) of Italy on 'Technological systems, research evaluation and innovation policies', from the IPTS-Joint Research Centre and European Commission-DGIII Project 'The Impact of Regulation on Innovation', from the MURST Project 40% (1988-2000) 'Infrastrutture, competitività, livelli di governo: dall'economia italiana all'economia europea'.

Last but not least, we are extremely grateful to Caroline Cornish, Desk Editor at Edward Elgar, for her meticulous work and assistance in the final editing of the book.

It must, however, be stressed that we bear the sole responsibility of any error, omission and misinterpretation.

This book is partly based on already published material, although all the chapters have undergone a process of revision to make them mutually coherent and internally consistent within the book.

Chapter 3 is partly taken from: Leoncini, R. (1998), 'The nature of long-run technological change: innovation, evolution and technological systems', *Research Policy*, vol. 27, no. 1, pp. 75-93.

Chapter 4 has been published as: Leoncini, R. and Montresor, S. (2000), 'Classifying technological systems: an empirical application to eight OECD countries', in Saviotti, P. and Nooteboom, B. (eds), *Knowledge and Innovation. From the Firm to Innovation Systems*, Edward Elgar, Cheltenham, pp. 152-173.

Chapter 5 has been published as: Leoncini, R. and Montresor, S. (2000), 'Network analysis of eight technological systems', *International Review of Applied Economics*, vol. 14, no. 2, pp. 213-234 (www.tandf.co.uk).

Chapter 7 has been published as: Leoncini, R. and Montresor, S. (2001), 'The automobile technological systems. An empirical analysis of four European countries', *Research Policy*, vol. 30, pp. 1321-1340. Reprinted with permission from Elsevier.

To Sabrina, Davide and Lorenzo

To Barbara

Introduction

This book is about long-run technological change and about that complex set of interrelated phenomena which goes under the heading of 'innovative processes'. Although it arrives at a time when the 'effects' of technological change[1] are extensively recognised and studied by an extensive literature, this book does not perfectly fit within it. Its focus is instead on the 'sources and procedures of innovation' (Dosi, 1988a), that is, on those factors, actors and relationships which enable (or hinder) technological change, and which make it evolve along different patterns, with highly context-specific characteristics. In so doing, the effects of technological change are something we aim at understanding and explaining, rather than detecting.

In spite of such a particular perspective, the book still fits into a large and influential body of literature which, from the early 1980s onwards, has seriously engaged to go 'inside', 'exploring the black box' of technological change (Rosenberg, 1982, 1994). Since then, several results have been obtained about what has become known as 'the economics of technological change': the importance of science, both pure and applied, the role of technological paradigms and trajectories, in explaining path-dependence and lock-in, the relevance of demand factors, for both the introduction and the diffusion stage, the incidence of firms and sectors, both in terms of scale and organisation, are only a few examples.[2] Among these results, one of the most relevant is the *system nature of the innovative process*, a result that is also the starting point of this book.

THE SYSTEM NATURE OF THE INNOVATIVE PROCESS

The introduction, the diffusion and the economic implementation of (absolutely and relatively) new products, processes and organisational forms occur neither linearly nor in isolation: feedback, spillovers and other more deliberate forms of producer-user relationships are at work. The innovative process thus involves complex systems of different kinds of organisations, such as firms, universities, public and private research institutes, banks, and insurance companies. Indeed, the innovative process calls for resources, capabilities and competencies of different kinds, which are not in general available to a unique, ultimate innovator, and which rather require the interaction of several qualified actors.[3]

Moreover, these innovative interactions, as every other kind of social relationships, do not occur in a vacuum. On the contrary, they need so-to-say a connective tissue of both formal and informal institutions to channel those information and knowledge flows which make the interactions themselves possible (Johnson, 1992). To be sure, in the case of innovative interactions the presence of an institutional set-up is even more crucial, as the innovative process involves radical forms of uncertainty – with respect to its outcome – high transaction costs – in the establishment of producer-user relationships – and substantial conflicts – particularly in appropriating innovative results (Edquist and Johnson, 1997).

Those institutions which make it possible to overcome (at least partly) these problems[4] are of course socially embedded. Indeed, they are deeply affected by the cognitive frameworks, ideologies and cultures from which they have emerged. It follows also that the innovative process, which is enabled by such institutions, is highly context-specific, that is, remarkably influenced by the social-cultural, historical and geographical environment within which it occurs.

The previous arguments have stimulated the search for conceptual tools of system nature, allowing these important features of the innovative process to be retained. Starting from the seminal idea of *national system of innovation*, and by emending (either extending or narrowing) its functional and geographical boundaries, different systems of innovation approaches (Edquist, 1997a) have been elaborated and applied. Although in some respects still 'conceptually diffuse' (Edquist, 1997a, p. 26), these approaches have turned out to be extremely helpful in investigating the innovative process, to the point that a handbook has recently been produced (Edquist and McKelvey, 2000).

Although our book is firmly placed within this research programme, the research trajectory we follow is parallel, but not alternative, to that of the systems of innovation. The differences emerge mainly in two respects, which are summarised by the two key words of the title of the book: the unit of analysis (the technological system), and the methodology (based on intersectoral innovation flows). As we will see, the two research trajectories are highly complementary, in both respects, so that their mutual integration provides a powerful approach in studying the innovative process from a system perspective.

TECHNOLOGICAL SYSTEMS AND SYSTEMS OF INNOVATION

As the title of the book clearly indicates, our unit of analysis is the *technological system*, rather than any of the systems of innovation concepts available in the literature, i.e. national, regional, local or sectoral. However, this choice does not presume the superiority of a sector perspective (typically associated with the technological system),[5] over a geographical one (implied by the national and sub-national systems of innovation approaches).

Our choice, instead, follows from the recognition that the technological system, meant as the set of organisations and institutions that gravitate interactively around a core of scientific and technological knowledge (and of the related techniques), has a quite broad interpretative power. Indeed, by referring to its inner epistemological foundations, and disentangling the evolutionary mechanisms occurring within and between its sub-systems, the notion of technological system emerges as a 'transversal', rather than a 'horizontal', variant of the system perspective we are considering.

First of all, its functional boundaries are quite wide, as they encompass: the institutional actors of the systems of innovation approaches (as described by Edquist, 1997b), the technological elements addressed by the 'large technical systems' approach (see, for example, Hughes, 1989), and the knowledge generation and diffusion mechanisms which are central to the evolutionary analysis of technological change. The functional boundaries of the technological system are therefore also flexible. Indeed, depending on both the role of the dominant institutional set-up, and on the structure of its constitutive techno-economic relationships, the technological system can take on different configurations among those stylised by the literature on the systems of innovation. This holds true with respect to both macro technological systems, whose internal connectivity degree is an important configurational aspect (this point will appear evident in Part Two), and with respect to sectoral technological systems, for which the extension and the nature of the relationships with other sectors play a crucial characterising role (an argument that will be developed in Chapters 7 and 8).

Also the geographical boundaries of the technological system we are referring to are flexible. Indeed, depending on the extension and on the structure of its external relationships, the degree of openness of a macro technological system can be measured, and its entailed configuration actually identified, rather than determined *a priori* (this point will be clearer in Chapter 4). The same holds true with respect to a sectoral technological system, whose international, transnational or national extension can be established by referring to the actual structure of its external techno-economic flows (this point will also be developed in Chapters 7 and 8).

Although the technological system is our 'broader' unit of analysis, its relationships with the systems of innovation are quite strong. Indeed, as we will see, the former overlaps in different ways with the latter depending on the characteristics of the innovative process under investigation. Further complementarities emerge when we look at the methodology through which such units of analysis are concretely applied in studying the innovative process.

INTERSECTORAL INNOVATION FLOWS AND TECHNOLOGICAL SYSTEMS

The second distinguishing feature of our approach is the way in which we investigate the technological systems, that is, by analysing their *intersectoral innovation flows*. In other words, what we actually do is to analyse the innovation flows exchanged by the economic sectors into which the technological systems can be broken down (in the case of macro technological systems), or through which they can be identified (in the case of sectoral technological systems).

At the outset, the intersectoral approach we have developed results from the search for a methodology for the empirical analysis, consistent with a system perspective. Given that a technological system exists as long as some kinds of relationships connect its components, our first search criterion has been the need to provide a suitable measure for its linkages. The focus on innovation diffusion, and in particular on embodied technological flows,[6] seemed to us particularly useful to this need. Indeed, although it does not catch the whole array of relevant relationships, this kind of diffusion process presupposes, and imposes, important techno-economic linkages between the actors of a technological system.

In choosing among the different levels of analysis of the diffusion process, a second search criterion has been the need to measure flows, which, consistently with our inspiring perspective, would account for both technological and economic relationships. Both these kinds of interactions are to a certain extent reflected by the inter-industry coefficients of an economy, which in turn depend on both the nature of the available techniques, and on the dominant production structure. Accordingly, the intersectoral level of analysis appeared to us consistent with the need to catch manifold kinds of relationships, and in particular techno-economic ones. This methodological choice can also benefit from the theoretical and empirical results of an emerging research program, which employs the input-output analysis to study the relationships between economic interdependence and innovative activity (DeBresson, 1996).

The intersectoral level of analysis we have adopted also satisfies a further requirement. It provides comparable measures of the linkages with respect to different technological systems. Indeed, given the uncertain and open-ended nature of the innovative process, technological systems cannot be evaluated with respect to any equilibrium or optimal configuration: a comparative perspective thus turns out to be crucial (Edquist, 1997a, p. 20). Among the possible alternatives, the sectoral level of analysis has appeared to us the most conducive to homogeneous comparisons, mainly, but not only, because of data availability reasons.[7] Furthermore, intersectoral innovation flows can be directly integrated with other intersectoral flows and variables which can be taken as proxies for other techno-economic and institutional relationships, both internal and external. Last, but not least, at an intersectoral level, the technological systems can be investigated by means of powerful analytical tools. In particular, as we will see, input-output analysis and network analysis can be fruitfully integrated to obtain a combined methodology with a high interpretative power.

The study of intersectoral innovation flows has several important implications. In particular, it allows us to move from a synthetic level of analysis, that is, the configuration of the technological systems, to an analytical one, that is, the exploration of their sectoral partitions and of the linkages that establish among them.

Nevertheless, such a methodological choice also suffers from some limitations. Apart from the technical problems (that will be discussed in Chapter 3), the crucial issue is that the specific intersectoral perspective we follow does not enable us to catch and measure all the relevant relationships of a technological system. Indeed, on the one hand, many interactions materialise in intersectoral flows whose nature is different from embodied technological flows.[8] This holds true, in particular, for those complex relationships referring to the institutional set-up that can be only partially proxied by synthetic techno-economic flows. On the other hand, the sectoral level of analysis prevents us from catching and mapping the dense network of relationships that are established among firms, both within and across sectors, and between them and other institutional actors.

The previous limitations are of course quite relevant. However, their incidence can be somehow attenuated by integrating closely our methodology with that of the systems of innovation approaches. Indeed, the latter is typically based on different tools of analysis, which are also more qualitative and therefore more suitable to the investigation of aspects of institutional nature.[9] It is also on the basis of this further argument that the present book aims at complementing, and should in turn be complemented by, the literature on the system nature of the innovative process.

THE FIELD OF THE ANALYSIS

The approach we have just outlined will be applied to a specific, but still quite wide field of analysis. Although the details of the application will vary to a certain extent from chapter to chapter, the reference will always be to the technological systems of countries classifiable as developed, that is, to the so-called OECD area.[10]

This choice has been driven by both methodological and practical reasons. At the outset, we aim at analysing and comparing technological systems which are not too dissimilar, and whose characteristics are not too heavily influenced by their different degrees of development. By filtering out structural kinds of gaps, we aim at catching the incidence of differently organised, rather than more or less mature, institutional set-ups, and of differently specialised, rather than unevenly developed, economic structures.

Indeed, as we will show, in spite of some 'conditional' form of convergence, the technological systems of the OECD area remain heterogeneous also because of the variety of their underlying models of capitalism and of the specificity of their production-technological specialisation patterns.

The field of analysis has been chosen also on the basis of practical reasons. First of all, the countries of the OECD area have been, in the last 20 years, the most dynamic in terms of technological change, showing both a greater involvement in research activities – as measured, for example, by R&D intensity – and a higher rate of innovativeness – as proxied, for example, by innovation counts and patents. In order to estimate this sustained pace of technological activities, the relevant statistical offices have recently built up wide databases on innovation for the OECD area, which can be directly matched with other more general economic data. For measuring the intersectoral innovation flows we have referred to above, two of these databases will be mainly used: the ANBERD database, containing data on the R&D expenditure of the major OECD countries by economic sector, and the OECD Input-Output database, reporting for some OECD countries different kinds of intersectoral production flows matrices.[11] The combination of these two sets of data has in a sense conditioned the other characteristics of our field of analysis: the number of countries, first of all, which actually consists of a sub-set of the OECD area.[12]

The second implication of the selected databases has to do with the sectoral disaggregation. All the sectoral disaggregations used in the book refer to manufacturing only. Given the increasing importance that technological change is acquiring in services, especially within the so-called 'new economy', this is of course a serious drawback of our analysis. However, data on innovation (that is, on R&D and on other proxies) for the service sectors are still too scanty to carry out extensive comparisons. Services are therefore forced to stay out of this kind of analysis, unless the focus is on one or a few technological systems at a time (see, for example, Leoncini and Montresor, 2001).

The combination of the selected data sources imposes on the field of analysis a third specification, concerning its temporal span. Apart from some non-systematic upgrading (as, for example, in the analyses of Chapter 7 and 8), the applications of the book mainly refer to the 1980-1990 decade. Although what we investigate is therefore as much as ten years old, two considerations make this limitation less severe. First, the two databases we use have a quite different nature. Indeed, while that on R&D expenditure is frequently updated, this is not the case with the input-output tables, for which it takes considerable time to collect and organise the data in a comparable way.[13] Secondly, as we will show, the phenomena we explore have a structural nature, as they depend on such factors as the relevant institutional set-up and the dominant production-technological structure. Indeed, these factors modify quite sluggishly, unless exceptional events or radical changes occur. Although the last decade (1990-2000) has been characterised by important structural changes (such as deep recessions, financial crises and important regionalisation processes), it seems to us secure enough to maintain that the technological systems we analyse have been affected by them in a less drastic way than others which have not been included (think, for example, of Mexico or of the East Asian countries). Therefore, the results we have obtained are expected to show a certain degree of persistence, and might have exerted some influence (if not even some sort of path-dependence) on those of the present decade.

OUTLINE OF THE BOOK

The book is organised into three parts that, although strictly integrated, have specific aims and characteristics.

Part One – *Theoretical Background and Methodology* – constitutes the conceptual skeleton of the book.

In Chapter 1 we provide a consistent argument for the process nature of technological change and we discuss its system characteristics. The way we approach the issue is somehow different from that of the 'textbooks' on the topic (for example, Lundvall, 1992a; Nelson, 1993a; Edquist, 1997b). First of all, we start from evolutionary theory and we illustrate the potential of its analogies – in particular the biological and thermodynamics – in studying the introduction and diffusion of new technologies, and the non-linear competition processes with those already available. Secondly, we focus our system analysis of technological change on the two most distinguishing system elements: the network of relationships among those actors and factors driving the innovative process, and the specific socio-cultural and institutional set-ups that host them.

Chapter 2 presents our unit of analysis, that is, the technological system. At least two elements characterise this presentation. First of all, as the growth of knowledge is pivotal in explaining the structure and the functioning of a technological system, a brief epistemological discussion is set at the beginning, along with a clarification about the distinction between science, technology and techniques. The system components and their dynamics are then analysed. More precisely, the system components are conceptually organised into interactive sub-systems, by referring to the variety generation and selection mechanisms of which they consist. Unlike the idea of a national system of innovation, which emerges as a sort of 'highest common divisor' of different system components, our idea of a technological system would therefore aim at constituting a sort of 'minimum common multiple' of several possible system configurations.

In Chapter 3 we review the 'toolbox' of analytical instruments we used to measure intersectoral innovation flows, upon which, as we said, our investigation of technological systems is largely based. From a theoretical point of view, different kinds of innovation flows (that is, embodied versus disembodied, direct versus indirect) can be taken to account for techno-economic relationships of different kinds. From an empirical point of view, instead, their measurement poses different degrees of difficulty. On the basis of both arguments we take embodied intersectoral innovation flows as the most consistent proxy of our system approach. Further methodological choices arise in building up those matrices that host the measurement of such innovation flows. In this last respect, the reference to vertically integrated sectors and the driving role of final demand constitute two additional specification elements.

Part Two – *Empirical Analysis: the Macro Perspective* – hosts the first and main set of empirical application in this book. It includes three chapters about the configuration and the exploration of what we have referred to above as 'macro' technological systems.

In particular, in Chapter 4, technological systems are first analysed by means of an internal connection indicator, that is, a measure of the polarisation/pervasiveness degree of (some of) their constituent relationships. The resulting internal configuration is then combined with the correspondent external one, obtained by applying to the relative international trade flows an appropriate external connection indicator. A fourfold taxonomy is thus derived, and the investigated macro technological systems are fitted within it by distinguishing the more pervasive system from the segmented, and the more nationally from the internationally oriented ones.

In Chapter 5 the internal flows of each technological system are analysed more deeply, by applying to the relative intersectoral innovation flows an array of network analysis indicators. Indeed, some of these indicators (that is, density and centralisation) allow us to establish the different degree of connectivity that innovation flows of different magnitude guarantee to each technological system. Some others, instead (that is, centrality indicators and the graph analysis) allow us to measure the relative importance of each sectoral node, and to map the intersectoral route of the corresponding innovation flows. In so doing, important qualitative differences in the structure of the investigated technological systems can be directly identified.

The innovation flows upon which we have based the analysis of Chapters 4 and 5 refer only to the economic sectors into which the technological systems can be broken down. No direct measure is provided for the connections which are established between the production-innovation sub-system proxied by these techno-economic flows – and which encompass the core of our technological system – and other sub-systems, namely those of the external market and of the institutional set-up. These are the focus of Chapter 6 in which the exploration of the technological systems is completed by retaining both core and extra-core relationships. Such an operation turns out to be extremely delicate, as the search for an adequate extra-core proxy has imposed a substantial reframing of the analysis. Indeed, both the institutional set-up and the foreign market can be fitted within each technological system by mapping their outward relationships towards the core sectors in terms of R&D financing, respectively, from public and foreign sources. Intra-core relationships can be recalculated accordingly, in terms of private R&D financing flows, thus obtaining a consistent and homogeneous picture of the complete technological system. However, this can only be done at the price of a substantial downscaling of the sectoral disaggregation, and of a limited (mainly qualitative) comparability with the results of the previous chapters.

Part Three – *Empirical Analysis: the Sectoral Perspective* – includes the second set of empirical application in this book, based on a sectoral perspective. The reference point is still represented by the embodied intersectoral innovation flows matrices and by other production flows matrices, from which a specific sector is properly isolated and examined. Indeed, although focused on a single sector, the analysis tries to investigate the extension of the corresponding technological system by measuring the structure and the direction of the different kinds of internal and external flows (that is, both productive and innovative), which come in and out of the sector itself. As for the macro perspective, in this last respect also, network analysis can fruitfully integrate standard industrial indicators by casting light on the structure of both productive and innovative flows.

Of course, in principle, this sectoral analysis could have been applied to each of the sectors considered in the previous chapters. In order to provide an exemplification, we have instead applied it to two: the automobile (Chapter 7) and the chemical (Chapter 8) technological systems. Although to a certain extent arbitrary, this choice has been driven by the following considerations: the very relevant and crucial role that these two sectors have for the innovative-productive capacity of a nation, the recognition of the complex networks of intersectoral relationships which constitute the innovation-production *filière* of these systems, and the high degree of internationalisation (if not even of transnationalisation) which nowadays characterises them. Both these facts make the potential of our system-sectoral analysis more apparent, especially if we concentrate on a group of structurally homogeneous countries where these sectors have constituted pivotal industries for several decades.

The conclusions of the book try to convey a synthesis of the results we have obtained from the different applications. The results are both general, providing insights that might possibly be extended to similar kinds of analysis, and specific, that is, strictly relative to the technological systems that have been investigated.

NOTES

1. Both at the macro level – for example, on economic growth/development, structural change, international competitiveness and employment – and at the

      micro/meso level – for example, on firm organisation, industrial structure and market (quasi-market) relationships.

2.   See, for instance, among the many surveys, Dosi (1988a), Dosi and Nelson (1994), Nelson (1995), Stephan (1996), Archibugi and Michie (1998), Hodgson (1998), Sankar (1998).

3.   The typical example is the mutual interaction between firms and research institutes. In implementing a new product firms draw on the scientific knowledge which the research institutes obtain also by taking into account the business needs expressed by the firms. The picture gets more complex when we just take into account the financing of new projects, which, because of radical forms of uncertainty, usually requires interaction with qualified financial intermediaries.

4.   As for the radical uncertainty of the innovative outcomes, let us think about public subsidies to research and development (R&D), about laws on innovation financing, and about the fiscal treatment of R&D expenditures. As for the transaction costs of innovation, let us think about those formal and informal channels of communication which exist both within and between firms. Finally, as for the appropriability of the innovative results, let us think about patent legislation and patent offices, and about norms on intellectual property rights.

5.   On the differences between these two perspectives see, among others, Edquist (1997a, p. 3). It must be briefly noted that the term 'sector' has here a broad meaning, as it refers to a technology which might encompass one or more economic sectors.

6.   As is well known, these are innovations exchanged, through both intermediate and capital goods flows in which they are incorporated.

7.   As we will show in Chapter 3, the ways the relevant data are collected make the intersectoral level of analysis the most reliable in studying the innovative diffusion process (see Papaconstantinou *et al.*, 1996).

8.   Let us think, for example, of the intersectoral mobility of qualified human capital. Other examples are discussed in Chapter 3.

9.   The different contributions collected in Nelson (1993a) are a clear example of this methodology.

10.   In particular, the number of OECD countries considered varies from four – France, Germany, Great Britain and Italy – in the sectoral applications of Chapter 7 and 8 – to eight – in the macro applications of Chapters 4 and 5 – Australia, Canada, Denmark, France, Germany, Great Britain, Japan and the Netherlands.

11.   For a detailed description of the coverage of these two databases see the web site: http://www.oecd.org/dsti/sti/stat-ana/index.htm. In addition to these two, other OECD databases will be used for some more specific applications of the book, notably that of the *Basic Science and Technology Indicators* (see Chapter 6).

12.   For example, Italy has been included only in the sector-wide applications of the book with a European focus (that is, Chapter 7 and Chapter 8), and in the attempt in Chapter 6 to extend the macro perspective, given that comparable input-output tables are available for one year only (that is, 1985). Similarly, the USA has been excluded because comparable input-output tables are only available with a specification which is not consistent with those of the other countries (for example, at current rather than at constant prices).

13. Although some of the countries we consider in our application have more updated input-output tables, those which are available for comparison within the OECD database do not go beyond the early 1990s.

PART ONE

Theoretical Background and Methodology

1. System view of the process of technological change

Technological innovation has always been acknowledged as one of the leading factors behind economic growth. By attaching a very wide meaning to technological change (ranging from new or improved artefacts, to knowledge and organisation) the classical economists were well aware of the crucial role of this element for the increase of the wealth of nations. The generation and the eventual bringing to the market of innovation was entirely due to heroic individual figures (the entrepreneur). This fact had the two consequences of both underestimating the socio-economic impact of innovation and of making it almost impossible to incorporate a theory of innovation within the mainstream of economic theory.

This pattern changed dramatically around the end of the nineteenth century, with the establishment of the first specialised R&D industrial laboratories. However, despite this crucial shift, still the 'first' Schumpeter (1934) did not realise the potentialities of this transformation. The institutionalisation of the process of discovery and development of invention was in fact fully accomplished by him 'only' lately (Schumpeter, 1943). It was only later, in fact, that he focused on the progressive process of internalisation of a big slice of scientific and technology activity within large corporations, which could provide a proper environment for both fundamental and applied research. Since then the potential for science and technology to contribute significantly to the process of economic growth has been clearly stated, although the inclusion of technical change in models of growth and its empirical analysis date only from the 1950s.

One of the earliest and most interesting efforts to explain the nature of technical change is due to Schmookler (1966). His contribution, focusing on market demand for new and improved products, started a debate on the origins of technical change: whether it was either 'pulled' by the demand prevailing on the market or 'pushed' by technological discoveries on the supply side. The main differences between these two approaches refer to the role of market signals in prompting innovation and to the firm's internal capability of linking them to its profitability

The demand-pull theory focuses, on the one hand, on the capability of the market to generate some form of needs for new products and of signalling them, and, on the other hand, on the ability of the firms to convey perceived market needs into a research project appropriate to satisfying them. The introduction of an innovation is thus seen as the firm's response to the perception of certain profit opportunities. The technological effort and the reaction of the firm must be rapid and flexible enough to respond to changes in market signals (movements in prices and quantities) that result from shifts in the elasticity of demand, in turn following changes in consumers' tastes and preferences.[1]

The technology-push theory, instead, depicts the firm as the promoter of technological innovation. The causal link between the various components of the firm and between the firm and the market is reversed with respect to the demand-pull theory. In this case the process starts from the research facilities of the firm: technical advances are strictly linked to the capability of the firm to carry out basic scientific research and to apply it to the available technology in order to improve the production process. There is here, therefore, a direct, linear causal relationship[2] from basic scientific knowledge to technology, leading to the production line, and finally to the market.

It seems natural to try to combine these two polar cases in order to capture both types of technical innovation: the incremental type, as a response by the firm to the demand side of the market, the discontinuous one, as a development coming from the supply side. However, a framework of this kind, in order to encompass both types of technical advance, needs to be intrinsically dynamic. In particular, it must deal with disequilibrium dynamics rather than converging ones, and must also allow for the differential behaviour of different agents.

This has been one of the preliminary tasks of the Schumpeterian theory of entrepreneurship, upon which the development of the evolutionary theory has subsequently heavily relied. The entrepreneur is pushed to introduce innovation because, in a situation of general equilibrium, this is the only way to gain a relative advantage with respect to competitors and to earn the 'monopoly' profits deriving from his/her deviant behaviour:[3]

> entrepreneurial gain may also be called a monopoly gain, since it is due to the fact that the competitors only follow at a distance. (Schumpeter, 1965, p. 52)

Therefore, the entrepreneurial function involves alertness to opportunity, and capability to impose a point of view:

> The entrepreneurial performance involves, on the one hand, the ability to perceive new opportunities that cannot be proved at the moment at which action has to be taken, and, on the other hand, will power adequate to break down the resistance that the social environment offers to change. (Schumpeter, 1947, p. 157)

As Schumpeter points out, there is a need for the entrepreneur to differentiate his/her behaviour in order to obtain differential advantages:

it is clear that if all people reacted in the same way and at the same time to the presence of new possibilities no entrepreneurial gain would ensue. (Schumpeter, 1965, p. 52)

If the first innovator proves to be successful, being rewarded by extra profits, a wave of imitators is encouraged to follow. Because of the relatively low risk involved in imitation, the bankers are willing to finance this stream of followers, and the process ends up when a new point of equilibrium is reached:

> Profit is temporary by nature: it will vanish in the subsequent process of competition and adaptation. (Schumpeter, 1939, p. 105)

The innovation brought about by the entrepreneur is radically new with respect to existing market needs, bringing into the economy a qualitative, structural change. The imitators, as Schumpeter (1939, p. 414) clearly stated, 'are still entrepreneurs, though to a degree that continually decreases to zero'. Therefore, it is reasonable to assume that their role is that of marginally improving already existing innovations, being more akin to satisfying market demand and revealed consumers' needs.

Two main points need to be further stressed. The first one is that Schumpeter recognises that innovations are to be considered autonomous with respect to the economic system,[4] very much like the technology-push kind of innovation, though they could also be stimulated by the desire to overcome scarcity. The second point is that, despite the broad similarities with the neoclassical vision, the Schumpeterian theory is essentially a disequilibrium dynamic theory. It stresses processes of change rather than convergence towards the equilibrium, and it focuses on the disequilibrium path that the economy follows during the diffusion process instead of defining the final equilibrium of the diffusion of an innovation. But, more than that, the concept of entrepreneurship is intrinsically unmanageable by an equilibrium theory, no rationale being furnished to explain behaviour outside of the equilibrium point. To consider it as a perturbation of a pre-existing equilibrium simply renders entrepreneurship an empty concept. Indeed, in equilibrium theory there can be no entrepreneurs.[5]

This pioneering vision of the role of technological competition elaborated by Schumpeter raised many important questions such as, for example, the differentiated role of invention, innovation and diffusion, the role of qualitative change in promoting long waves of socio-economic development, etc. However, many issues still remained to be analysed (to mention a few, relationships between equilibrium and disequilibrium forces, international aspects, the role of the various institutions), some of which have been subsequently tackled by the evolutionary theory, to which we now turn our attention.

1.1   MR DARWIN OR MONSIEUR LAMARCK?

Schumpeter's focus on differential entrepreneurial behaviour and on disequilibrium paths of development has been 'rediscovered' by the evolutionary theory of technical change, whose main champions are surely Richard Nelson and Sidney Winter. In their words:[6]

> the term 'neo-Schumpeterian' would be as appropriate a designation for our entire approach as 'evolutionary'. More precisely, it could reasonably be said that we are evolutionary theorists for the sake of being neo-Schumpeterians. (1982, p. 39)

Evolutionary thinking has undergone different revolutions, from Lamarck, to Darwin, to the neo-Darwinians. Therefore, we will briefly sketch these three different approaches and then point out the analogy with technological change.[7]

Evolution is the term that indicates a phenomenon according to which groups of a certain population undergo, over time, a transformation process (that is, variations in the genotype). This process gives rise to the formation of groups with brand-new characters (that is, new phenotype) in the constituent units.[8] According to Darwin, biological evolution occurs because a passive environment selects certain new varieties of characteristics in a species destined to become permanent (hereditary). The basis of the mechanism of evolution lies therefore in the appearance of variations, transmissible to the offspring, in groups of individuals struggling for life. The survival of some individuals instead of others is due to the fact that the environment selects some variations: the individuals with those variations best suited to the selective device will survive, while others will not. Variance of transmittable characters, struggle for life, and selective environment are thus the relevant characteristics of this approach. In other words, as Darwin put it, natural selection is the 'presentation of favourable variations and the rejection of injurious variations' (Darwin, 1859, p. 131).

It is however necessary to distinguish this view of the evolutionary drive from the so-called Lamarckianism. Lamarckianism is a much-modified version of the theory of the French biologist J.B. Lamarck. His explanation of the adaptive nature of evolution is alternative to the Darwinian one. Indeed, changes are adaptations (that is, changes in the phenotype) that make individuals fit to survive: they are responses to the particular environment that individuals face during lifetime. In order for these adaptations to become relevant for the evolutionary process they need to exert their effects also on the nature of the offspring. If this is so, the evolution of new and improved adaptations is granted over time.[9]

Finally, it is necessary to point out a successive step in the development of the Darwinian theory. The neo-Darwinian theory, starting from considerations about the stochastic nature of the variations, reinterpreted the

Darwinian theory of natural selection in terms of differential reproduction, identifying thus the population as the unit of evolutionary analysis. The population is defined as the integrating level between the individual level and the species. Once the population is assumed as the unit of analysis, there is the need to shift from the Platonic idea of reducing phenomena to their essential characteristics, and to explain them by means of these latter only. That is, all the features not common to all the elements constituting the universe under examination are to be considered as superfluous for the description and the study of the phenomena. This perspective is known as essentialism. The understanding of the world is made by means of the analysis of a few characteristics that define every phenomenon (for example, the representative agent).

There is, therefore, the need to shift towards a different approach, that is, a populationist approach that privileges distributions of phenomena. In this case, diversity and variety of behaviour are of interest to explain the evolutionary drive.[10] The change in perspective has far-reaching consequences:

> First, the behaviour of the population is a statistical construct, to be explained in terms of levels and changes in the mean, variance and higher moments of the population distribution. Secondly, the performance of any population member is only significant in terms of its position in the overall distribution of behaviour. Thirdly, the behaviour of the population aggregate needs not be reducible to the behaviour of the corresponding population members. (Gibbons and Metcalfe, 1986, p. 11)

In order to explain the process of change by means of these concepts, it is important to distinguish between transformational and variational change. The former deals with changes in the characteristics of a single entity (for example, the firm). Different theories can explain this type of change. For instance, it is possible to imagine an explanation based on rational behaviour of economic agents, on fixed *ex ante* rules, on analogies with the life cycle, etc. The latter deals with variations in the structure of the population, obtained through modifications in the relative weight of the different units of the population itself. The Darwinian theory of natural selection is a classical example of variational change. A model of technological diffusion, showing how the structure of a population of technologies changes over time, belongs to this category. The two concepts are complementary, in that it is not possible to have the latter without the former. Variational changes depend (by means of the selection mechanism) on the existence of different behaviour, which, in turn, is explained by means of a transformational change theory (Matthews, 1984; Metcalfe, 1989 and 1998a; Metcalfe and Gibbons, 1989).

The analogy with economics can thus be pursued, though some precautions must be taken.[11] Firms operate in a dynamic environment characterised by uncertainty, struggle for profit (or market share), and continuous transition. A firm's behaviour is not that of a maximiser but rather that of a 'satisfier' (Simon, 1982). The technique of production is therefore not unique and each firm has its own organisational rules and targets (Nelson and Winter, 1982). Variety among firms, as far as these attributes are concerned, is the essential mechanism that pushes the economic change of a certain industry. The level and proportion of input utilisation, the level of efficiency, the rate of profit, the level of unit costs, and the level of output are all different among the firms, and are all differently targeted by the firms. The overall rate of technical advance is thus determined not only by the performance of individual firms, but rather by the interactions of the firms' behaviour, or, in other words, by the covariances of their relevant functional variables. In fact, firms with a higher degree of technological capability will create a differential growth rate with respect to the less capable. Firms more inclined to change readily their actual situation will expand their production and their market share. This will force less innovative firms to imitate the more innovative ones. The result is a dynamic setting, where no firm has a definite advantage – unless it becomes structural – characterised by micro instability, inherent disequilibrium behaviour, multiple equilibria and open-ended processes (Metcalfe, 1998a).

The main concepts on which evolutionary theory is based are thus diversity, selection and developmental processes. The first refers to: (i) efficiency (that relates to production); (ii) fitness (relating to the propensity to grow); (iii) creativity (relating to technical skills). The second refers to: (i) the rate of growth of the market; (ii) the price structure of the market; (iii) the frequency of the market process (in turn determined by the degree of ferocity with which the various firms react to changes in market conditions, and the degree of homogeneity of this reaction) (Gibbons and Metcalfe, 1986). The third refers to the fact that, for evolution to occur (that is, in order to have cumulative genetic changes), a transformation process is needed that transforms natural selection (which is ahistorical) into a fully cumulative, historical evolutionary account. In other words, evolution is the dynamic process of variation accumulation over time of both phenotypic selection (by the environment) and genotypic response (in terms of genetic combination and mutation).

The evolutionary process is thus driven by the interaction of four different types of variational phenomena: (i) phenotypical changes without genotypical relevance; (ii) mutation, for example, a change in genotype; (iii) changes in gene frequency or dispersion of existing information; (iv) very few mutations that result in speciation (Mokyr, 1990b, p. 351). The first refers to variations of incremental type, equivalent, for instance, to alterations of factor proportions with a given technology of reference, the second to the discovery of an invention that needs a process of technological (and social as well as political) refinement to acquire economic weight, the third to the spread of a minor innovation in the population of business units.[12] The fourth type of variation represents the most extreme case of Darwinian evolution: the speciation. In this case we assist a discrete alteration of the socio-cultural and scientific reference framework. The productive structure of a firm is now dramatically altered in order to gain a relevant advantage over its competitors, implying a discontinuity in technological progress.

It is possible to apply this taxonomy to social science and revive the controversy between Lamarckianism and Darwinism. Indeed, because the transmission of information can be directed and inherited, Lamarckian evolution is to be interpreted as technological competition of the incremental type for a given 'technological design'. The environment is active with regard to the units of the population and generates phenotypical alterations of some characters. Therefore, firms improve their performance marginally as a result of a process of feedback and interaction with the surrounding environment.

Darwinian evolution instead allows 'only' a passive role for the environment. Genetic alterations are produced 'randomly' (with respect to the selection mechanism), and after a 'checking' period some of them survive. According to this analogy, firms produce innovations independently of the environment (that is, of demand conditions) by means of their techno-scientific knowledge base. In order to establish themselves on the market, these mutations must produce superior, radically different performances in the process of production. Depending on their impact on the market, they can be classified either as mutations (case (ii) above) or speciation (case (iv) above).

1.2   PARADIGMS AND TRAJECTORIES

As already mentioned, one of the main points that a truly dynamic theory of qualitative change has to face is the balance between centrifugal and centripetal forces, that is, the relationship between the dynamic (disequilibrating) forces and the equilibrium ones. A theory must in principle be consistent with the simple observation that chaotic micro-behaviour can, and indeed does, generate ordered socio-economic patterns. This problem is particularly pressing in the case of evolutionary theory,[13] which by construction does not have a built-in mechanism for so-to-say synchronising micro with macro behaviour and thus achieving stability.

Several contributions have addressed this issue by referring (either implicitly or explicitly) to the Kuhnian notions of paradigms and trajectories. A surely non-exhaustive list must comprehend the notions of dominant design (Abernathy and Utterback, 1975), technological imperatives (Rosenberg, 1976a), technological regimes and natural trajectories (Nelson and Winter, 1977), technological paradigms and technological trajectories (Dosi, 1982 and 1984), technological guideposts (Sahal, 1985), techno-economic paradigm (Freeman and Perez, 1986), chreodes (Clark and Juma,

1987), design configuration (Metcalfe and Boden, 1991). The usual borrowing from Dosi defines paradigms as:

> 'models' and a 'pattern' of solution of selected technological problems, based on selected principles derived from natural sciences and on selected material technologies. (1984, p. 83)

That is, a paradigm imposes a technological horizon for the solution of certain techno-economic needs. Firms are constantly trying to differentiate themselves from one another, given the 'initial endowment of technological culture' defined by the paradigm. Paradigms mould technological expectations of a community of practitioners in such a way that inside the horizon of the paradigm a very large array of technological solutions is at hand. A paradigm thus simultaneously sets both the limits and the opportunities for further development. Indeed, within a paradigm there exist many technological trajectories, along which every firm tries to marginally improve its performance in order to be positively selected by the market. However, only if some technological improvements prove to be such as to create a new 'standard of reference', may a new paradigm emerge. This will thus be followed by a stream of imitators, who will again try to develop marginal improvements, and so on.

The analogy is here with the scientific paradigm elaborated by Kuhn as:

> universally recognised scientific achievements that for a time provide model problems and solutions to a community of practitioners. (1970a, p. viii)[14]

Within a paradigm, the role of the scientists (that is, of normal science) is that of 'puzzle-solver', that is, to solve problems posed by the scientific paradigm, for which, by the way, it happens that the existence of a solution is normally assured. The normal scientific activity is therefore, in Kuhn's view, no more than 'a test of ingenuity or skill in solution' (1970a, p. 36). It is interesting to point out that in contrasting the Popperian scientist (defined as 'problem solver'[15]) with his own definition, Kuhn writes:

> I use the term 'puzzle' in order to emphasise that the difficulties which ordinarily confront even the very best scientist are, like crossword puzzles or chess puzzles, challenges only to his ingenuity. He is in difficulty, not the current theory. (1970b, p. 5)

This is a very important characteristic to be underlined, because the exclusion effect of a paradigm is an essential feature in the definition of the agenda of relevant scientific problems. The 'puzzle-solving' activity implies in fact a limited (in relative terms, of course, for solving a puzzle can be greeted as a relevant step forward in absolute terms), marginal capability of developing alternatives to the dominant paradigm. Thus, the concept of paradigm has proved to be very useful for a better understanding of the self-regulatory, self-organising nature of the economic system. The following statement by Kuhn is indeed very appealing. His book, he says:

> portrays scientific development as a succession of tradition-bound periods punctuated by non-cumulative breaks. (1970a, p. 208)

Nevertheless, the transfer of this idea from philosophy of science to economics has partly undermined its capability of a deeper understanding of the nature of technological change. Indeed, in Kuhn's vision the paradigm is a regulatory framework of scientific research. Crisis, instead, can only arise from within, when the piling up of unresolved puzzle makes the paradigm crumble:

> the emergency of new theories is generally preceded by a period of pronounced professional insecurity. As one might expect, that insecurity is generated by the persistent failure of the puzzles of normal science to come out as they should. Failure of existing rules is the prelude to a search for new ones. (Kuhn, 1970a, p. 67)

However, as far as economics is concerned, the existence of more than one competing paradigm cannot be ruled out as an exception, but rather is the norm. That is, a technological paradigm cannot crumble by internal contradiction, because the milestone is not the advancement of knowledge but profits: as long as a paradigm allows for profits, it prevails. Thus, a dominant paradigm, by definition, is always able to supply the 'right answer' to every problem coming from within. Only another, already existing, paradigm, that proves to be more profitable, can successfully challenge, coexist, and eventually substitute the old one. But, in so doing, the new paradigm is creating an external contradiction to the incumbent one. It is the invention of something new that causes a change in paradigm, if and only if it produces either better or cheaper goods or both. For instance, when the paradigm of horse riding was dominant in the society, there was no alternative to it, nor was it conceivable. That is, the idea of moving people or materials more quickly and cheaply was not a need, because it had no economic meaning at all. When it becomes possible to make a choice (or even to think reasonably about making a choice), this is possible because another paradigm is available. Then, and only then, the change of paradigm is prompted. Within the paradigm nothing can create a piling up of unresolved puzzles, just because the puzzle is resolved naturally in its economic meaning. This problem leaves, thus, unanswered the question of why and how a paradigm should undergo such a structural change.

Moreover, once a scientific paradigm has been overcome by another, it simply disappears, becoming food for the historians of science. This does not happen for technological paradigms, because it is possible for more than one paradigm to coexist. Indeed, there is a great variety of transportation means, from cart to flight, and they all survive, carving their own economic niche. On the contrary, in no part of the scientific community of astronomers shall we find a subset of this community still believing in geocentrism and teaching Ptolemaic astronomy to their students!

One final point to stress is about the 'closedness' of paradigms. The self-contained nature of a paradigm is such that it operates as an excluding device, focusing the scientists' attention on certain problems while hiding some others, focusing on certain methods and goals while others are simply not seen in the context of the every-day puzzle-solving activity. The metaphor used is often that of people working inside a cave, and Kuhn himself describes the change of paradigm 'as if professional community had been suddenly transported to another planet' (1970a, p. 11). However, this metaphor holds if only one paradigm is allowed to exist, while, if the existence of more than one paradigm is possible, we are back to a closed system analogy. That is, when some unknown socio-cultural and economic circumstances have brought a paradigm to dominate in its economic field, the trajectories become the analogy of a *ceteris paribus* context for 'laboratory experiment'. This has implications for both the kind of processes (closed versus open-ended) established within a paradigm, and on the very important issue of flows exchange among different systems, and thus on the kind of equilibria (possibly) resulting from such dynamics.

1.3   A SYSTEM VIEW OF TECHNOLOGY AND ECONOMICS

The concepts of technological paradigm and trajectories, although useful, proved to be a limited tool of analysis. There is the need, at this early stage, to develop a fully-fledged system theory, which can complement and overcome an evolutionary account of techno-economic change based on evolutionary theory and paradigms.

Therefore, the next stage starts from the definition of technological change as a multidimensional phenomenon in which several factors, internal and external to the firm, all jointly determine the technological outcome (see, for instance, Sahal, 1981a, cap. 2 and 1981b). In such a context technology is the result of the continuous interactions between internal and external factors (Saviotti, 1986, 1988, 1996). By advocating system theory (von Bertalanffy, 1968; Laszlo, 1972) it is thus possible to define three relevant dimensions of a system: (i) the external environment; (ii) the internal environment; and (iii) a series of linkages. The characteristics of the current technology thus depend on the interactions among these dimensions. There are three main issues to focus attention on: (i) the definition of the relevant characteristics of the environment external to a certain technology (the local environment); (ii) the changes in the local environment; and (iii) the relative speed with which the external and the internal environment change. In such a framework it is possible to borrow and adapt concepts from thermodynamics such as that of entropy, and the degree of openness of a system with respect to the flows exchanged with the environment.

On these premises, it is possible to understand the process of techno-economic change by analysing the relationships established both within the system and between different systems. Hence, the core of the analysis is constituted by the interactions among units of systems. Obviously, a related and crucial issue is about boundary definition. In fact, in its simpler definition a system, or, as we will call it, a *technological system*, is about technological creativity, technology transfer and/or acquisition in different forms and under different 'transaction rules'. Hence, the core of the activity of a system lies in the types and quantities of transfers taking place within and across the system's boundaries. In other words, the explicit focus on connections among actors is what system theory is mainly about, and this, in turn, implies the definition of a system's boundaries.

Moreover, since we will argue that technological systems are socially constructed systems, some additional interesting features are added to the picture. In particular, given that, as a result of the interactions, the agents' behaviour changes over time, a technological system is historically rooted at least in two senses. First, the capabilities of the agents to innovate the system (that is, the Schumpeterian capacity to produce, diffuse and appropriate material and immaterial technologies to identify and exploit profitable opportunities) evolve over time as a result of the interactions with other agents. Secondly, certain institutions grow out of certain environments rather than others, exactly because of the shifting configuration of a certain system over time. This is particularly true if a national dimension is associated with the technological system. In fact, the institutional infrastructure is in this case quasi-endogenous, because cultural identity and language (but also different standards) all contribute to the shaping of the dynamic properties of the technological system in terms of its ability to adapt and respond to outside changes.

1.3.1 System Theory and Thermodynamics

The concept of entropy defines the quantity of unavailable energy in a system at a certain moment of time, the opposite concept being potential energy. Potential energy, once transformed into heat, cannot be transformed back into energy without a further use of energy. That is, the available energy in a closed system continually decreases and evolves into unavailable energy until exhaustion. In physics the growth of entropy is linked to a tendency towards a relatively higher degree of disorganisation (disorder) of a system (Georgescu-Roegen, 1976). In a closed system entropy tends to increase and to reach a maximum corresponding to the thermodynamic equilibrium. Given that the system is isolated, every variation away from equilibrium will decrease the entropy, but this is a violation of the second law of thermodynamics. On the contrary, an open system cannot define its degree of entropy independently from the interactions with the environment. Therefore, an open system cannot gain a state of equilibrium because of the continuous exchange of energy and matter with the environment. It can however reach a stationary state where the level of entropy remains constant in the face of continuous exchange with the external environment. While in a closed system entropy increases continuously to reach its maximum value (the equilibrium), in an open system entropy can decrease by increasing that of the system with which it exchanges flows of entropy (that is, being a net exporter). Thus, an open system can tend, by moving from a stationary state to another, towards configurations characterised by an increasing degree of order, while a closed system inevitably tends towards an ever-increasing degree of disorder (of entropy).

A far from equilibrium open system is associated with an ordering principle that Prigogine (1976) defines as 'order through fluctuations'. Its representation is defined by three interacting components: a functional structure, a time-space structure, and a fluctuation component. The first two define the deterministic (Newtonian) part, the third is the element determining the peculiar dynamics of an open system (it is not indeed a correction mechanism that tends to re-establish the equilibrium). In practice, the analytical structure of this kind of model is made up by two logically inseparable parts: a deterministic one (that is, an equation describing the background dynamics of the system), and a stochastic one (describing the fluctuations by means of a non-linear stochastic equation). The stability of the system is therefore the result of the interactions between these two components. This is the concept of self-organisation. Its application to socio-economic systems allows for the description both of the deterministic behaviour of economic agents and of small historical events. These latter show either the willingness of single agents to deviate from consolidated types of behaviour, or small casual events of limited quantitative relevance. In a Schumpeterian (evolutionary) perspective, the two components can describe both average and deviant behaviour.

Self-organising systems (see, for instance, Silverberg *et al.*, 1988) are evolutionary when the results of economic activity are selected by the environment and the successful variations are retained and accumulated over time. Such systems are characterised by non-linearity and irreversibility. An evolutionary settlement is characterised by 'historic' time (that is, irreversible and non-deterministic), while classical physics dynamics is not evolutionary because the implicit notion of time is reversible and deterministic (logic time). Innovations are non-linear qualitative changes. Furthermore, those that are successful tend to perpetuate themselves and, becoming dominant, to forbid a return to past situations. Innovations cause the system to fluctuate away from the stationary state, interacting with a given historical and institutional structure.

The introduction of non-linearity (the innovation) in a self-organised system, composed of functional and time-space structures, can overcome the limits of the Newtonian vision typical of general equilibrium models. According to the latter, in fact, the relevant behaviour is implicit in the initial conditions and cannot undergo qualitative evolution. In Prigogine's words:

> There is a close analogy between the 'invention' of new techniques and the structural instability leading to new chemical mechanisms. Of course, there is no question of classifying societies according to a single criterion such as their energy or entropy production. This is merely a characteristic of evolution, but a very important one because of its universality. In contrast, our approach clearly shows the rather oversimplified nature of theories of 'progress' (linear progress, cycles, etc.). (1976, p. 125)

The possibility of qualitative changes is tightly linked to the non-linear nature of the economic system. Therefore, the nature of the particular equilibria varies according to the particular state and moment of time. In particular, the development path is subject to sudden bifurcations: the system dynamics is univocally defined with respect to time until it reaches one of these points where two alternative paths are open. In the neighbourhood of each bifurcation point the alternative actually chosen may well depend on small casual events. They thus can determine the outcome of the system by forcing one path or another. In such cases it becomes extremely difficult to define the causal relationships among the variables and to make any kind of forecast other than a random one. Thus, system behaviour will be determined by different sets of relevant variables, depending on the distance from the bifurcation points. It is thus possible to explain why a system shows stable behaviour for (quite) long periods of time, along stable and well-defined techno-economic trajectories, while in other periods (that is, in the neighbourhood of a bifurcation point) it will choose, in an apparently random way, certain directions instead of others because of certain individual (and apparently irrelevant) choices. And it may be very difficult to predict the relevance of these choices at the very moment in which they are made.

By incorporating increasing returns to scale, or more generally externalities, it is thus possible to explain certain phenomena that are apparently paradoxical if analysed within the framework of rationality and maximisation. For instance, Arthur (1989) and David (1985) have shown how, during the diffusion process of competing technologies, one may come to dominate (even if it is inferior from the point of view of absolute efficiency) because of small historical accidents that are apparently irrelevant, or by the sequence of single adoptions.

1.3.2 The System Approach

If, as Boulding frivolously stated, a system is 'anything not in chaos', it is fairly clear that, on the positive side, we are left a bit unclear on many important issues. So far, many scholars have contributed to the clarification of many important issues relevant to a system approach, and it is not this chapter's aim to go in this direction. However, a few points will be highlighted in order to clarify which are the most important problems at stake, with particular reference to what follows, and with no pretence for completeness.

In particular, the focus will be on the fact that a system view is based on the following points:

1. The process of change is based on linkages, that is, on the exchange of flows among networks of agents. The focus on linkages must be properly addressed because it has far-reaching consequences on several aspects of the system dynamics, on its empirical approximation, etc. To put it more strongly, it is the existence of the flow exchange among nodes that makes for the existence of a system perspective at all. And the establishment of a network of relationships among agents and institutions and their feedback generate the process of dynamic change. Therefore, systems differ, first, because they have differently shaped institutions, but, secondly and more importantly, because even with identical institutions it is still possible to get different kinds of connections among them. They are historically determined and conditioned, so that systems' behaviour will be rather different, although at a superficial glance they appear to be composed of equivalent building blocks.
2. The process of change is institutionalised, that is, heterogeneous agents play the game at different stages, with frequent and important non-linearities and feedback, thus calling for institutions. Again, to put it strongly, agents and institutions are embedded in social and cultural dimensions which condition their response to incoming signals.
3. The definition of system must be properly spelled out because, otherwise, there is the risk of using *ad hoc* definitions with undesired effects on the kind of analysis (in particular on the empirical analysis) performed. For one, the importance lies in the problem of how the balance between import and export of entropy is determined. With respect to systems of innovation and technological systems, the utilisation of the label 'national' usually solves the problems of the boundaries of a system. This is a sort of compulsory path to escape these difficulties. Indeed, as Hughes (1989) and Carlsson and Stankiewicz (1991) have shown, it is quite difficult to come up with a satisfactory and meaningfully operational definition once the national boundaries are removed.

Having said that, it is fairly obvious how systems differ along at least five dimensions which it is extremely important to investigate as we argue in what follows.

1. It is important to consider the historical state of a system's connections. Within certain systems, certain channels of transmission may develop rather

than others,[16] they may develop at different historical moments in response to different stimuli and therefore, although formally similar (or morphologically equivalent), they could well exert different consequences and thus different outcomes.

2. We need to consider the direction and intensity of the connections. Each system has its own network of linkages which is characterised by several facts such as: that one connection exists or not, that a connection links the same couple of agents or institutions and the direction of their connections; that in one system one connection carries more flows than another, while the reverse holds for another system (that is, the intensity of the linkages); that the connections and the flows travelling along them coincide or not; that one connection is mediated or not by the institutional interface. All these are crucial factors determining the system dynamics.

To the previous two, at least three further arguments should be added. However, before turning to these subsequent arguments, some considerations are still necessary about the second argument concerning such issues as: (i) connectivity degree; (ii) flow direction; (iii) system structure and behaviour; (iv) flows and information channels; (v) institutional interface. Let us briefly examine each of them in turn.

(i) Connectivity degree. This is a crucial 'property' of a system approach. In fact, a system exists insofar as nodes are connected. And, by definition, the set of linkages defines the system's boundaries. Therefore, the way linkages have developed historically has a very clear impact on the different structural properties of a system. Different agents or institutions may well be linked in different ways (in some cases directly, in some others indirectly). This implies that there is a bi-directional relationship among the system's components: their properties and behaviour influence that of the whole system, which in turn affects a single unit through at least another unit. Therefore, the disappearance of a linkage has by definition an impact on the system's performance. Moreover, if the system is not robust, the same disappearance of a node may well cause the system to disappear. Indeed, a system may crumble if an element is subtracted and the system results in being unable to replicate its functions by means of a different subset of elements and linkages.

(ii) Flow direction. Flows have a direction, so that there are two possible types of relationship among nodes: either unidirectional (both ways), or bi-directional. In this last case, a process of feedback is at work. Feedback is the dynamic element of the system performance. Without reciprocal interaction, the system does not evolve, but undergoes a sort of one shot (static) game (a 'wave' propagates across the system from a certain starting point to the last element, and that's all). Instead, a process of feedback makes the system intrinsically dynamic and capable of evolving over time by a recursive mechanism. Obviously, the direction of change is not definable *a priori*.

(iii) System structure and behaviour. Different systems may be equal in terms of structure (nodes and linkages) but still behave differently. On the contrary, systems with either different nodes or different linkages may well behave in the same way, according to the intensity distribution of the interactions that may lead to the same overall result. It all depends on the intensity with which nodes interact. This is a differentiating and crucial property of systems' behaviour. In fact, since the overall behaviour is an emergent property of the system, each system may evolve differently, given certain historical conditions. Thus it will develop some linkages rather than others, and produce the same output by connecting different nodes with different intensities. Moreover, connections that are frequently used get reinforced for the sole reason of their more intense usage, while, on the contrary, connections that are not frequently utilised tend to die down. Therefore, there appears to be a cost involved in keeping linkages alive. These costs are in terms of both material and immaterial structures, hardware and software, matter and people.

(iv) Flows and information channels. The distinction between flows and channels along which information travels has very important implications. Indeed, first, there are many different types of channels related, for instance, to people mobility, research projects, etc. All of them concern different behaviours, rules and strategies, all of which involve different sub-sets of relationships (nodes, directions and intensity) within the system. Secondly, very relevant implications derive from the existence or not of the distinction between channels and signals. For instance, if channels and flows coincide, we may well think of tacit knowledge being transferred between nodes, while, if they do not coincide, the knowledge flows relate to transfers of codified knowledge.

(v) Institutional interface. A final important point is related to the existence of an institutional interface. Indeed, in every social system, and therefore also in a technological system, two elements must be kept in mind. First, the direction of change is not 'right' by definition and mechanisms such as focusing devices, technological guideposts, technological trajectories and the like work only at the level of single technologies, but not at the level of the whole system. Secondly, a social system is historically rooted and it is also the result of many accidental and unintentional actions coupled in various and complex ways with intentional ones. Therefore, a role for an institutional interface emerges from within the system as the only way so-to-say to drive the process of change in certain directions rather than others. This emergence is however triggered by completely different and differently shaped social forces. They act with different directions, intensities and timing, with the sole common purpose of keeping a 'suitable' degree of stability, which pushes forward the forces of change (of 'progress') in a certain direction. The direction is obviously socially determined and depends on the distribution of the balance of power among the various agents within the system.

As we said, the previous points are in fact sub-points of the second argument. Let us now move to consideration of the other three differentiating dimensions of a system.

3. It must be recognised that an (evolutionary) system view of relationships among agents excludes by definition a sort of comparative statics approach (or better a comparative dynamics one). In fact, a crucial element in system dynamics is that it is not possible to disconnect one element from the others to analyse it. Without invoking a holistic approach, it is possible to say that within a system view the behaviour of the whole system exceeds that of the single constituencies, while every unit still keeps its identity (DeBresson, 1996). Indeed, given that a system is based on connections between nodes, two things clearly emerge. First, each node is at least connected to another one and thus its behaviour depends at the very least on that of another one. Secondly, given the interdependence existing within a system, when a node is taken out of the system, all the other remaining nodes will change their set of characteristics. Thus, removing one node has implications which range from the redefinition of the system's relationships, to the disappearance of the system itself if the node has a very 'central' position. The only impossible outcome is the system maintaining its pace unaltered. In this sense, a system cannot be interpreted only by looking at its single units, while a 'system view' is also required, pertaining to the particular behaviour that can be referred only to the system itself as a unit of analysis. Hence a twofold analysis is required, at both levels.

4. A system may therefore be hierarchic. Apart from the possibility of equally distributed and parithetic connections (in terms of both direction and intensity), some nodes will turn out to be more strongly connected. This implies that not only all the nodes within a system have the same importance, but also, and more importantly, that some nodes are connected only indirectly. Thus, the dynamics of a system may be more dependent on a certain subset of linkages rather than others.[17] Conversely, there are limited opportunities for certain blocks to influence the dynamics of the system with respect to others.

5. A definite step towards a system methodology requires that the analysis of the linkages of the various building blocks is pursued according to their statistical distributions. This means that if we are evaluating the different flows among building blocks, they must have certain characteristics, one of which is, for instance, that there are no bottlenecks (or reverse salient, according to Hughes, 1989). Indeed, while if evaluated at a micro level such bottlenecks might be beneficial for innovative activity by establishing development potential (Dahmén, 1989), at the system level the appearance of a reverse salient cannot be overcome by single micro-activities, but needs a sort of more co-ordinated and strategic point of view. In this sense indicators of statistical distribution, such as mean and dispersion, might give a

reasonable description of the existence of bottlenecks which can prevent flows from travelling from one block to another one.

1.3.3   Systems and Institutions

Although it is widely believed that a system perspective has been present in economics since Adam Smith, an explicit acknowledgement of the relevance of the interrelationships among economic agents and institutions, and their evolution over time as a cumulative process of adaptation and feedback, is to be fully found in institutionalist theory.[18]

Starting from a critique of the foundations of neoclassical economics (about rationality, information, absence of history, and the role of institutions), a theory is then developed based on a holistic approach with reference to both individual behaviour and the whole system. Indeed, as far as the individual is concerned:

> the cognitive and cerebral processes are best regarded as a complex and multi-tiered system, and [...] actions themselves take place in regard to different levels of thought. (Hodgson, 1988, p. 9)

This is equivalent to the adoption of an approach, well developed in cognitive psychology, of considering perception as mediated through culture and with a conscious and unconscious (or subconscious) dimension. This represents a clear challenge to the neoclassical principle of maximisation, in fact:

> the argument for conceiving the mind and consciousness as multiple-levelled and hierarchical is compelling. The argument about whether 'economic man' is entirely rational or non-rational is a false dichotomy. Human agents are both rational and sub-rational at the same time. (Hodgson, 1988, p. 110)

With this mixture of rational (in terms of explicit calculation) and customary (even in terms of conditioned response) actions, institutions develop as ways of structuring thinking and habits common to the majority of people, imposing a degree of coherence upon human activity:

> we can define a social institution [...] as a social organisation which, through the operation of tradition, custom or legal constraint, tends to create durable and routinized patterns of behaviour. (Hodgson, 1988, p. 10)

The importance of well-established habits is twofold, as a stable action in the present, and as a basis for future action:

> the relevance of the study of social institutions is underlined. Precisely because such actions are not fully flexible and deliberative, and are habitual in the context of a given structure, it is important to examine social institutions to see how

habits and routines are formed. The study of institutions offers a means of examining the basis of routinized action from the viewpoint of the system as a whole. (Hodgson, 1988, p. 10)

In this regard it is important to stress the fact that:

One important consequence of the system view adopted here is that it is possible to focus on the processes of transformation of both individual tastes and productive technology through time. By bringing these into the system their evolution and change become legitimate and major topics of enquiry. (Hodgson, 1988, p. 17)

The evolutionary nature of the process of technological change, the existence of multiple levels of analysis, the holistic approach, the importance of tacit knowledge and its connection to firm's routines, all constitute points of contact between institutional and evolutionary theories (North, 1990). The two approaches that have been developed autonomously show a progressive convergence (Hodgson *et al.*, 1994), although evolutionary theory has maintained a more technologically oriented focus.

We can now refer specifically to the process of technological change. Indeed, the relevant institutions provide guideposts along which individuals and collective agents try to achieve their goals, such as: the generation of scientific and technological knowledge, its utilisation as an input of some production process, and finally in the adoption of the results of a certain technological activity. In particular, agents pursue technological and organisational change to produce a structural change in the prevailing conditions in order to benefit from the (temporary) degree of monopoly that the innovation may create. In so doing agents must face strong uncertainty regarding, first, both technological and economic results, secondly, the structure of incentives, thirdly, how to solve conflicts eventually arising. To this end, in fact, sets

of both informal rules (constraints, taboo, customs, traditions, and codes of conduct), and formal rules (constitutions, laws, property rights), [...] have been devised by human beings to create order and reduce uncertainty in exchange. (North, 1991, p. 97)

The institutional framework provides societies with basic behavioural patterns with which agents conform their interactions. Institutions thus exist to provide the system with the degree of stability necessary for change (Johnson, 1992). However, institutions are not static, but their structure changes over time and 'as that structure evolves, it shapes the direction of economic change toward growth, stagnation, or decline' (North, 1991, p. 97). In so doing, they 'have merely changed with changes in economic conditions, and they may today be even more mandatory than the decrees of a dictator' (Commons, 1931, p. 649).

Far from trying to accomplish a full analysis of the role of institutions in systems of innovation, which is beyond the scope of this chapter,[19] only two points are worth briefly mentioning: the twin nature of institutions, and their relationships with innovative activity.

Institutions are usually referred to as both patterns of behaviour, such as habits, routines, codes of conduct (see, for instance, the citation from North), and hierarchical structures with explicit purposes, that is, organisations. Indeed, institutions 'range [...] all the way from unorganized custom to the many organized going concerns, such as the family, the corporation, the trade association, the trade union, the reserve system, the state' (Commons, 1931, p. 649).

This distinction accounts for wide differences (and sometimes misunderstandings) in how institutions are perceived and incorporated into various theoretical frameworks. For instance, Nelson's interpretation of a national system of innovation is rooted more in the latter definition, while Lundvall's is rooted in the former.

For the sake of this book, this distinction will be dealt with by acknowledging that formal organisations work as interfaces between institutions and 'society', that is, formal purposive structures are the organisational result of the 'cultural' environment at large. Hence, organisations differ among countries exactly because they translate 'in solid' the weight of 'imponderable' rules.[20]

As a result of this definition, institutions acquire an operational meaning: the concept used will be that of institutional interface. On the one hand, theoretically, it refers to the norms, culture, etc. that characterise and differentiate the various technological systems. On the other hand, operationally, it refers to how norms, customs and the like are made explicit and translated into hierarchical structures.

As far as the second point is concerned, that is, the relationships between institutions and innovation, for now it is only worth saying that

> innovation activities are so uncertain and conflict ridden that they need strong institutional support in order to become an important activity to which more than marginal resources are allocated. (Edquist and Johnson, 1997, p. 55)

Hence, only institutions can create order and reduce uncertainty thus supplying enough stability to trigger techno-economic change:

> institutions [are] collective action in control, liberation and expansion of individual action. (Commons, 1931, p. 649)

And this is true of both private[21] and public[22] organisations.[23] It is thus the interplay of the various and multidimensional institutional set-ups that is largely responsible for the wide differences we observe in the techno-economic performance of different technological systems.

1.3.4   Technological Change as a Complex Phenomenon

The consequences of the above-mentioned way of dealing with technological change, as part of a system of complex interrelationships,[24] are important for the definition of the concept of innovative activity, at both industrial and national level.

At the outset, the innovative process is not a single act, but rather it implies a series of successive innovations and developments.[25] It is fairly intuitive that these are direct consequences of the first innovative impulse, but the same can be said at a higher, more general, level. In fact, because technology is partly a firm-specific asset, each firm directs its innovative efforts in precise directions trying to make extensive use of the material and immaterial knowledge base already at its disposal. In normal conditions, technical change tends to be local, because it is directed, for instance, by rules of thumb (Cyert and March, 1992) or routines (Nelson and Winter, 1982). This means, to a certain extent, that past history can address present activity towards certain directions rather than others. Past decisions are thus a constraint for the future ones and path-dependency is a specific feature of the whole process (Dosi, 1988a). A typical incremental process is therefore set in motion, which can hardly gain global *optima*, but local ones will have a higher probability of being reached and maintained over time. Only successful innovations (and not the best from an abstract technological point of view) confer competitive advantages[26] upon the firms that implement them, and this represents the basis for the successive innovative activity (Nelson and Winter, 1982; Sahal, 1985). Technical progress is seen as a cumulative process. Indeed, a firm experimenting with a successful innovation gains higher profits and market shares and, at the same time, it has a higher probability of maintaining this differential competitive advantage. In going in specific directions, each firm strengthens its competitive position with respect to its rivals, the latter being based on competence and skills acquired throughout a costly process of learning (Malerba, 1992) which is multidimensional (learning-by-doing, Arrow, 1962; learning-by-using, Rosenberg, 1976a; etc.).

This is fairly clear once it is recognised that a certain level of productivity is associated with physical factors not *per se*, but only by means of the co-ordinating activity of human competence. Hence, the concept of economic competence expresses the capacity of an enterprise to identify, expand and exploit profitable opportunities by combining selective, organisational, technical and learning capabilities (Carlsson and Eliasson, 1994). From this viewpoint, economic competence becomes the centrepiece of the micro level upon which the perspective presented here is based.[27] Therefore, firms are characterised by the uniqueness of their organisational form, as derived from the uniqueness insight upon which the managerial activity is based. For one, because material structures depreciate and skills atrophy, this is truer in a dynamic setting with ever changing technologies and markets making them obsolete. Hence, differences in firms' competence are differences in the technological skills, complementary assets and organisational routines and capabilities that determine the degree of their techno-economic performance (Teece, 1988).

Innovative activity, by its nature, implies a process of discovery during which it is not possible to know *ex ante* the set of possible events and outcomes which would thus determine a probability structure. The process is rather characterised by strong uncertainty (Dosi and Egidi, 1987; Dosi, 1988b). This is particularly true not only of radical innovation (as a result of specific innovative activity such as, for example, R&D), but also, though to a lesser extent, of incremental innovation (as a result of improvements derived from experience and interaction with users). In other words, agents do perceive the existence of important opportunities, on the basis of specific elements such as market and technical knowledge, the capability of gathering information, and that of learning from the surrounding environment. The different degree of perception of such opportunities is the key element in explaining the innovative choices of a certain firm.

This idea of innovative process has given rise to several contributions, such as, for instance, the idea of technological paradigm already discussed, and those related to sectoral patterns of innovative activity and to national innovation systems.

The former approach is due to Pavitt (1984) who, in an empirical work, derived a taxonomy for the different types of innovative behaviour depending on the specific sector to which a firm belongs. The following classes are thus identified: supplier dominated, production intensive (in turn divided into scale intensive and specialised supplier), and science based. The first category is constituted mainly by traditional sectors (such as agriculture, textiles, clothing, etc.) and is characterised by cost-reducing process innovation embodied in intermediate and capital goods acquired from other sectors. The typical dimension of the innovative firm is small and medium, while innovative activity is generally the result of incremental innovation produced outside the sector. The scale-intensive category refers to (big) firms in manufacturing sectors such as durables, chemicals (partly), transportation, etc. Innovations are produced internally, mainly by exploiting economies of scale (for example, R&D). Firms invest considerable amounts of resources in formalised innovative activity and tend towards vertical integration. Appropriability is linked to know-how, secrecy and patents. The specialised supplier category refers mainly to sectors, such as machinery and instrumentation, typically oriented towards product innovation that diffuses as capital equipment and is bought by firms in other sectors. Small dimension, endogenous production of innovation, close links to final users, high appropriability due to tacit and cumulative technological competence are the main characteristics. Finally, the science-based category is constituted by firms of big dimension in sectors such as electronics, chemicals and the like. Innovation is generally mixed and is frequently directed towards the creation of new technological paradigms due to substantive advancements in scientific knowledge. Innovative activity is therefore codified and formalised, carried out in laboratories, typically with high spillover, and with a high degree of patenting (especially in the chemical sector).

1.3.5   The National Dimension of the System Approach

The concept of a national system of innovation is a more complete (but also complex) account of the various techno-economic relationships established within a system. It describes all the peculiarities of the innovative process as derived from the national character of the various agents and institutions that contribute to generating a 'socio-cultural' environment catalyst of particular techno-economic performances. This process refers to a particular historical moment and to specific institutional settings, producing a certain performance, in terms of international competitiveness. The structure of a national innovation system is thus the result of an idiosyncratic historical process and, as such, it is neither easily (if at all) transferable nor appropriable from abroad. The convergence of the contribution of different institutions, their incentive structure, their competence, user-producer interactions, all determine the speed and direction of technological learning. In this way a proper national 'socio-cultural' identity determines, in turn, the different characteristics of the innovative processes within nations. These characteristics are thus a constraint on the process of international technological transfer and, more generally, on learning from and among nations. In particular, these historical, cultural, social and linguistic differences will correspond to differences among nations relating to categories hardly analysed in the orthodox literature. To this literature we will now turn an idiosyncratic eye.

A national approach to the study of the co-evolution of the technological, economic and institutional performances of a system has existed for a long time. According to Freeman (1995), it dates back at least to Frederich List at the beginning of the nineteenth century, although according to others (for example, Dosi, 1999) it existed even before that period.

However, in most recent times, and with more coherently specified aims, a system approach has been developed, starting from the early contribution by Gille (1986), only in the last fifteen years. The contributions have ranged very widely and thus many different concepts related to a system view of techno-economic relationships have been elaborated so far. The best known is certainly the concept we have referred to above, that is, the national system of innovation, developed from the seminal contributions of Freeman (1988) and Lundvall (1988), and then further refined in Lundvall (1992a) and Nelson (1993a).[28] According to their definitions, a national system of innovation is identified by the set of institutions (the institutional infrastructure) that supports, influences, shapes and determines the rate and direction of technological learning (Lundvall, 1992a, p. 10; Nelson and Rosenberg, 1993, p. 3; Patel and Pavitt, 1994, p. 12).[29]

Such a conceptual construct has been developed, as a piece of what Nelson (1995) termed appreciative theorising. The starting point has been the observation of a certain degree of stability and persistence over time of the distribution, among countries and sectors, of techno-economic performances,[30] as derived from particular patterns of competencies, organisational forms, types of relationships and material and immaterial infrastructures. Therefore, the limited aggregate convergence rates which have been observed on average, in spite of the existence of (sometimes marked) differences in company performances, suggest the relevance of certain national characteristics: the so-called institutional context, a very powerful player in determining the rate and direction of the techno-economic activity.

Therefore, the system approaches defined above have, generally speaking, a geographically bounded dimension, which is usually associated with the national borders. However, different specifications can be found in the literature, such as, for example, regional systems of innovation, industrial districts and innovative milieux (for a recent survey, see Howells, 1999).

The boundaries of a techno-economic system might also be defined from a sectoral focus. In this case, definitions different from those of a national system of innovation may lead to different concepts such as those of: 'technological system' – if the clustering of activities defining the system can be either wider or narrower than a sector and can encompass more than one of them, as in the definition of Carlsson and Stankiewicz[31] – 'large technical system' – as described by Hughes[32] – 'technology support system' – as described in De Liso and Metcalfe (1996).[33]

However, the distinction between national system of innovation and technological system is quite blurred. As Carlsson and Stankiewicz put it: 'when the boundary is defined in terms of the national institutional infrastructure, the technological systems, as defined here, have much in common with the concept of "National System of Innovation" as defined by Freeman [...] and Nelson' (Carlsson and Stankiewicz, 1991, p. 49).

Indeed, the problem of the boundaries of a system is not merely one of definition. Given that systems can be bounded in several different ways, this has far-reaching implications for a set of features that define and characterise the system's identity (that is, different functions, different kinds of stability, problems of adaptability and the dynamics of a system). Indeed, the boundary is not only a red line delimiting the system extension, but it is also a coherence/compatibility principle. If national borders define the boundary of a system, they do not define only a physical limit, but also a connecting principle, which is quite different if we define the boundary starting from a functional (for example, sectoral) perspective. For instance, let us think of stability. We have already said that if a relevant component of the system is taken out, a system might well crumble. However, it is easy to see that this is possible only for the latter definition of system (the sectoral), which is based on a certain definition of boundary. If the 'largest' actor within a cluster of firms moves elsewhere, or goes bankrupt, then the rest of the system may disappear as well. For instance, all the remaining firms in the cluster may undergo a restructuring process so intense as to lead to a substantial re-orientation of their strategies towards different production lines (one historical example, might refer to the Italian chemical industry after the Second World War).

However, the possibility of a mere breaking down of the technological system could not arise if the unit of analysis considered is the national technological system, rather than the sectoral one. In fact, the national dimension of a technological system implies that the disappearance of a very big firm (even the biggest ones) cannot bring with it the disappearance of the national economic entity to which the technological system in this case refers. Obviously, this will imply (even major) restructuring of the national system components and in turn of their connections, but will never cause the system to crumble and disappear. Therefore, a very important aspect emerges quite clearly: different degrees of adaptability characterise the different forms along which the technological system functions are defined. And conversely, certain 'functional forms' exclude *a priori* certain responses to qualitative changes, be they from within the system or from the external environment. This, in turn, has very strong implications for the dynamics of the system itself.

In some cases, the analysis might well be focused on a sort of life-cycle analysis, while in some other cases this would simply be meaningless. But a more interesting approach could be related to issues such as structural change and the response to shocks (the analysis being focused on characteristics proper to the system such as flexibility, adaptability, reverse salient (Hughes, 1989), bottlenecks, development blocks (Dahmén, 1989), etc.). This is not to deny that the national and sectoral levels are interconnected, but that they have obviously different implications, focuses and instruments of analysis. It has thus been shown how the definition of the system boundaries is not a simple matter of 'ad hocness', but rather a substantial problem.

The concept of national system of innovation (but the same can obviously be said for the equivalent concept of technological system) implies conceptual and analytical problems which are related to the national dimension. Indeed, there are related key issues that impinge on the development of the literature on the subject. In the following, some concepts will be dealt with briefly in order to sketch the broad framework within which they must be analysed.

There are evidently some apparent contradictions in using a term like national systems of innovation in times of intense globalisation. Globalisation indeed has been used and abused as a catch phrase to describe many different aspects of the intense pushes that nation states are facing towards a rapid convergence in all their constituent aspects: that is, in inner components, rather than in external performance.

However, it must be briefly noted that, first, globalisation is an ongoing process that has very differentiated patterns, some of which lead to international convergence, while some others call forth a national characterisation of techno-economic performance.

Indeed, globalisation is quantitative rather than qualitative. Therefore, on the one hand, it is quite easy to detect increasing degrees of globalisation by inspecting increasing shares of trade and foreign direct investments, which is further enhanced by the recognition that the latter are far more dynamic than the former. On the other hand, less 'convincing' quantitative evidence seems to corroborate the qualitative way in which globalisation is acting. A first example is the strong link between sectoral specificity and product global differentiation: in some sectors products are more easily conformable to international standards than others, and not all sectors are alike in the degree of product customisation. This fact, in turn, leads to a degree of customisation, sometimes strong, that transnational corporations usually implement to comply with the particular characteristics of the local markets. Let us also observe that the relationships between firms and national market size are not very unambiguous: while, on the one hand, it is true that big companies based in small countries are naturally forced to base part of their activities abroad, thus increasing the degree of globalisation, it is also true that at a more 'aggregate' level this is more difficult to understand. Indeed, problems of demand have been frequently advocated to explain the poor EU technological performance with respect to that of the USA and Japan (see, for instance, Eaton *et al.*, 1998). Finally, we cannot forget the evidence on the scarce (although increasing) spreading of transnational corporations outside the main (few) industrialised countries, which is coupled to the not very clear-cut evidence on the degree of R&D activities that transnational corporations locate abroad (Patel and Pavitt, 1991).

This is not to mention the usual and frequently abused argument about national idiosyncrasies based upon culture and language. All these aspects act as a push and pull device determining the degree of internationalisation of an economy, but they are far from acting in only one direction.

NOTES

1. This approach, which is well rooted in neoclassical micro-foundations, has nonetheless many flaws (among the many criticisms see, for instance, Freeman, 1979; Mowery and Rosenberg, 1979; Kamien and Schwartz, 1982; Dosi, 1984). However, for the sake of the argument, it suffices to remark that, on the demand side, it is difficult to accept that shifts in prices and quantities can define such a precise pattern of needs that lead to the definition of the direction and the extent of the technological efforts.

2. The so-called linear model (invention, innovation, diffusion, market) was (and still is in some regards) a well-established model that has dictated science and technology policy since the Second World War. See, among the innumerable contributions, Freeman (1982) for a discussion and a critique, and Wise (1985) for a historical account.

3. Schumpeter repeatedly emphasised the necessity for forms of imperfect competition to prevail, in order to have a dynamic world in which there exist incentives to invest in superior products, new technologies, new sources of supply and new forms of organisation (Schumpeter, 1943, p. 84). The crucial point is the difference between static and dynamic efficiency: in a world where agents are always maximising static efficiency (such as neoclassical perfect competition), it is impossible to invest resources in technology (and it is thus impossible to outperform competitors and to create higher economic growth); as a result there will be dynamic inefficiency. That is, the long-run performance will be inferior exactly because the conditions for static efficiency are continuously satisfied. In passing, it is worth noting that this is the main route followed by neoclassical endogenous growth theory (for example, Romer, 1990, Aghion and Howitt, 1998).

4. See Ruttan (1959) for an interesting attempt to merge Schumpeter's theory of innovation with Usher's theory of invention.

5. The relationships between static competition and equilibrium have been debated for a long time. See, for instance, Stigler (1957), McNulty (1968), Nelson and Winter (1974), Georgescu-Roegen (1976), Kaldor (1985), Loasby (1989) and (1991).

6. But see also Freeman (1994). We will not enter the discussion whether Schumpeter was 'truly' evolutionary, and whether his approach was Darwinian or not. On this see more, for instance, in Hodgson (1993b), Magnusson (1994) and the Kelm (1997)–Hodgson (1997) debate in the *Journal of Evolutionary Economics*.

7. An intense debate and a huge amount of literature have been devoted to this theme. Nitecki (1988), Hahlweg (1991), Tuomi (1992) and Young (1993) are a good starting point.

8. The phenotype is meant to be the 'exterior' appearance of an organism (its visible characteristics), which results from the genetic information inherited (that is, the genotype) and from the interactions of the organism with the environment. In other words, the genotype represents the potentialities of an organism, while the phenotype represents the realisation of one of these potentialities as mediated by the interactions with the external environment.

9. The big debate arising from the clash of these two alternative explanations of evolution is not of interest here. As will be shown in the following, in fact, much of the debate loses importance once applied to a social context.

10. It is necessary to briefly recall that the neo-Darwinian theory, based on a frequency population approach (Hirschleifer, 1977; Witt, 1993), has given rise to many interesting arguments, which, however, refer in some ways to a reductionist vision of the evolutionary process. According to some authors (Hodgson, 1993b; Khalil, 1993), the latter would not be well suited to deal with the intrinsically open-ended processes typical of evolutionary theory.

11. It is necessary to warn against a straight application of evolutionary biology to the social sciences. For example, intentionality in human behaviour, co-evolution of agents and environment, learning and co-operation, and the more rapid and

discontinuous nature of technological change with respect to biology, are all elements to be borne in mind, since they may cause distorted interpretations. See Khalil (1992) for a methodological discussion of some related questions. See also Knudsen (1998) for a thorough discussion of the viability of the application of the concept of natural selection to economics.

12. All these kinds of variation are compatible with a state of competition in a market characterised by a relative uniformity of production performances.

13. The neoclassical theory, instead, does not have this problem, given that micro-optimisation is the rule that once consolidated obtains macro-stability.

14. We will not make reference here to the much improved version of the Postscript to the second edition of *The Structure of Scientific Revolutions*, because for the purpose of this chapter the concept of paradigm works equally well. Moreover, it is not the purpose of this section to investigate the various meanings that have been attached to such a concept. Masterman (1970) found almost two dozen different meanings of the term paradigm in Kuhn's book only.

15. '[S]cience starts only with problems. Problems crop up especially when we are disappointed in our expectations, or when our theories involve us in difficulties, in contradiction' (Popper, cited in Kuhn, 1970b, p. 5).

16. An example is given by the completely different role that insurance has in countries such as Great Britain and the USA, with respect to countries such as Germany, France or Switzerland. In the former case, insurance is, so-to-say, about 'betting' on future states of the world, while in the latter case it is the socio-cultural product of historically developed mutual aid societies.

17. Obviously every node is important for the systems dynamics, but it turns out that some are more important than others, and contribute more to the overall performance.

18. The reference is here to the line connecting Veblen, Commons and Mitchell to the more recent contributions by Coase, North, Williamson and others. See Hodgson (1993a) for an assessment and a discussion of the main differences between the 'old' and 'new' institutionalism.

19. For comprehensive surveys see, for instance, Samuels (1989), Hodgson (1993a), Hodgson *et al.* (1994). For the relationships among institutions, technological change and system approach, see Johnson (1992) and Edquist and Johnson (1997).

20. The opposite case, that is, institutions resulting from organisations, means that some organisations are hosts to specific institutions. However, either the resulting institution is not an institution in the proper sense, because it constrains only a subset of the whole population of agents (thus on the basis of a more general rule), or it is the result of an organisation which determines the constraints to action (for example, quality standard-setting). This occurs on the basis again of broader principles (such as minimum level of customer satisfaction) which could however be made explicit and implemented in many other different ways.

21. That develop competencies relating to routinised search activities for the creation (or the absorption) and the exploitation of new knowledge.

22. Providing and implementing technology policies (such as patents, procurement and patronage policies), standards, etc.

23. Other differences can be singled out among various types of institutions, in relation, for instance, to the production and distribution of knowledge, etc.

24. A similar approach is social constructivism, which develops a sociological point of view about the idea of a technological system. See, for instance, Pinch and Bijker (1984), Bijker *et al.* (1989). There is also another very important related field of inquiry, which will not be touched upon here, linked to the political role of technology (Mumford, 1964). On this see, for instance, MacKenzie and Wajcman (1985), and in particular Winner (1985), and Feenberg (1991).
25. For instance, on the concept of post-innovation performance, see Georghiou *et al.* (1986).
26. Because of the possibility for a particular configuration to dominate not merely in technological but rather in techno-economic terms, this last might not be the most desirable outcome in terms of global results (David, 1985; Arthur, 1989 and 1994).
27. For more thorough accounts see, among many, Pelikan (1988), Teece (1988), Foss (1993) and (1996), Carlsson and Eliasson (1994).
28. Given that this is a very idiosyncratic summary, focused only on some specific topics related to these system concepts, no thorough coverage is here provided of the literature.
29. It must be strongly stressed that the various concepts of NSI developed are quite different (see, for instance, McKelvey (1991) for a review of the differences among the various notions proposed). However, here the focus will be on common elements and definitions rather than on differences. An attempt at building a unitary framework of analysis has been recently put forward by Edquist (1997a) under the more general heading of Innovation Systems.
30. In terms of differential rates of efficiency in production and innovation and relatedly in the rates of adoption, of market shares, income and employment.
31. '[A] technological system may be described as a network of agents interacting in the economic/industrial area under a particular institutional infrastructure and involved in the generation, diffusion, and utilisation of technology' (Carlsson and Stankiewicz, 1991, p. 94).
32. 'Technological systems contain messy, complex, problem-solving components [and] include organizations, such as manufacturing firms, utility companies, and investment banks, and they incorporate components usually labelled scientific [...] Legislative artifacts, such as regulatory laws, can also be part of technological systems' (Hughes, 1989, p. 51).
33. '[A technology support system] is reflected in an institutional division of labor between organizations that respond to different incentives and that are effective in developing technology only to the extent that they are connected or bridged together' (De Liso and Metcalfe, 1996, p. 89).

2. The technological system

Let us briefly review the main points up to now. First of all, technological change has a mixed nature. It comes out neither as pure autonomous supply push, nor as a pure endogenous product of consumers' needs. Hence, a framework is needed to cope with the complex nature of technological progress. Furthermore, the scope for technical advance is to be seen as a consequence of the competition between agents struggling for a safe and unassailable position. These goals can only be reached by constantly pursuing differential behaviour. The only way for an entrepreneur to gain economic ground in a territory already conquered and divided is to destroy the preceding situation in order to create the opportunity for gaining a newly created dominant position. Focusing on diversity and ever-changing situations leads us to move from the representative agent, who, from this point of view, no longer represents anything. Furthermore, the transmission and elaboration of information is of crucial importance. Agents share common beliefs and recognise the exchange of (and the access to) flows of information as strategically important.

These ideas can boil down to the idea that firms and the related technologies are multidimensional entities interacting with their 'internal' and 'external' environment, by exchanging flows of matter and information in a complex way: hence the necessity for a system approach to the analysis of techno-economic change. The system analysis developed in the previous chapter will now form the basis for the construction of the concept of technological system (TS). Two final pieces of methodology need to be spelled out in order to proceed to the construction of the TS and an explanation of its dynamics. The first concerns the use of an evolutionary methodology. Indeed, as has already been said, the TS is based on a methodology which allows for an explanation of how diversity is first generated and then selected to determine the evolution of the system. This is done by resorting to an evolutionary epistemology which describes the patterns of the growth of knowledge. In fact, as the process of technological change is mainly focused on how knowledge is translated into market performance, the growth of knowledge becomes the central epistemological issue for the construction of a system perspective on the process of techno-economic change.

The second methodological step to construct the TS is related to the distinction between science, technology and technique. This is done in order to separate logically, rather than practically, the *loci* of tacit and codified knowledge. This is central to the construction of the TS proposed and has implications for the cognitive and instrumental contents of the activities related to the various building blocks of the TS.[1]

2.1   ON METHODOLOGY

2.1.1   Evolutionary Epistemology

The process of technological change unfolds with the translation of abstract knowledge into revealed market performance. Different processes are at issue: the genesis of technological and scientific knowledge, its transformation into technical constructs and their development into saleable artefacts through a process of interaction with market forces.

The growth of knowledge is therefore a central epistemological issue which amounts to explaining the continuities and discontinuities shaping the historical evolution of human knowledge. A shift from physics, a metaphor we used in the previous chapter, to evolutionary epistemology is called for:

> Evolution is a process in which information regarding the environment is literally incorporated, incarnated, in surviving organisms through a process of adaptation. Adaptation is [...] an increment in knowledge. (Bartley, 1987, p. 23)

According to this view, scientific knowledge grows and develops as a result of variation and selective retention (Campbell, 1987b) or, in Popper's words, by conjecture and refutation.[2] Human knowledge is a result of two interacting factors: biological and social evolution. Indeed, a theory must undergo a process of 'natural selection':

> How and why do we accept one theory in preference to others? The preference is certainly not due to anything like an experimental justification of the statements composing the theory; it is not due to a logical reduction of the theory to experience. We choose the theory which best holds its own in competition with other theories; the one which, by natural selection, proves itself the fittest to survive. This will be the one which not only has hitherto stood up to the severest tests, but the one which is also testable in the most rigorous way. A theory is a tool which we test by applying it, and which we judge as to its fitness by the results of its applications. (Popper, cited in Campbell, 1987a, p. 49)

But there is also a process of 'social selection':

> We do not know: we can only guess. And our guesses are guided by the unscientific, the metaphysical (though biologically explicable) faith in laws, in regularities which we can uncover-discover. Like Bacon, we might describe our own contemporary science – 'the method of reasoning which men now ordinarily

apply to nature' – as consisting of 'anticipations, rash and premature' and as 'prejudices'. (Popper, cited in Campbell, 1987a, p. 53)

Therefore, two components define the nature of the evolution of scientific and technological knowledge: its testability, and the socio-cultural nature of the community of its practitioners. Furthermore, for the process of variation and selective retention to gain meaningful results, three mechanisms are vital: (i) a mechanism for the generation of variety, (ii) one for generating a consistent selection process, and (iii) a mechanism for the preservation and the diffusion of the characteristics selected. What is noteworthy is that selection mechanisms are ordered in 'nested hierarchies' (Campbell, 1987a). These different mechanisms of selection act with a multi-layered perspective, from the system level (that is, the organism-environment interactions) to more elementary ones. Different kinds of selection are also at work: from the physical elimination of the deviant, to trial-and-error adaptation (that is, from natural selection to adaptive learning). To be sure, a significant number of trials and of consequent errors is needed at each level for the process of selection to operate.

Selection mechanisms are thus acting at different levels (system, organisation, individual) with feedback and interactions, both vertical (the level of selection) and horizontal (different kinds of selection), defining the final result of the process (or better, its disequilibrium dynamics).

2.1.2 Variety, Unit of Selection and Selection Mechanism

Focusing on variety and selection mechanism means, first of all, to define the unit of analysis. Every system (and consequently each of its sub-systems) is defined on the basis of a bounded set of elements developing mutual relationships among them. This definition implies a degree of consistency among the elements of the system in order to establish its separateness from the surrounding environment (comprising other systems and related sub-systems as well). Furthermore, because a TS is characterised by multi-dimensionality, every sub-system has the same general properties (isomorphism). Therefore, it seems useful to rely on an analogy with the concept of autopoietic systems which:

> are systems that are defined as unities as network of production of components that recursively, through their interactions, generate and realize the network that produces them and constitute, in the space in which they exist, the boundaries of the network as components that participate to the realization of the network. (Maturana, cited in Luhmann, 1990, p. 3)[3]

Therefore, the system dynamics emerges as the self-organised result of a multi-layered process of selection.[4] The selection mechanism can be seen as a push-and-pull device made up of positive and negative inducements. The most important negative inducement is obviously the degree of market competition faced by the firms. Several dimensions are related to it: the price structure, the speed of other firms' reaction to deviant behaviours and, of course, the number of firms that actually react to it. The rate of growth of the market is an important mechanism too: related to the degree of competition itself, but to other variables as well. The positive inducements are represented by incentives such as: the degree of monopoly to be eventually obtained, again the price structure of the market, and the perspectives of locking out rivals by undertaking certain actions earlier. It must however be stressed that positive and negative inducements are more a matter of subjective than objective perception. That is, the firm may attach greater value to a certain loss than it would attach to a gain of equal amount. This has obvious implications for the firm's behaviour in terms of either its conservativeness or progressiveness, and, of course, it is another source of variety in the firm's behaviour.

2.2   SCIENCE, TECHNOLOGY AND TECHNIQUE

In order to define science, a distinction must first be made between analytical and empirical sciences. The difference between the two lies in the possibility for direct experience to accept or refute the validity of certain statements. Analytical sciences (for example, mathematics and logic) do not allow in principle this role to practical experience, while empirical sciences do. This latter can in turn be divided into pure (physics, chemistry, etc.) and applied sciences (engineering, medicine, etc.). While a distinction between pure and applied sciences is fairly arbitrary, it can be said that in some ways they fulfil both a cognitive and an instrumental task, but these two tasks are mixed together in different proportions. Therefore, cognitive elements are preponderant in pure sciences, while instrumental elements are preponderant in applied sciences. Indeed, in pure science, statements are assumed to have a sufficiently high degree of reliability despite the fact that their specific usefulness may be questioned. On the contrary, applied sciences assume usefulness as a landmark, while the degree of reliability may, in principle, not necessarily be high (that is, theoretical understanding plays a less important role). Although there obviously exists neither an absolute nor a generally accepted boundary line between the two, ultimately the difference can be summarised in the following two statements: 'believing for the sake of knowing' or 'believing for the sake of doing' (Mattessich, 1978).

The definition of technology with respect to applied science is puzzling. These two closely related notions can be seen either as the two poles of a continuum with boundaries fairly impossible to define, or as synonymous. At the very least they both refer to the same concept of 'applicability' of scientific ideas. For the sake of the argument of this chapter, it is useful to distinguish the two by attributing to technology a more 'pragmatic' nuance, while to applied science a more 'rational' nuance. Therefore, statements scrutinised for the sake of doing so in a technological domain can be referred to a very experimental setting, while in the applied science domain they are closely linked to the truthfulness of the statement itself. Focusing on different nuances allows technology and science to be dealt with as separate but largely overlapping bodies. The common area is the *locus* where the information exchange from one to the other implies very deep interrelationships, extensive reformulation of problems, of consequent solutions, and seldom sparks of creativity. In this 'common space', problems and individuals are often mixed, thus creating a great deal of information transfer. Furthermore, a great deal of work for the maintenance of the communication channels is related to it. The community of technological practitioners is very mixed and comprises manufacturers, civilian and military users, governmental agencies, scientific organisations related to government, private agents, university and non-profit organisations.

Referring to technology mainly as a body of knowledge overlooks two other related dimensions of technological activity: skills and artefacts. We will therefore refer to these two further dimensions under the separate heading of technique. The definition of technique is then simply inferred from that already given for technology: that is, a bunch of skills and of practical knowledge necessary to translate technological knowledge into marketable artefacts.

Partitioning technology and technique in such a way is a useful methodological device that helps in highlighting some interesting features of TS. However, it is fairly obvious that, as with the boundary between science and technology, we are confronted with moving borders, crossed by multidimensional flows of energy and matter in both directions. It must thus be clearly stated that, rather than proposing a 'pipeline' view of science, technology and technique (in this regard, as already said, the TS view strongly emphasises the existence of non-linear mechanisms), the separation of the two concepts of technology and technique is a methodological tool that serves the purpose of building the concept of the TS. Thus, technology and technique are frequently mixed together in a common physical space (for example, the firm), but even so different functions of the firm can be assigned to different scopes. In so doing, it is possible, for instance, to assign a technological role to the firm's R&D department and a technical role to the firm's production line, subject of course to loops and feedback. Technology and technique must thus be perceived as pertaining to different conceptual, if not physical, domains.

Having assigned to technology a knowledge dimension, the conversion of knowledge into artefacts implies the design of a project, starting from the generation of an idea, passing through a multilevel and hierarchical complex web of skill-knowledge relationships, and arriving at the realisation of a marketable artefact.[5] Loops and feedback take place during the unfolding of such a process. The unintended, involuntary result of the interactions between the various components of the system (engineers, scientists and some components of the economic sub-system) contributes to the construction of what can be referred to as standard reference practice.

2.3   THE SYSTEM COMPONENTS

Having delineated all the background elements, it is now possible to define the composition and the behaviour of the TS. The TS is composed of a certain number of interacting blocks, the focus being on linkages and feedback processes rather than on the number and the consistency of the various building blocks. In fact, although there is a close relationship between the number and the consistency of the blocks and the number and the intensity of the linkages, this relationship is neither univocal nor fixed. The state of a TS is indeed the result of a complex historical process, which continuously shapes the relationships among blocks, according to the factors and forces mentioned in the previous chapter. They happen to be at work with different timings and different degrees of synchronisation, thus determining very singular self-reinforcing processes of change over time. Moreover, because of the inherent non-linearities characterising the system relationships, the building blocks are both determinants and results of the overall dynamics, so that peculiar macro-processes of feedback are continuously at work in such a hierarchical context. Therefore, as already said, a multi-layer evolutionary process is constantly pushing the TS morphology.

A TS is constituted by four main building blocks: (i) a hard core of technological and scientific knowledge, (ii) a constellation of technical systems, (iii) the market environment and (iv) the institutional interface (Figure 2.1).

These building blocks are open sub-systems, constantly exporting entropy in order to maintain stability. Their behaviour is the self-organised result of micro-diversity. Flows of matter and information are thus the main determinants of the system's behaviour (Saviotti and Metcalfe, 1991, p. 8).

The TS is therefore composed of four different hierarchically related interacting blocks, with the hard core of scientific and technological knowledge at its centre. This last building block exchanges flows of matter and information with a constellation of firms, which are related to each other by functional relations (both horizontal and vertical). These clusters of firms, which may or may not extend beyond sectoral boundaries, are here termed technical systems in order to stress the different nature of the 'knowledge base' (as it has been made clear in the preceding paragraph) of this building block with the hard core. Four different clusters of firms (four different technical systems) are, for instance, depicted in Figure 2.1. The technical system also has a set of relationships with the market, while the hard core is only related to the technical systems, thus depicting the TS as a hierarchical structure.

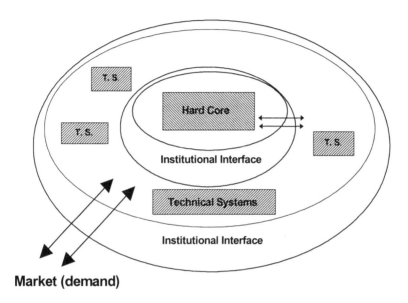

Figure 2.1   The technological system

A further dimension that characterises the technological system is given by the presence of the institutional interface. This building block is the most difficult to sketch out, since it has two simultaneous functions. On the one hand, it is a proper building block that interacts with the rest of the system, and it has the peculiarity of being the only one for which it is possible to establish linkages with all the other blocks. On the other hand, it is also the connecting principle regulating the exchanges between the various building blocks. Indeed, since it defines the basic principles according to which signals travel among blocks, it constitutes a common set of agreed fundamental rules regulating the transmission of signals within the technological system. In particular, it refers to the set of rules to which the establishment, activation, deactivation and maintenance of the linkages must conform, or are required to conform, as a prevailing custom or standard.

This brief description of the main elements of the TS will now be integrated by a further description, first, of the characteristics of the various building blocks, and secondly of the system's dynamics.

2.3.1   The Hard Core

The hard core is made up of two overlapping halves: science and technology. Its main organisations (universities, other non-profit research centres, and private and public R&D laboratories) carry on different stages of production, testing and experimentation of knowledge. Consistency is the focus of their activity. The process of evolution refers to the already mentioned process of conjecture and refutation of knowledge. The methodological discipline is defined as a set of consistent rules (research programmes), such as positive and negative heuristics agreed by a community of practitioners (Lakatos, 1978).

The production of knowledge follows a process of evolution that is context-dependent, based on different institutional arrangements with moving boundaries between science and technology. A scientific research project develops into a codified, widely appropriable technological base, according to a process of co-evolution between the hard core and the constellation of technical systems. The technical systems ask for very particular and very applied solutions, while the hard core moves from very general and fundamental principles. The resulting flows exchange (which is highly dependent on the institutional context) is the dynamic solution to these two contradictory pushes. Only if the technical system can appropriate a subset of these flows, can a process of innovation start.

2.3.2   The Constellation of Technical Systems

This sub-system refers to a complex web of interrelationships between knowledge and skills, aimed at producing saleable artefacts. The relevant organisations adopt knowledge inputs from the hard core, process it by means of their own body of skills and knowledge, and, after a process of loops and feedback with the market, they transform knowledge from public and codified into appropriable and tacit.

The process of evolution (in contrast to that undergone by the hard core) is deployed at a twofold level. On the one hand, the technical system must display enough competencies to be positively selected with respect to the scientific and technological knowledge made available by the hard core. On the other hand, it must be able to cope with the market, and, ultimately, to generate such a productive performance as to be positively selected by it. This twofold process attains different domains. Among these, the ability to cope with the hard core confers long-run technical perspectives (dynamic efficiency), while the ability to cope with the market forces confers short-run economic perspectives (static efficiency).

2.3.3 The Market

The market environment is made up of institutions that select firms within the technical system (buying certain goods instead of others) and, in turn, are selected by the technical system (that employs and remunerates some units instead of others). The institutions involved (that is, households and the government) adopt and select technical change, as embodied in the artefacts they decide to buy and in the jobs they are involved in. Indeed, the power of positive or negative selection is effective only if members of the market have the necessary means for forcing the (money dependent) selection process.[6] The selection mechanism generates multidimensional flows, to which the technical systems react by trying to 'cope with and absorb' the stimuli coming from the market.

2.3.4 The Institutional Interface

As already said, the institutional interface is a very complex sub-system because of its twofold nature. On the one hand, it is a proper sub-system, with its own institutions (for example, the government and the public administration), internal rules and processes of evolution. On the other hand, it is the bridge connecting all the other sub-systems. It has the crucial role of conveyor of all the signals travelling from one sub-system to another, and as such, it may have different effects on the flows exchange: slow-down,[7] acceleration, deflection, etc. Therefore, as a combination of these two aspects, the main features of the institutional interface lie in the possibility of creating and modifying flows. It may be either complementary or subsidiary to the flow exchange, it may contrast or favour lock-ins, and it may or may not sponsor some technical solutions instead of others.

2.4 THE SYSTEM DYNAMICS

The TS dynamics results from the interactions among the building blocks. Flows are thus both the results and the determinants of the system's behaviour in a complex process of loops and feedback. Structural tensions among sub-systems, like the differential voltage between electric components, may act as catalyst of both continuous and discontinuous change. The direction and the consistency of the flows are thus relevant features, but although the former is definite, the latter is not. Indeed, the hard core supplies the technical systems with flows of science and technology, and the technical systems supply the market with goods. The reverse holds for the market that supplies information about the relevant characteristics of the consumer goods, and for the technical systems, supplying information about the relevant characteristics of the production processes adopted. What is important for the TS dynamics is the idea that differences in the consistency of these flows are the fundamental driving force, and, in this regard, the institutional interface plays a major role.

The hard core and the technical systems links aim at techno-economic performances, which are the result of two different, contrasting, needs. On the one hand, the technical systems are constantly looking for innovative actions with the highest possible degree of tacitness and appropriability. On the other hand, the intrinsic scientific nature of the hard core drives research towards fundamental and general results. Innovation is thus the result of this trade-off (Leoncini, 1997).

The interactions between market and technical systems are the driving force of the canonical diffusion stage. At this level, diffusion has the twofold nature of radical and incremental, according to the degree of overflowing that the market can exert on the technical systems. For instance, structural change occurs if an increasing number of firms are unable to satisfy an increasing number of market signals in order to start a feedback process with respect to the hard core. If this process is large enough, in terms of both strength and number of flows involved, it may force a redefinition of the science and technology relationships (that is, the science and technology base on which the firms build their economic performance). What is thus needed is a clustering of firms increasingly more in search of a yet unknown solution to certain market needs. And this puzzle can be resolved only in the higher instance constituted by the hard core.

At this stage, technicalities take the lead with respect to technology, and the parameters of reference become essentially those relating to some index of performance. Yet, marginal improvements are continuous in order to tune up the relationships of the system. Both positive and negative bottlenecks can take place at this stage, such as, for instance, reverse salient (Hughes, 1989) and/or functional failures (Constant, 1980). Some components of a larger whole may lag behind in terms of technical efficiency. Alternatively, the whole system may encounter limitations in its performance at a level not foreseen by the technological knowledge that has generated it. These facts may well start a feedback process with the technological side in order to eliminate the bottlenecks.

Depending on the tightness of the systemic relationships between different components, the development of a new component can imply either no cross-effects (the two components are disjoint), or weak cross-effects (one component marginally influences the other, implying that they are complementary, at least to a certain degree), or strong cross-effects (co-evolution). The latter is typical of a system type of relationship.

It must be underlined that the two processes of production and marketing of an innovation are interrelated and mostly contemporary. There is neither a linear sequence of steps from the hard core to the market, nor a process leading to the 'discovery' of consumers' preferences, but rather technical systems face continuous push-and-pull mechanisms.

On the market side, the relationship is between the capability of satisfying consumers' needs with an adequate heterogeneity of supply, and the speed of absorption of the internal market with respect to the foreign one. On the hard core side, there is a link between the number and the intensity of signals that the firms can process for their technical needs, and the degree to which the technological change produced by the hard core can be incorporated into new production processes. Feedbacks are thus acting to constantly reshape relationships. This fact determines a double selection mechanism (economic and technological), which co-evolves according to the strength of the flows, and is in turn determined by the interactions between these building blocks and the institutional interface. Depending on its characteristics, the TS develops different structural and institutional configurations for, as already mentioned, the main traits of a TS depend on the types and consistency of flows linking the sub-systems.

The institutional interface acts as both a bridging and a catalyst institution, insofar as it creates and modifies, boosts and tampers with the strength and the direction of the signals from one block to another. Thus, *ceteris paribus*, two TS, differing only in institutional interface behaviour, will show completely different dynamics and completely different techno-economic performances. This feature seems interesting in that it allows for an explicit embodiment of the role of institutions (and of institutional change). Indeed, it is possible to discuss how a certain institutional set-up is related to a certain performance, that is, for example, to connect national characteristics to models of capitalism.

Finally, as far as the stability of the various building blocks is concerned, the hard core is to be regarded as the most stable of the components of the TS. Its own nature (in terms of capability of absorbing shocks) and the surrounding institutional interface (presuming that it is usually in the institutional interface interest to preserve the hard core from crumbling easily) ensure a very high degree of stability to the hard core. The technical system is less stable, having to deal with two kinds of different (and sometimes contrasting) signals, coming respectively from the hard core and from the market. Technical systems are therefore forced to fluctuate between 'hard core pushes' and 'market pulls'. Finally, the more volatile of the building blocks is the market. In fact, it has direct linkages with the technical system (through the institutional interface) and, furthermore, it is only through this last mediation that its signals can influence the hard core.

2.5   HOW THE SYSTEM WORKS

It is now possible to describe in detail how a TS works. During 'normal' periods, the clusters of firms in the constellation of technical systems behave according to certain, more or less fixed techno-economic rules. These rules have been defined and agreed upon by a community of techno-scientific practitioners. They should, in fact, have previously targeted a certain research project and, in the course of its development, they implicitly define conditions for it to be transferred, by means of certain technological criteria, to the technical side. In this way, the importance of the role that a certain research project exerts on the hard core side is confronted with the need for a certain degree of appropriability, which is necessary for the cluster of firms to expect potential profits.

As already noted, the relationships between science and technology, and between technology and techniques are non-linear. Therefore, a research project can be generated without a previous sound scientific base, while some technical conditions that have to be satisfied may constrain the whole process (for example, reverse salient and/or functional failure). However complicated the genesis of an innovation is, the non-linear 'science push' stage of the process starts once an agreed set of relationships between the hard core and the technical system has been established, and once a process of evolution and selection, based essentially on the capability of generating and processing knowledge, has taken place.

The firms in the technical system are thus trying to adapt themselves (through a process of copying and absorbing shocks) to the ever changing market environment by making use of their internal resources: essentially skills and, to a lesser extent, practical knowledge. The mechanism of variation and selective retention in this case is intrinsically economic and confers differential profitability on the different technical configurations (in a broad sense, including organisation).

The 'demand pull' stage is thus an incremental one, essentially based on the limited capability of the various firms constituting the technical system to give satisfactory answers to the challenges coming from the market side. The set of possible answers is bounded by definition. This holds true because it is a characteristic of the technical system to apply practical and organisational skills to a body of scientific and technological knowledge produced outside it.[8]

Radical changes can thus originate only in the body of knowledge produced in the hard core, either as an endogenous non-linear process, or as a reaction to increasing pressure from the technical system. In this case, the interactions between hard core and technical systems may lead either to radical innovations, or to structural changes in the knowledge base of the whole TS (if the feedback process starts to involve an ever-increasing number of units). In fact, on the one hand, the level of stress is due to rise because the technical system does not succeed in coping with the market pressures. Thus, while the economic prospects keep fading, the inability of the technical system to modify such a situation will be completely transferred to the hard core. This, in turn, will try to produce the new (radically different) body of knowledge required. On the other hand, it may well be the case that, if the unmet demand of a certain technical system has a certain degree of generality, other technical systems will experience fading profits too, related to the same technological bottleneck. This is the case in which a structural change in the hard core may be due to happen. In this case, the theoretical and methodological premises upon which a certain research programme is based collapses, to be substituted by a new set that (in a Kuhnian sense) will both replicate the old results and cope with the new challenges.

Finally, an example is provided to better explain the working of a TS. Let us consider the problem of pollution and the environment. Apparently, on the demand side, there is a growing consensus that something should be done in order to avoid natural resources depletion, pollution and health-related problems. There is also a growing concern about future generations. This concern must become so-to-say very relevant, in order to force significant changes in the technical systems, and so as not to be significantly altered by the social institutional interface. Indeed, the firms have started to adjust marginally to these 'demand-pull' *stimuli*, trying to cope with the challenge and absorb it into the next generation of technical practices. However, the technical systems' reaction is generally that of reducing pollution given a more or less invariant technological knowledge base. Alternatively, technology might adjust according to slightly different criteria (for example, design for recycling, design for dismantling, etc.), but being still locked in a sort of 'hard core mentality' that looks at these problems as an unsolvable trade-off between environment and well-being. Only a discrete, structural change in the knowledge base is likely to produce new environment-compatible technologies (which are those required by the market). Indeed, this is a challenge to the hard core of the system, rather than to the single firms of the technical system itself.

However, a major, qualitative change in technology will eventually be produced only if firms become more and more unable to cope with the present situation, thus starting an increasing feedback process towards the hard core. Also in this case, the social institutional interface is likely to intervene in order to mediate and to smooth out the signals. This happens to keep the hard core as stable as possible, rather than contributing to send additional feedback signals to the hard core,[9] on the assumption that a likely target would be that of maintaining the hard core internal structure stable. A radical shift in environmental policy and technology would therefore be provoked only if the level necessary to trigger a structural change in the technological knowledge of the hard core were to be overcome on the market side.[10]

NOTES

1. As will be clear in the following, this distinction is logical and relates to functions that in some cases can hardly be separable. In spite of this, it is always possible, *in principle*, to apply the same distinction.

2. For a recollection of Popper's influence on economics, see, for instance, De Marchi (1988) and Caldwell (1991).

3. It is not the purpose of this chapter to pursue the argument further. It is only argued here that since communication is an essential feature of an open system: 'communication is an evolutionary potential for building up systems that are able to maintain closure under the condition of openness. These systems face the continuing necessity to select meanings that satisfy these constraints. The result is our well-known societies' (Luhmann, 1990, p. 13).

4. Although we are actually interested in the whole system as a unit of analysis, eventually undergoing the process of selection, the unit of selection can also be defined at different levels. A technology, a technique, a firm's organisation, etc., can all undergo such a process. For instance, the firm's organisation level appears to be useful in studying how technical change is brought about and in turn brings qualitative changes. Indeed, by defining firms as social organisations, for instance, we are building another level at which selection occurs. It is thus possible to take into account the interactions between people inside and outside the firm: these are structured by the organisation of the firm and in turn determine how the various functions are assigned, how the decision processes are undertaken, etc. A process of trial-and-error and of learning how to cope with the outside environment is thus incorporated in firm behaviour.

5. A related point is that of technological styles (Hughes, 1989, p. 69). Clearly, there are historical, geographical, institutional and national reasons for the existence of different technological styles, but one powerful explanation can be found in the separation drawn between technology and technique. Once a body of knowledge has been generated, agreed, refined and published on books and scientific journals, it obviously relies everywhere on the same principles. However, the actual implementation and the technical performance refer to a body of skills that are less general, frequently tacit, and refer to contingent environments and values. It has to be noted, incidentally, that the concept of technological style can account for another powerful source of variety.

6. It has to be noted that almost all the literature on this subject neglects the twin role of the market, by focusing almost totally on the supply side.

7. See, for instance, Cantelon (1995) for an account of the crucial role of the USA Federal Communications Commission in blocking post-war commercial development of microwave telephony for nearly a quarter of century, by favouring AT&T backward cable technology.

8. It must be stressed again that the distinction between hard core and technical system is horizontal, and still holds in the case of large corporations with R&D facilities producing basic research (that is, with a vertical integration of the different functions related to technology). In this case there are still selection (the appropriate technology, on the hard core side, and the appropriate technique, on the technical side) and limited capability. A feedback process is in fact needed, between the different levels of a corporation, to overcome eventual bottlenecks, or to go beyond very limited technological capabilities at plant level. Indeed, at this level, operations are carried out in a technical way through skills and organisation.

9. This fact is obviously possible. However, it depends on political rather than on purely economic criteria.

10. Just as an aside, it seems that, at the end, a very relevant issue has surfaced: the relationships between technology and the democratic control of its design (for very interesting insights on this problem see Winner, 1985).

3. Intersectoral innovation flows

As we stressed in the Introduction, a methodology for the empirical analysis of technological systems (TS) should first of all be consistent with a system perspective, and therefore focused on linkages. In this chapter we will argue that a great and important part of the linkages of the TS concept we have developed in the previous chapter can be caught by referring to the innovation diffusion process, in particular to *embodied innovation flows*.

In general terms, embodied innovations can be defined as innovations that materialise in new and/or improved artefacts, which also act as carriers for their diffusion. Our point is that the corresponding innovation flows are extremely important for the analysis of technological systems, both from a theoretical and an empirical perspective. First of all, we will argue that these kinds of embodied flows identify a powerful proxy for those techno-economic interactions framing the notion of TS we are referring to (Section 3.1). Secondly, we will show how, at an intersectoral level, these flows can be measured consistently with respect to different contexts (Section 3.2), thus proving to be functional to the comparisons we will carry out in the next chapters. Finally, we will illustrate the hypotheses and the analytical steps leading to the measurement of such flows in consistent intersectoral matrices (Sections 3.3 and 3.4).

At the beginning it should be pointed out that, although extremely relevant, the embodiment channel is not the exclusive means of diffusion for innovations. On the contrary, they also spread in a disembodied way that operates through what we will call 'pure knowledge spillovers'. These latter flows will not be employed in this book, but their relevance and their specific nature with respect to the former (embodied) flows will be dealt with, for reasons of completeness and differentiation.

3.1   EMBODIED AND DISEMBODIED INNOVATION FLOWS

The distinction between embodied and disembodied technological flows is one of the key issues in studying the innovative diffusion process. The rationale of this distinction can be sketched following the well-known OECD *Report on Technology and the Economy*:

[There is] a fundamental conceptual distinction between two types of technology diffusion. It is the distinction between *disembodied* and *equipment-embodied* technology diffusion. The former is the process whereby technology and know-how spread through channels other than embodiment in machinery. It originates in the *externalities* that characterize the innovation process and the *research spillovers* that occur when the firm developing a new idea or process cannot fully appropriate the results of its innovation. Equipment-embodied diffusion on the other hand is the process whereby innovations spread in the economy through the purchase of technologically-intensive machinery, components and other equipment. (OECD, 1992, p. 48)

The basic idea underlying this distinction is quite clear. Unlike the disembodied one, the embodied diffusion process is driven by a material 'support'. Accordingly, an innovation reaches its user in the form of an artefact, typically a capital good, newly created or simply improved by the innovation producer. The classical example of this process is that of firms with high R&D intensity, in general active in high-tech sectors (e.g. electronics), which sell technologically sophisticated intermediate and/or capital goods to firms which operate in 'downstream' sectors (typically in the services sectors), and which employ these goods as inputs to realize their final output.[1] The destination of a new or improved commodity as one of the components of the final demand represents another example of embodied diffusion.

A first important element therefore emerges. Embodied innovation flows are typically material flows, pertinent to a technological dimension that, following De Liso and Metcalfe (1996), we might refer to as 'artefacts'. As we will see, the adoption of an intersectoral perspective makes it possible to measure also immaterial kinds of flows, which are pertinent to another technological dimension that can be referred to as 'knowledge'.[2]

A second relevant point has to do with the 'techno-economic' nature of embodied innovation flows, at least in two respects.

1. First of all, by definition, these flows are strictly correlated with those 'economic' flows which occur within the 'structure' and the 'transformation apparatus' of the production system (Quadrio Curzio and Scazzieri, 1983), that is, one of the constitutive component of the TS. Indeed, embodied innovation flows are the result of interactive relationships between producers and users (in the present approach, basically firms) which are mainly, although not exclusively, of an economic-productive nature (Montresor, 1996). Recalling the well-known 'interactive-learning' approach developed by Lundvall (1992a), the economic distance between producer and user is, in this kind of process, at least as relevant as other forms of distance (that is, 'geographical', 'organisational' and 'cultural'). Accordingly, the input-output structure of one economy, measured by the corresponding national accounting tables, and studied through the tools of the intersectoral analysis, becomes a crucial element in studying a TS:

In an extended input-output table (a table where deliveries of capital goods are included and where organisations, producing science and technology, are represented as sectors), the economic distances between different activities are indicated by the prevailing set of input-output coefficients. [...] Actually, the unit of analysis discussed so far, the user-producer dyad, is defined as the combination of units, as close to each other as possible, measured in this dimension. (Lundvall, 1992a, pp. 54-56)

The reference to the 'producer-user' approach allows us to stress the interactive nature of the embodied diffusion process, and its relevance for system analyses such as that of the present book. With respect to the embodiment channel, the boundaries between innovation diffusion and production are in fact more blurred than with respect to the disembodiment channel. Indeed, the techno-economic interaction with an actual or a potential user is not a mere pre-condition for an innovative producer to be able to transfer his/her innovation. On the contrary, the user plays an extremely important role both in the development of an innovation, by disclosing to the producer his/her needs and his/her desiderata, and in its implementation, for example, through 'reverse engineering' processes.[3] Among the possible users of an innovation, final consumers have to be considered too. Indeed, they are able to affect the diffusion process both through 'advanced' and specialist requirements (Porter, 1990), and through their influence on the total production coefficients which determine the economic distance between producer and user firms (Miller and Blair, 1985). Indeed, as we will see, this is a further techno-economic characterisation of the embodiment diffusion process.
2. In addition to the 'conducive' role played with respect to them by the production system, a further element which makes of the embodied diffusion a techno-economic kind of flow is the influence of the relevant market structure. Furthermore, as the market structure within which innovative actors operate is also affected by the relevant institutional context (such as, for example, the legislation on firms' competition, and the anti-trust authorities), embodied flows allow us to refer, although only implicitly, to a further constitutive sub-system of our TS notion, namely the institutional set-up.

While embodied innovation flows have the twofold techno-economic nature we have sketched above, disembodied ones are usually identified as purely technological. However, in our opinion, the 'standard' equivalence, between disembodied flows and spillovers, on the one hand, and embodied flows and equipment transfers, on the other, is not entirely accurate, as it neglects some other relevant aspects of the diffusion process.[4]
As far as the disembodied diffusion process is concerned, the reference to 'anonymous', that is, agent-independent spillovers cannot neglect the fact that the effective diffusion of public forms of knowledge requires that the

innovative user builds up an adequate 'absorptive capacity' (Cohen and Levinthal, 1989) also through deliberated R&D. R&D investments are in fact extremely relevant also in the diffusion, and not only in the innovation production process.[5]

As far as the embodiment diffusion process is concerned, a particular kind of spillover can be identified also with respect to them, so that spillover phenomena are not only exclusive of the disembodied process.[6] The crucial point in this last respect is the distinction between 'pure knowledge spillovers', such as those we have referred to above, and 'rent spillovers', which instead are typical of the embodied diffusion process. Following Griliches (1979), the latter would consist of those economic advantages granted to those firms which acquire an 'innovated' intermediate or capital good as a result of the fact that their producers are not able to appropriate entirely the 'surplus' embodied in the good itself.[7] The classical example is that of the productivity advantage acquired by a firm through an 'innovated' capital good. In fact, such an advantage cannot be entirely counterbalanced by the price increase which reflects the performance improvement of the capital good (Verspagen, 1997). This occurs because the producer is not able to charge the user a price which fully covers this performance improvement. In so doing, he/she grants the user a special 'rent spillover', in the form of an improved quality-price ratio, whose extent depends on the competitiveness degree of the industry (or the economic system, following an intersectoral perspective) in which the exchange occurs. Indeed, the less competitive the market, the greater the monopoly power of the producer, and the lower is the entailing 'rent spillover'. This last observation therefore introduces a further element in the techno-economic characterisation of embodied flows. Such innovation flows do not exclusively depend on the magnitude and direction of the production flows by which they are carried – the former of the two techno-economic aspects we have analysed – but also on the inner structure of the market (and of the institutional apparatus which influences the market) within which they occur.

On the basis of the previous theoretical insights, it appears evident that the reference to the embodied (intersectoral) diffusion process of innovation allows us to retain some of the crucial elements of the 'broad' notion of TS we are dealing with. On the other hand, it would be as important to consider those innovation flows which have a more genuine technological nature, as they are less dependent on producer-user relationships, such as the 'pure knowledge' spillovers we have referred to above. This latter extension would also be necessary in the light of the need to integrate the analysis of material technological aspects – such as those represented by embodied flows – with that of immaterial elements. As we have previously said, these latter flows will not be directly considered in the applications of this book. Their relevance, along with the problems entailed by the construction of the relative matrices, will however be discussed only for reasons of completeness and distinction.

3.2   INTERSECTORAL EMBODIED INNOVATION FLOWS: A
        CONCISE REVIEW OF THE EMPIRICAL LITERATURE

As we have shown, embodied innovation flows constitute a good 'theoretical' proxy of the interactive relationships of a TS. The choice of an intersectoral perspective makes them convenient also from an empirical point of view. Indeed, not only do intersectoral flows reflect the production structure of an economy, and the linkages entailed by the nature of the available technologies, they can also be more promptly and properly measured than at other levels of analysis, such as, for example, at the firm level. This latter point has been clearly recognised by the empirical literature on innovation diffusion, which has stressed several conceptual and practical problems of measuring innovation flows from one firm to another.[8] Such problems become particularly relevant when inter-firm innovation flows are analysed comparatively with respect to different technologies and/or different national contexts. For reasons of data availability, cross-sectional measurements are instead handier to carry out at an intersectoral level. Much of the empirical work on the topic has therefore focused on the intersectoral innovation diffusion process, following different perspectives and techniques.

In what follows, we briefly review the relevant empirical literature in order to show how the reference to embodied intersectoral innovation flows is most consistent with the comparative system focus of our approach. Indeed, the measurement of disembodied intersectoral technological flows can be carried out only under severe assumptions. Also on the basis of this further argument, our choice to focus on embodied, rather than disembodied, flows appears legitimate. Let us consider how these flows can actually be measured.

The first technique we refer to is a direct kind of technique, based on the so-called 'technology surveys' (Papaconstantinou *et al.*, 1996). As is well known, these are surveys which, through the opinion of experts and professionals (that is, scientists, engineers, etc.), aim at identifying the most relevant innovations 'produced' in a certain context (that is, within a country). They then assign them, on the one hand, to those industries, which represent the main economic activity of the innovative firms, and, on the other hand, to those industries in which their 'first' users operate. The most popular example of this technique is still represented by the innovation flows matrices built upon the basis of the famous 'SPRU database' of the University of Sussex (Robson *et al.*, 1988).[9] A more recent example of the same methodology is the study carried out by DeBresson *et al.* (1994). In this study, the results of the ISTAT-CNR Italian innovation survey (1981-1985) are employed to build up 'rectangular' matrices, referring to the producer and user sectors of the innovations 'declared' by the firms in the survey itself.[10] Further examples of the same technique applied to other countries (and regions) are collected in DeBresson (1996, Ch. 6).

The results of these and other similar applications are, of course, extremely useful in mapping the innovative activity of one economy along its constituent sectors. However, the analysis of the firms in a certain survey is necessarily partial, as it is exclusively based on a selected number of 'important' innovations, which are also mainly connected to their principal economic activity.[11] In addition to this 'technical' disadvantage, the corresponding matrices are not entirely consistent with the approach we are developing, for at least two reasons. First of all, at a methodological level, their construction is empirically quite burdensome. The relative data are in fact collected by a limited number of national statistical offices (in the previous cases, Great Britain and Italy), and according to methodological choices which are not perfectly homogeneous and comparable.[12] Furthermore, at a conceptual level, the flows of the corresponding matrices have a 'spurious' nature. Indeed, although they occur on the basis of certain 'economic' relationships, they are also affected by the public nature of the corresponding 'technological' knowledge. The following example, taken from a recent study by Verspagen (1995), helps to better clarify the point:

> the approaches mentioned so far tend to ignore important aspects of the spillover process. [...] because they are based on user-producer relationships, they tend to overlook spillover relations that are more explicitly based on technological linkages between sectors. For example, the technical knowledge in a patent on fertilizers may be useful to a broad range of economic sectors, although the fertilizer itself will probably not be applied outside the agricultural sector. One may think of sectors such as rubber and plastic products or the glass industry, which, by the chemical nature of their technology base, may benefit from technical knowledge on fertilizers, although their relations in terms of user-producer interactions with the fertilizer industry will be marginal. (Verspagen, 1995, p. 2)[13]

The last argument represents the starting point for tackling the complex issue of an adequate measurement of innovation flows which are actually 'direct', so that we will come back to it later in this section.[14] Before that, we should however observe that the same 'spurious flows' problem arises also with respect to a second measurement technique of intersectoral innovation flows. Indeed, this problem also affects those matrices which are based on the use that the firms of a certain sector make of the patents (rather than of the innovations) obtained by firms operating in other industries.

The most popular example is that of the intersectoral technology flows matrix built up by Scherer, mapping the patenting activity of a group of large American companies in the late 1970s (Scherer, 1982, 1984). To be sure, this is an intersectoral R&D flows matrix, obtained by distributing the innovative investments of the companies themselves, disaggregated according to a first sectoral classification, over an opportune (normalised) intersectoral patent matrix.[15] This latter matrix, in turn, is constructed by identifying (through experts' evaluations) the 'sectors' of origin and of potential use of the patents obtained by the same group of firms. As patents are classified in a 'functional' way, that is, according to detailed product codes, their concordance with R&D investments, which are instead classified by industrial sectors, has represented and still represents one of the major problems in using these kinds of patent matrices.[16]

To be sure, this last 'technical' problem has been partially overcome in a more recent application, that of the so-called 'Yale matrix', using the data collected by the Canadian Patent Office. Indeed, this is one of the few Patent Offices assigning each granted patent to those sectors (one or more) which are considered as potential producers of the patented innovation. As each patenting firm is also asked to declare to the same Patent Office the potential user sectors (up to a maximum of three) of the patent, an intersectoral patent matrix, of the kind employed by Scherer, can be obtained straightforwardly. Indeed, the number of patents allocated to a certain sector, and to be used by another sector, has just to be divided by the total number of patents 'produced' by the former, and the procedure repeated for each of the relevant sectors. Following the same 'distribution' technique employed by Scherer, such a matrix has been used, for example, to build up an intersectoral technological flows matrix for the USA (Evenson and Putnam, 1988) and for Italy (Putnam and Evenson, 1994).[17]

Although the problem of the concordance between different classifications can be solved in some way, resorting to patents in the construction of intersectoral innovation flows matrices remains affected by other important technical and conceptual problems. First of all, unlike the innovation matrices we have considered before, those technological exchanges that are measured by patent matrices are potential, rather than actual. Furthermore, as in the previous case, these matrices strictly refer to specific national contexts (in the two studies we have referred to above, the USA and Italy), and their application to different TS, according to the usual 'distribution' technique, is only partially acceptable, as the patenting propensity is presumably different in different countries.[18] In addition to these technical problems, an important conceptual question still affects the use of intersectoral patent matrices. The corresponding flows are even more spurious than in the previous case, as the reference to patents introduces the possibility of 'rent' spillovers which are indistinguishable from 'pure knowledge' ones. The previous example discussed by Verspagen (1995) is still of some help in clarifying the point:

> at least in as far as patent data are used to construct the spillover matrix, the underlying technological knowledge is actually appropriated by the knowledge producer. Using, again, the example of fertilizers, the producer of the innovation, if the patent application is granted, may claim the sole use of the knowledge in the patent, and will therefore be able to charge a mark-up over marginal costs to cover R&D costs. If, in such a case, there would be spillovers (between producer and user of the innovation) at all, they would most certainly contain important rent-spillovers in addition to pure knowledge spillovers, because they are related to the economic transaction, rather than a pure technological link. [...] however,

one may argue that a 'Yale' or Scherer-type matrix captures at least some aspects of pure knowledge-spillovers, if only because economic linkages in the form of user-producer relationships may 'guide' technological efforts by firms to a certain aspect. (Verspagen, 1995, pp. 2-3)

As the quotation suggests, the nature of the flows of a patent matrix remains quite blurred.

Both technical and conceptual problems get substantially attenuated by a third measurement technique of intersectoral innovation flows, based on the use of the input-output tables of a certain country.[19]

The basic idea, originally put forward by Brown and Conrad (1967), is quite simple. Indeed, it consists of mapping technological flows by assuming that the innovations 'produced' by the firms of a certain sector spread to the other sectors, proportionally to the corresponding production flows, as measured by the relevant input-output tables.

In the study by Brown and Conrad the reference is to 'direct' production flows of intermediate goods.[20] More precisely, sectoral R&D expenditure (or employment), taken as an innovation proxy, is 'distributed' intersectorally on the basis of the corresponding matrix of direct production requisites.[21] However, in other subsequent applications, namely that by Terleckyj (1974), the same input-output methodology is applied by assuming that the carriers of intersectoral technological flows are more realistically represented by flows of capital, rather than intermediate, goods. Further refinements are then introduced by Momigliano and Siniscalco (1982), who stress the need to consider both direct and indirect intersectoral production requisites, following the notion of 'vertically integrated sectors' proposed by Pasinetti (1973). Accordingly, the sectoral variables taken as innovation proxies (either R&D or patents) are distributed on the basis of the total requisite matrix derived from the Leontief inverse. Finally, among the other extensions, let us observe that the input-output methodology is not exclusively employed to measure the diffusion process within a certain country.[22] Indeed, further refinements have been introduced to analyse intersectoral innovation diffusion at an international level, mainly by referring to import coefficient matrices.[23]

As is shown by the large number and variety of applications,[24] this third methodology can be more readily implemented than the previous two, based on, respectively, innovations and patents. Indeed, the corresponding matrices can be built up with respect to different countries, by employing input-output tables, which are nowadays available in a homogeneous format, from different international agencies, such as OECD and Eurostat. Furthermore, these input-output tables are available at a sectoral disaggregation level that can be directly matched with that used to measure the relevant innovation proxies. The concordance problems between different sectoral classifications that we have found with respect to the previous techniques are therefore overcome by this third methodology, so that the corresponding flows are both comparable and consistent. However, as we will see, this methodology is not free from other limitations which have to do with the typical hypotheses of input-output analysis, and with other more specific assumptions introduced in building up the relevant innovation matrices.

As far as the nature of these latter flows is concerned, the hypotheses we have discussed above make it clear that they are unequivocally embodied, that is, of the kind we have seen in the previous section. In fact, they are techno-economic flows, based on producer-user relationships of an economic-productive nature. Accordingly, in these latter flows the 'confusion' between spillovers of different kinds is less apparent than with the previous techniques, as the unique spillover typology that can be admitted for them is that of the rent spillovers.

On the basis of the previous argument, it seems to us possible to conclude that the opportunity of founding the TS investigation on embodied intersectoral flows emerges as clearly as from the theoretical analysis of the previous section. This conclusion is also supported by the technical problems one faces in measuring disembodied innovation flows, which are truly direct technological flows. In what follows, some remarks will be provided on this point, as we said, mainly for reasons of completeness and distinction.

The first attempt to measure 'pure knowledge spillovers' can be considered that of Jaffe (1986). Although at a firm level, it was Jaffe who first introduced the idea of 'potential spillover pool' as that generic knowledge stock which cannot be appropriated by the firm that produced it. In spite of its public good character, the benefit that a firm can draw from the knowledge in the pool is however not unlimited. On the contrary, it is the greater, the closer are the firms in technological, rather than in economic terms. In other words, pure knowledge 'spills' more intensively over firms which are more technologically similar. On the basis of this idea, Jaffe tried to develop a way to measure such a technological kind of distance between firms. More precisely, he referred to the distribution of their patents in certain technological areas, and identified their technological proximity by comparing their relative shares.

The seminal approach developed by Jaffe has been later further refined, and its rational has been also extended to intersectoral studies.[25] Among these, we should at least mention that carried out by Goto and Suzuki (1989). In trying to evaluate the R&D impact of the Japanese electronic sector on the other Japanese industries, they tried to measure their relative distance by referring to a product classification of their R&D investments, and by comparing their relative share in a way similar to that proposed by Jaffe.

Although both the techniques we have sketched above refer to spillovers which are more clearly technological than those of the previous matrices, their practical implementation is affected by some drawbacks. The lack of sectoral classification schemes with a suitable level of disaggregation, and the limited possibility of coherently replicating their application in different national and temporal contexts, represent the most crucial disadvantages.[26]

A substantially different approach to the measurement of pure knowledge spillovers is that suggested by Verspagen (1995, 1997). Indeed, in his empirical studies,[27] Verspagen proposes to build up direct technological flows matrices by referring to the patenting procedures of the main international patent offices: the European Patent Office (EPO) and the United States Patents and Trademarks Office (USPTO). More precisely, on the basis of their datasets, Verspagen (1995) constructs three kinds of matrices. The first two, relative to the EPO dataset, are particularly relevant for our analysis. They are identified on the basis of the following instructions provided by the International Patent Classification (IPC) system, according to which:

> Patent documents
> (a) comprise 'invention information', i.e. technical information as defined by the claims, with due regard given to the description and the drawings (if any). The classification symbols allotted should not be restricted to the place or places in the Classification, which cover only one aspect of a technical subject identified. Due regard should also be given to further places in the Classification where non-trivial other aspects of that technical subject may need to be classified;
> (b) may comprise 'additional information', i.e., non-trivial technical information given in the description, which is not claimed and does not form part of the invention as such but might constitute useful information to the searcher. (WIPO, 1989, p. 26, analysed in Verspagen, 1995, p. 3)

The first matrix refers to the distinction contained in point (a). The idea is that 'invention information' which is claimed by the inventor improves not only the technological knowledge, which characterises the invention itself, but also other knowledge fields (that is, codes) which are relevant (that is, non-trivial) for it. The relative matrix is therefore obtained on the basis of a twofold kind of argument. On the one hand, those codes to which the 'principal component' of the claimed information refers, translated into sectoral terms,[28] are considered as proxies of knowledge-producer sectors. On the other hand, the codes referred to by the 'secondary component' of the claimed information (always translated into sectoral terms) are instead taken as proxies of knowledge-user sectors.

Evidently, the resulting matrix has a different nature from those analysed before. Indeed, the technological principle followed in its construction makes it more coherent with the 'pure knowledge' spillover concept we have previously described, while the contamination with other producer-user relationships diminishes.

The pure knowledge spillover nature of these flows appears even more evident in the second EPO matrix, built up by referring to the distinction between points (a) and (b) of the previous quotation. Accordingly, the main 'invention information' of a certain patent is supplemented by 'additional information', which, although not to be claimed by the inventor, might however improve knowledge fields other than that specific to the invention itself. The resulting matrix is therefore obtained by considering the codes to which the information of points (a) and (b) refers, opportunely translated into sectoral terms, as proxy, respectively, of knowledge producer and user sectors.

Unlike the previous two, the third matrix constructed by Verspagen is based on the US patenting system, and on the so-called 'cross citations' practice. As is well known, in this latter case the patent document contains a list of citations of different kinds of scientific sources, and of other patents previously issued by the USPTO, which are deemed relevant by the inventor. Accordingly, each patent is assigned to two series of codes, different from those of the previous matrices: the former, relative to the class of all the 'original' patents; the latter, relative to both original and quoted patents. These two series offer the opportunity to build up an intersectoral innovation matrix by simply considering the codes of the patents, once again translated into sectoral terms. More precisely, the codes of the latter series can be taken as a proxy of producer sectors, and the codes of all the patents series (both original and quoted) as proxy of user sectors. [29]

In spite of the different technique employed, the nature of the flows measured by this third matrix appears quite similar to that of the other two EPO matrices, and distinct from that built up on the basis of the previous input-output techniques.

Once they have been normalised, these matrices, such as the innovation and the patent matrices we have seen before, can also be employed to distribute over them some sectoral innovation proxy (typically the R&D expenditure), and to obtain intersectoral matrices of direct innovation flows with respect to different national contexts. For this reason, also in the present case, the comparability requisite between flows is only partially satisfied. Indeed, although the reference to an international patent office eliminates the problems due to different national patenting procedures, the external patenting propensity remains differentiated, being more or less stimulated by both strategic and structural characteristics. Nonetheless, for the reasons that we have exposed above, this kind of matrix appears the most appropriate to catch flows whose nature is clearly distinct from that of the embodied flows. Accordingly, a possible extension of the approach we have developed in this book should try to explore the potential of this latter technique.

3.3   BUILDING UP INTERSECTORAL EMBODIED INNOVATION FLOWS MATRICES

The analytical procedure we will use to build up embodied intersectoral innovation flows matrices is quite straightforward. Following the rationale of the previous section, we will 'distribute' a suitable sectoral innovative proxy over an adequate intersectoral structure of relationships (Marengo and Sterlacchini, 1990). However, in doing this, two delicate issues arise: (i) the measurement of sectoral innovations; (ii) the construction of a significant and consistent map of their intersectoral distribution.

(i) As far as the first point is concerned, we will assume that the innovations introduced by a certain sector at time t can be proxied by the R&D expenditure of the corresponding firms in the same temporal span. Accordingly, the 'innovative production' of a certain TS can be represented by the diagonal vector $\hat{r}_t(n \times n)$ of the R&D expenditure of its n sectors.[30]

A few comments are due about this first methodological choice. First of all, the innovative perspective we will adopt is an *input* one, as it is based, in addition to the embodiment hypothesis, on an input kind of indicator such as R&D. In this way, we claim, we are able to capture relationships of a wider nature than by using other proxies. Indeed, if the intersectoral innovation flows matrix was obtained by means of output indicators (for example, either patents or innovation counts) – as in some of the procedures we have described in the previous section – the relative flows would be less representative of techno-economic relationships such as those on which we intend to focus. A certain user sector might in fact not have very significant economic links (in terms of intermediate or capital goods transactions) with the patenting producer sectors to which it pays the corresponding royalties. On the contrary, as we have already said, the development of a new R&D program is more likely to stimulate interactions between actors that are also close in economic terms (that is, of input-output coefficients). Let us also remember that, in general, although both output and input indicators suffer from serious limitations (Griliches, 1990; Patel and Pavitt, 1995), the latter are less affected by problems of scale than the former which are mainly significant for those economic units that can afford a patenting effort. Finally, data availability reasons are also relevant. Indeed, R&D figures can be obtained at the same disaggregation level of the input-output tables that we will use in the following, while patents are classified using slightly different 'product' based and functional categories.[31]

A few comments are also due about the 'flow' rather than 'stock' nature of our input proxy, that is, about the adoption of current (that is, at time t), rather than cumulated (over time) R&D expenditure. This choice is due to the substantial problems that still affect the selection of the most suitable temporal lags and depreciation rates for the construction of the so-called 'R&D capital stock' (Papaconstantinou *et al.*, 1996). However, this implies that the embodiment of innovative efforts in the goods produced by different sectors is both 'complete' and 'immediate', while a certain intersectoral diversification and a temporal delay of the embodiment process are on the contrary more plausible.[32]

(ii) Let us now consider the structure of the intersectoral relationships over which the previous R&D diagonal vectors, $\hat{r}_t$, have to be distributed. In formal terms, these relationships can be represented by a certain input coefficient matrix, either embodied, $\mathbf{R}_t^E$ ($n \times n$), in the case of embodied innovation flows, or direct, $\mathbf{R}_t^D$ ($n \times n$), in the case of 'pure knowledge spillovers'.

We should stress here that, for the 'the distribution' of $\hat{\mathbf{r}}_t$ over $\mathbf{R}_t^E$ ($n \times n$) $\mathbf{R}_t^D$ ($n \times n$) to be possible, the former vector and the latter matrices need to be conformable, that is, to have the same order, $n \times n$. This condition inevitably requires us to identify n as 'a sort of minimum common multiple' of the sectoral disaggregations at which data on R&D expenditure and input coefficients are available. A crucial trade-off thus emerges between the attempt at considering as many sectors (that is, technological partitions of the TS) as possible and that of referring to a common homogeneous classification. This trade-off will often emerge in the applications of this book.

Accordingly, the corresponding intersectoral innovation flows matrices of a certain TS, that is $\mathbf{F}_t^E$ ($n \times n$) and $\mathbf{F}_t^D$ ($n \times n$), are given by the following expressions:

$$\mathbf{F}_t^E = \hat{\mathbf{r}}_t \mathbf{R}_t^E \tag{3.1}$$

$$\mathbf{F}_t^D = \hat{\mathbf{r}}_t \mathbf{R}_t^D \tag{3.2}$$

Evidently, the number of sectors n to which the above vectors and matrices refer results from an important trade-off, between the attempt to consider as many sectors (i.e. technological partitions) as possible and that of referring to a common homogeneous classification.

Coming to a closer analysis of the input coefficient matrix, that of embodied input coefficients, $\mathbf{R}_t^E$, takes on different formulations depending on the kind of production flows in which technological embodiment is assumed to occur. In this last respect, the simplest hypothesis is that innovation flows among the sectors of a TS through the corresponding *direct* flows of either intermediate or capital goods. Accordingly, the 'amount' of innovation that a certain sector j receives from another sector i of the same TS would be proportional to, respectively, the intermediate and capital goods that j acquires from i to produce one unit of its output. In the former case $\mathbf{R}_t^E$ coincides with the standard input coefficient matrix of input-output analysis, $\mathbf{A}$, that is:[33]

$$\mathbf{R}^E = \mathbf{A} = \mathbf{X}(\hat{\mathbf{x}})^{-1} \tag{3.3}$$

where $\mathbf{X}$ is the intersectoral matrix of intermediate commodity flows, while $\hat{\mathbf{x}}$ is the diagonal vector of total sectoral production.

In the case of capital goods, instead, $\mathbf{R}^E$ would be given by a capital input coefficient matrix, $\mathbf{Z}$. Such a matrix can be obtained by normalising the intersectoral capital formation matrix, $\mathbf{K}$ – in turn adjusted to make it square $(\mathbf{K}^{ad})$ – with respect to the corresponding sectoral output, that is:[34]

$$\mathbf{R}^E = \mathbf{Z} = \mathbf{K}^{ad}(\hat{\mathbf{x}})^{-1} \tag{3.4}$$

Although, in principle, it is more realistic to assume that innovation flows among sectors embodied in capital, rather than in intermediate goods, the latter adjustment procedure makes (3.4) less practical to be implemented than (3.3). Furthermore, the matrix one should refer to in describing the embodiment process is an intersectoral capital *stock* matrix rather than a capital *formation* (i.e. investments) one. However, as is well known, the construction of the capital stock matrix is still affected by serious technical problems, and is hardly available for more TS on a comparable basis.

A common problem of the previous two formulations is that they both refer to a direct kind of flows. In so doing, they neglect the fact that innovation gets embodied also in production 'rounds' subsequent to the first one, that is in those inputs that are needed to produce further intermediate inputs. In order to overcome this problem, in what follows we will rather stick to another formulation for $\mathbf{R}^E$. Indeed, we will assume that innovation gets embodied in the intersectoral production flows that are activated, both directly and indirectly (that is, in subsequent production rounds), by the sectoral components of final demand. As we have previously observed, this amounts to considering innovation flows embodied in 'vertically integrated sectors' (Momigliano and Siniscalco, 1982). In analytical terms, the corresponding matrix $\mathbf{R}^E$ is given by the following expression:

$$\mathbf{R}^E = (\hat{\mathbf{x}})^{-1}\mathbf{B}(\hat{\mathbf{d}}) \tag{3.5}$$

where, in addition to the notation defined above, $\hat{\mathbf{d}}$ is the diagonal vector of the sectoral final demand, while $\mathbf{B}$ is the standard Leontief inverse matrix, in turn defined as:

$$\mathbf{B} = (\mathbf{I} - \mathbf{A})^{-1} \tag{3.6}$$

where $\mathbf{I}$ is the identity matrix and $\mathbf{A}$ the direct input coefficient matrix.

As far as (3.5) is concerned, let us remember that the generic element of $\mathbf{B}$, b_{ij}, represents an 'output-demand' multiplier which, for simplicity reasons, can be indicated as follows:

$$b_{ij} = \frac{\Delta x_i}{\Delta d_j} \tag{3.7}$$

where x_i and d_j are, respectively, the i and the j elements of the $\hat{\mathbf{x}}$ and $\hat{\mathbf{d}}$ diagonal vectors.

Accordingly, in (3.5), the post-multiplication of **B** by $\hat{\mathbf{d}}$ yields a matrix which indicates the intersectoral production flows activated, both directly and indirectly, by each sectoral component of final demand. The pre-multiplication of **Bd** by $(\hat{\mathbf{x}})^{-1}$, instead, operates a direct normalisation by row of these production requisites. Indeed, it transforms them into shares, so that the sum by row of the correspondent $\mathbf{R}^E$ matrix yields the unit:

$$\sum_j R_{ij}^E = 1 \qquad (3.8)$$

Also in the present case, it would appear more realistic to apply the direct/indirect requisites rationale to capital, rather than to intermediate inputs, and to consider an $\mathbf{R}^E$ matrix such as the following:

$$\mathbf{R}^E = Norm\left[(\hat{\mathbf{x}})^{-1}\mathbf{BZ}\right] \qquad (3.9)$$

where, in addition to the above-defined variables, a proper by-row normalisation (*Norm*) is needed to transform the corresponding requisites into unitary shares, so that (3.8) still holds. Apart from the technical problems we have stressed above, concerning the capital formation matrix, **K**, let us observe that the **Z** matrix itself can be considered a particular intersectoral 'explosion' of (3.5) in which investments are the only component of aggregate demand to be considered. As it can be traced, at least to a certain extent, to (3.5), the formulation of (3.9) will not be considered in the applications of this book.

In discussing the most proper formulation of the embodied input coefficient matrix, $\mathbf{R}^E$, a last remark is due about the role played by final demand in (3.5). Indeed, final demand is crucial, as production flows, and those innovations which are embodied in them, are driven by final demand itself. In this last respect, it would have been alternatively possible to consider technological flows embodied in total (that is, both direct and indirect) production coefficients that are consistent with sectoral production outputs (taken as given) rather than with sectoral final demand. In other words, it would have been possible to consider the linkages which are established in subsequent production rounds by keeping total sectoral production constant. This could be done by ruling out the fact that, because of indirect requisites, sectoral production outputs increase with respect to their current values. Accordingly, the correspondent $\mathbf{R}^E$ matrix could be represented as follows:

$$\mathbf{R}^{E} = \left\{ x_1 \left[\mathbf{b}_1^* \right], x_2 \left[\mathbf{b}_2^* \right], ..., x_n \left[\mathbf{b}_n^* \right] \right\} \tag{3.10}$$

In (3.10), apart from the notation defined above,[35] $\mathbf{b}_j^*$ represents the *j*th column of the matrix $\mathbf{B}^*$. Such a matrix is usually defined as the 'output-output' multiplier matrix (Miller and Blair, 1985, p. 328), and its generic element, $\mathbf{b}_j^*$, can be simply denoted as follows:

$$b_{ij}^* = \frac{\Delta x_i}{\Delta x_j} \tag{3.11}$$

and more precisely defined as:

$$b_{ij}^* = \frac{b_{ij}}{b_{jj}} \tag{3.12}$$

where b_{ij} is the generic element of the Leontief inverse $\mathbf{B}$.

The meaning of the previous two definitions can be immediately obtained from the generic element of the Leontief inverse. By recalling equation (3.7), the generic element of its principal diagonal can be defined as:

$$b_{jj} = \frac{\Delta x_j}{\Delta d_j} \tag{3.13}$$

By dividing (3.7) by (3.13) we therefore directly obtain that:

$$b_{ij}^* = \frac{b_{ij}}{b_{jj}} = \frac{\Delta x_j}{\Delta x_j} \tag{3.14}$$

According to (3.14), therefore, b_{ij}^* measures how much the production of sector *i* should increase in order to meet an increase of Δx_j in the production of sector *j*, rather than of its final demand.

On the basis of the previous definitions, each column of the matrix implicitly indicated in graph brackets in (3.10) has a consistent meaning. Indeed, it represents the total production requisites of each row sector, which are consistent with the current production of each column sector. Again, the pre-multiplication by $(\hat{x})^{-1}$ transforms the total production requisites of each row sector into shares of their total output. Accordingly, the elements on the principal diagonal of the corresponding $\mathbf{R}^E$ matrix are meaningless, while the sum by row of the non-principal diagonal elements does not yield the unit. Indeed, the intersectoral acquisitions are related to the diffusing sectors, but they are consistent with the production output of the acquiring sectors. As the sum of the former does not return the total output of the latter, a proper normalisation, with respect to the non-diagonal elements, is therefore needed in order to use (3.10).

Although consistent with the same total requisites rationale, the $\mathbf{R}^E$ matrix of (3.10) is substantially different from that of (3.5). As it considers the current production levels as exogenous, by 'cutting out' the linkages with final demand, it reveals the particular relevance in the construction of R&D direct and indirect capital stocks (Papaconstantinou *et al.*, 1996, pp. 33-34), as it eliminates problems of 'double-counting'. However, as the market represents one of the constitutive elements of our TS, the reference to total production coefficients which are activated by the final demand itself appears more appropriate.

According to the previous evaluation of all the possible alternatives for the embodied input coefficients matrix, $\mathbf{R}^E$, in the applications of this book we will exclusively refer to the formulation defined in (3.5). By distributing $\hat{\mathbf{r}}_t$ over such a matrix, the *intersectoral embodied innovation flow matrix* we will consider, that is, $\mathbf{F}^E$ ($n \times n$), can therefore be written as follows:

$$\mathbf{F}^E = \hat{\mathbf{r}} \mathbf{R}^E = \hat{\mathbf{r}} \left\{ (\hat{\mathbf{x}})^{-1} \mathbf{B} \hat{\mathbf{d}} \right\} \qquad (3.15)$$

The meaning of such a matrix is quite immediate. Its generic element, f_{ij}^E, measures the R&D expenditure of sector i, which is directly and indirectly embodied in the production of the final good j. In particular, the principal diagonal elements measure the R&D expenditure of a certain sector, which 'remains' in the final goods produced by the sector itself. Marengo and Sterlacchini (1990, note 7) retain these latter elements to be representative of a process kind of innovations, as opposed to the product ones, instead represented by the non-principal diagonal elements. In our application, however, whose focus is on relational, interactive aspects, these intra-sectoral diffusions will be left out and the analysis will be exclusively referred to intersectoral ones.

Before turning to the specific procedure through which we propose to analyse such matrices, a few words are due about the construction of *intersectoral direct innovation flows matrices*. Although we are not going to use them, some comments are in fact useful to approach their integration within the methodology of the present book.

As we have said in the previous section, in order to measure truly direct innovation flows it might be useful to consider as the relevant direct coefficient matrix, $\mathbf{R}^D$ ($n \times n$), a matrix based on the patenting procedures of the main international patent offices, such as the EPO and the USPTO. Indeed, if a $\mathbf{G}$($n \times n$) matrix is available, whose generic element, g_{ij}, represents the number of registered (that is, issued or applied for) patents of sector i whose 'pure knowledge' spills over to sector j in one of the three ways described above, the corresponding $\mathbf{F}^D$ ($n \times n$) matrix can be defined as follows:

$$\mathbf{F}^D = \hat{\mathbf{r}}\mathbf{R}^D = \hat{\mathbf{r}}\left\{\mathbf{G}(\hat{\mathbf{g}})^{-1}\right\} \tag{3.16}$$

where $\hat{\mathbf{g}}(n \times n)$ is the diagonal vector of total sectoral patents.[36]

As we have said, these matrices will be not considered in this book, because of the severe assumptions that have to be maintained in building up $\mathbf{G}$ with respect to more TS.[37] The analysis will instead be exclusively based on the intersectoral embodied innovation flows matrix of (3.15). Accordingly, whenever we will speak of intersectoral innovation flows, the reference will be to that formulation.

3.4   SOME USEFUL TRANSFORMATIONS

Although the intersectoral embodied innovation flows matrix of (3.15) remains the main reference of our methodological approach, in the empirical parts of this book we will often find it convenient to consider some transformations of it.

Apart from specific adjustments to which we will refer as occasion arises, two kinds of transformations will be used in general. The first one simply serves to depurate $\mathbf{F}^E$ from the scale effects introduced by the reference to sectoral innovation expenditure (that is, by the diagonal vector $\hat{\mathbf{r}}$). In order to do that, we will consider a matrix, $\mathbf{F}^{E,\ Rel}$, defined as:

$$\mathbf{F}^{E,\mathrm{Rel}} = \mathbf{F}^E(\hat{\mathbf{f}}^E)^{-1} \tag{3.17}$$

where $\hat{\mathbf{f}}^E$ is the diagonal vector of total sectoral innovation acquisitions, that is, of the total by column of the $\mathbf{F}^E$ matrix.[38]

A second transformation is obtained by dichotomising the previous matrix (or some further transformation of it) with respect to a certain cut-off value k. This amounts to considering dichotomised matrices, $\mathbf{F}^{E,\ Dic}$, which are binary transformations of the original matrices, that is, $\mathbf{F}^{E,Rel}$, made up of 1s and 0s according to a 'greater than' test performed with respect to k itself:

$$f_{ij}^{E,Dic} = 1 \ \text{if} \ f_{ij}^{E,\mathrm{Rel}} > \mathrm{k}; \quad f_{ij}^{E,Dic} = 0 \ \text{if} \ f_{ij}^{E,\mathrm{Rel}} \leq \mathrm{k} \tag{3.18}$$

As we will see, this latter kind of transformation turns out to be extremely helpful as it allows us to work out some typical network analysis indicators, to which it is possible to apply an interesting 'technological' meaning.

Indeed, the sectors of our embodied innovation flows matrix can be thought of as the nodes of a 'valued network', that is, one whose edges, given by the flows themselves, measure linkages of different magnitude. Accordingly, their analysis calls for a dichotomisation, such as that of (3.18). Although mainly developed in economic sociology (Scott, 1991), network analysis indicators and techniques can be applied to examine the structure and the characteristics of a TS in the way we will show in the following chapters.

NOTES

1. The Pavitt taxonomy (1984), especially as far as the distinction between 'specialised suppliers' and 'supplier dominated' sectors is concerned, draws on the same idea.
2. As far as the last technological dimension is concerned, which, still following De Liso and Metcalfe (1996), can be referred to as 'skills', its measurement is not directly feasible within the present approach. Although a certain kind of relationship can be envisaged between intersectoral goods and human capital, its measurement remains a point which deserves an attention beyond the scope of this book.
3. For a deeper analysis of the relationships between the intersectoral innovation diffusion process and the interactive approach developed by Lundvall, see Montresor (1996).
4. In this last respect, the relevant argument can be identified, in the initial quotation of this section (OECD, 1992, p. 48), in the terms 'research spillover' and 'externality'. Apparently, following this quotation, the occurrence of positive externalities, in the form of knowledge spillovers, would be an exclusive feature of the disembodied diffusion process. Indeed, following the same quotation, the innovative knowledge produced by firms, mainly through their R&D activity, would take on the typical properties of a public good, as it would be both non-rival and non-excludable. For a wider discussion of the notion of 'spillover' see, among the others, Griliches (1979) and Romer (1990).
5. As we said, the distinction between these two 'steps' cannot be pushed beyond an illustrative scope.
6. In our opinion, therefore, spillovers and innovative interactions are not necessarily mutually exclusive. An opposite position is supported by DeBresson (1996), who maintains that the spillovers rationale is incompatible with that of interactivity, as the former would be for him a natural expression of the methodological individualism of the neoclassical school.
7. In a more recent formulation of the concept, Griliches (1992) suggests that the term 'spillover' would not be entirely appropriate to indicate this kind of economic advantage. More precisely, he argues that, as long as a good exchange between producer and user can be found, it is not possible to speak of a pure externality. However, in what follows, we will refer to the expression 'rent spillover' in order to distinguish it from the other kind of spillover, that is, the 'pure knowledge spillover' (Verspagen, 1997).
8. For a critical discussion of this issue, see Papaconstantinou *et al.* (1996).

9. This database collects data about more than 4000 'significant technical innovations' commercialised in Great Britain between 1945 and 1983.

10. The rectangular shape of these matrices is due to the possible mismatch between producer and user sectors. Indeed, many of the sectors whose firms employ 'external' technologies do not produce any innovation. Furthermore, user sectors also encompass the acquisitions of the final demand sector. Although such matrices can be examined with powerful methodologies, such as cluster analysis, square matrices, as we will see, allow us to accomplish helpful transformations and operations more straightforwardly.

11. As Marengo and Sterlacchini (1990, p. 31) observe, numerous secondary (usually incremental) innovations are therefore neglected, along with other 'important' (that is, radical) innovations obtained by the surveyed firms in economic activities other than their principal one.

12. To be sure, the recent design and implementation of the so-called 'Community Innovation Survey', extended to all the countries of the European Union, provides an important contribution to overcome this last problem. Its implementation is however still at an infant stage, and the use of the relative data in the construction of comparable intersectoral matrices is still to be evaluated to date.

13. To be sure, the approaches 'mentioned so far' to which Verspagen refers are those based on the use of patents, which we will discuss later. However, the argument also extends to those approaches which, although based on innovation surveys, share with the former the emphasis on the producer-user principle.

14. On the same issue see also van Meijl (1994), Los and Verspagen (1996), Los (1997), Verspagen and De Loo (1998).

15. The precise meaning of this 'distribution', that by now can be simply taken as an intersectoral allocation, will be clarified in the next section, where we will illustrate the techniques to build up intersectoral innovation flows matrices.

16. The methodology to construct such a kind of matrix is in fact much more complicated, as a series of quite delicate questions have to be solved, such as, for example: the assignment of a patent to more originating sectors, the degree of exclusiveness of patents attributed to several user sectors, and the intersectoral distribution of patents of 'general use'. For a detailed discussion of these and further issues see Marengo and Sterlacchini (1990, pp. 27-29).

17. Let us note that, in order to make the Yale matrix usable also in the intersectoral 'distribution' of the patents granted in other national contexts, Putnam and Evenson have built up a concordance scheme between the international classification system of patents – International Patent Classification (IPC) – and the industrial classifications used by the Canadian Patent Office (Evenson and Putnam, 1988).

18. The use of these matrices with respect to different national contexts is quite diffuse in those studies which aim at quantifying the impact of the so-called 'indirect' R&D stock on total productivity (see, for example, Coe and Helpman (1995) and Verspagen (1997)).

19. Nonetheless, as we will see, this methodology suffers from other kinds of limitations.

20. The term 'direct', this time, has to be understood according to the language of input-output analysis, that is, by looking at the relationship established between

one sector and another because the latter requires some production inputs from the former. The demand for intermediate inputs in turn required to produce these inputs – that is, indirect production flows – is instead neglected.

21. These and other input-output concepts are used here quite informally. Their meaning will appear clearer in the following section, where they will be presented in a more technical and rigorous form.

22. Among the first national applications let us remember that of Marengo and Sterlacchini (1990), with respect to Italy, and, more recently, that of Virtaharju and Akerblom (1993), with respect to Finland.

23. For an application to the technological exchanges between the USA, Canada and Japan, see Davis (1988).

24. In addition to those mentioned above, we should also consider the notable application recently carried out by Papaconstantinou *et al.* (1996) with respect to 10 OECD countries in the decade 1980-1990.

25. Among others, see Jaffe (1988, 1989), Adams (1990) and Park (1995).

26. Some of these problems can be solved through the measurement procedure suggested by Los (1997), in which the technological distance is measured by the cosine between pairs of input production coefficient vectors. Nonetheless, in this case too, the relevant application is exclusively based on the US input-output tables for 1987.

27. The studies carried out by Verspagen belong to that research line whose aim is that of investigating the relationships between spillovers and growth, and to which the construction of these matrices is just functional.

28. For the concordance table, see Verspagen *et al.* (1994).

29. As observed by Verspagen (1995), this procedure suffers from a certain over-estimation. Indeed, as it is impossible to distinguish, in the series of all the patents, between original and quoted patents classes, a flow which is revealed might actually not exist.

30. To be sure, n is the number of sectors of a TS which can actually be observed by looking at its intersectoral framework, a point we will develop later.

31. Let us also observe that the study of the economic structure of innovative activity from an output perspective is usually undertaken by comparing, with specific techniques, on the one hand, input-output tables (current flows matrices, input requirements matrices, and so on), and, on the other hand, innovation matrices as such (DeBresson, 1996), in turn based on patents.

32. These and other problems are discussed by Marengo and Sterlacchini (1990, pp. 36-37), who also propose a more realistic model to overcome some of them. Its practical implementation in an empirical comparative study, such as the present one, is however extremely difficult with the data available at the moment on innovations. For a critical discussion of this issue see also Montresor (1996).

33. In what follows, the temporal subscript will be omitted and retained implicitly.

34. As we have previously said, this adjustment is necessary because the standard capital formation matrix is a rectangular one, given that not all the sectors which use capital goods are also engaged in their production.

35. Let us observe that x_i, that is, the production output of sector i, is a scalar.

36. As far as (3.15) and (3.16) are concerned, let us remember that Marengo and Sterlacchini (1990, p. 37), who identify direct innovation flows with intersectoral patent matrices, stress how total R&D expenditure should be distributed between

embodied and direct flows according to specific sectoral coefficients. Apart from the problems of estimating such coefficients, especially with respect to different sectors and innovative contexts, the 'alternative' nature of the direct flows we have previously referred to makes this distribution less crucial, as the same R&D unit can generate both embodied and direct flows.

37. For a preliminary attempt to combine the analysis of both embodied and direct flows see Montresor (1998). In this application, the relevant **G** matrix is that built up by Verspagen (1995) with respect to nearly 60% of all the patents yielded by the EPO in the period 1979-1994.

38. The relativisation by column is used because that by row would have given back the underlying $\mathbf{R}^E$ matrix.

PART TWO

Empirical Analysis: the Macro Perspective

4. The technological system configurations

The aim of this chapter is to analyse the configurations the TS assumes on the basis of its constituent relationships. Such relationships will be identified by combining the structure of the internal relationships among its building blocks and that of its external relationships with the outer environment. Following the analysis of Chapter 3, we argue that intersectoral innovation flows are the most suitable proxy of the former kind of relationships, while sectoral foreign trade flows can be taken as a proxy of the latter.

Combining these two dimensions, a TS can take one of the following configurations: a pervasive TS (that is, what could be defined as a system of innovation), either outward or inward-oriented, or a segmented TS (or trajectories-based), which again can be either outward or inward-oriented.

This approach is applied to a group of eight OECD countries for three temporal spans (early 1980s, mid 1980s and early 1990s). It is thus shown that Japan and Canada are, respectively, the most pervasive and the most segmented inward-oriented technological systems. The rest of the countries instead identify different outward-oriented configurations: pervasive, in the cases of Germany and France, and segmented, in the cases of Great Britain, Denmark, Australia and the Netherlands. All these configurations are quite stable, except for the case of Denmark, which undergoes a structural change over time, moving from the cluster of the inward-oriented segmented TS, to that of the outward-oriented segmented TS.

4.1 METHODOLOGICAL BACKGROUND

As already said, our analysis is concerned with the determination of an internal and an external dimension of a TS, and with the identification of their connection degree through a proper indicator. The former is derived by calculating the dispersion of the elements of a proper matrix of intersectoral innovation flows, while for the latter we utilise the well-known Balassa index of revealed comparative advantages (4.1.2). By mapping the TS with respect to these two indicators, it is possible to characterise different TS in terms of structure and specialisation.

4.1.1   The Internal Connection Indicator

The kind of intersectoral innovation flows we refer to here is the normalisation by column, $\mathbf{F}^{E,Rel}(n \times n)$, of the relative matrix $\mathbf{F}(n \times n)$, as defined by equation (3.19). Hence, its generic element f_{ij} represents the percentage of the whole intersectoral innovative acquisitions that sector j gets from sector i. The intersectoral focus of these matrices makes them suitable for mapping the structure of the internal relationships of a TS as follows:

1. If each sector j 'acquires' innovation from a unique sector i_{j*}, we define this case as *maximum polarisation*. The $\mathbf{F}^{E,Rel}$ matrix is characterised as follows:[1]

$$f_{ij}^{E,Rel} = 1 \text{ if } i = i_{j*}; f_{ij}^{E,Rel} = 0 \text{ elsewhere} \qquad (4.1)$$

2. If the intersectoral acquisitions of each sector are equally distributed among the others, we define this case as *maximum pervasiveness*, and the $\mathbf{F}^{E,Rel}$ matrix is characterised as follows:

$$f_{ij}^{E,Rel} = \frac{1}{n-1} \text{ if } i \neq j; f_{ij}^{E,Rel} = 0 \text{ elsewhere} \qquad (4.2)$$

Given that (4.1) and (4.2) are the two extremes of all the possible feasible maps, we can consider the distribution of the elements of the maximum pervasiveness matrix as a reference term and characterise all the others as deviations from it. An internal connection indicator can thus be obtained for a TS as follows:

$$TS_{IN} = \frac{\sum_i \sum_j \left(f_{ij}^{E,Rel} - f_{ij}^{E,Rel^+} \right)^2}{n} \qquad (4.3)$$

where f_{ij}^{E,Rel^+} is the general element of $\mathbf{F}^{E,Rel}$ in the case of maximum pervasiveness. The domain of (4.3) is thus in-between the two extreme cases of maximum pervasiveness and of maximum polarisation:[2]

$$0 < TS_{IN} < \frac{n(n-2)}{n-1} \qquad (4.4)$$

Finally, (4.3) is normalised, and its complement to *1* calculated:

$$TS_{IN}^* = 1 - \frac{TS_{IN}(n-1)}{n(n-2)}, \quad 0 < TS_{IN}^* < 1 \qquad (4.5)$$

In so doing, low/high values will give evidence of a low/high degree of internal connection for the corresponding TS, within a [0;1] domain.

If TS_{IN}^* is high, the structure of the TS will be characterised by a high degree of innovative pervasiveness, which we denote as 'systemic'. If, on the other hand, TS_{IN}^* is low, the same interrelations denote a high degree of polarisation. This case is associated with more localised innovative processes, depending on a more segmented set of users and producers, which reminds us of the nature of technological trajectories.

4.1.2 The External Connection Indicator

Although quite helpful in studying internal links, an input-output analysis of innovative activity cannot properly face the question of the external (international) relations of a TS (Lundvall, 1996). It must be noted here that we are not interested in the international innovative penetration of a country, for which there is an abundance of indicators (balance of technological payments, foreign direct investments in high-tech sectors, patents obtained abroad, multinationals' diffusion, technological agreements, etc.). Our aim is instead that of examining the structure of the techno-economic relationships through which a TS realises such international penetration.

Accordingly, we decided to adopt an indicator describing the intersectoral extension of the commercial specialisations (despecialisations) of a country, by calculating the dispersion of the comparative advantages (disadvantages) of its sectors, as from the Balassa index. An external connection indicator can thus be obtained as follows:

$$TS_{EX} = \frac{\sum_i (\beta_{ic} - \overline{\beta_c})^2}{n} \qquad (4.6)$$

where:

$\beta_{ic} = \dfrac{EX_{ic}}{\sum_c EX_{ic}} \Bigg/ \dfrac{\sum_i EX_{ic}}{\sum_i \sum_c EX_{ic}}$ is the Balassa index of revealed comparative

advantages for sector i of country c, in which:

EX_{ic} are the total exports of product i by country c;
$\sum_c EX_{ic}$ are the total world exports of product i;
$\sum_i EX_{ic}$ are the total exports of country c;

$\Sigma_i \Sigma_c EX_{ic}$ are the total world exports;

and $\overline{\beta}_c = \sum_i \beta_{ic} \Big/ n$ is the average value of the comparative advantages

(disadvantages) of the n sectors of country c.[3]

Very high values of (4.6) are consistent either with very high specialisation or with very high despecialisation. In the former case, very high comparative advantages are presumably the result of quite well-developed national capabilities. In the latter case, the impossibility of catching up with the average world practices and of exploiting international relationships – that is, very high comparative disadvantages – presumably results from national capabilities that are not sufficiently developed. In both cases, although for opposite reasons, an inward-oriented (at most national) configuration seems thus appropriate. Very low values of (4.6) are instead the outcome of revealed comparative advantages that are quite closely aligned to the average. Therefore, they indicate that national capabilities are neither so high as to guarantee 'self-sufficiency', nor so low as to prevent the country from penetrating foreign markets: an outward-oriented (at most international) configuration is thus the most suitable in this case.

4.1.3   The Taxonomy

By combining the previous two pieces of analysis, each TS can be defined by the distribution of the values of (4.5) and (4.6). Accordingly, each TS might be located in one of the following configurations: (i) pervasive/inward

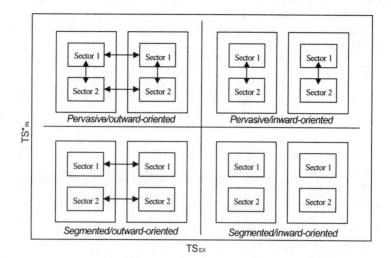

Figure 4.1   The technological system taxonomy

oriented (high TS^{*}_{IN} and TS_{EX}); (ii) pervasive/outward oriented (high TS^{*}_{IN} and low TS_{EX}); (iii) segmented/inward oriented (low TS^{*}_{IN} and high TS_{EX}); (iv) segmented/outward oriented (low TS^{*}_{IN} and TS_{EX}).

It is quite handy to visualise the same taxonomy through a scatter diagram such as that of Figure 4.1.

4.2   THE EMPIRICAL CONFIGURATIONS OF THE TS

In this section we use the previous taxonomy to investigate the configurations of eight TS for the following three periods: early 1980s, mid 1980s, and early 1990s (Table 4.1), using a 15 manufacturing sector disaggregation (Table 4.2).

Table 4.1   Dataset characteristics

	Internal connection		External connection
	I-O Tables	R&D Exp.	
Australia	1986, 1989	1986, 1989	1985, 1989
Canada	1981, 1986, 1990	1981, 1986, 1990	1981, 1985, 1990
Denmark	1980, 1985, 1990	1980, 1985, 1990	1981, 1985, 1990
France	1980, 1985, 1990	1980, 1985, 1990	1981, 1985, 1990
Germany	1978, 1986, 1990	1978, 1986, 1990	1981, 1985, 1990
Japan	1980, 1985, 1990	1980, 1985, 1990	1981, 1985, 1990
Great Britain	1979, 1984, 1990	1979, 1984, 1990	1981, 1985, 1990
The Netherlands	1981, 1986	1981, 1986	1980, 1985

Source: OECD (1994a); OECD (1994b); UN (various years).

This empirical analysis is aimed at comparing the TS of different countries in the different periods considered. However, it should be stressed that such a comparison cannot be exhaustive. Indeed, by its nature, this kind of analysis only partially describes the complexity of a system, and should therefore be complemented with other system approaches in order to embed our results within complex production and institutional set-ups. The exclusive reference to intersectoral innovation flows matrices to describe TS limits the TS complexity to its production structure (although complemented by the R&D components) as reflected in an input-output context. In so doing, a crucial trade-off cannot be neglected. While, on the one hand, we can compute the position of each TS in a single diagram, on the other hand, we miss the institutional characteristics of the TS analysed. In order to take into account the full complexity of a TS we thus decided to cross data sources and to parallel the synthetic treatment made available by the utilisation of intersectoral innovation flows matrices with more traditional types of data, especially in respect the structural characteristics of a TS. As will be clearer in the following, certain peculiarities of the TS configurations can be better understood in the light of such characteristics (as, for instance, country size and economic dimension). For instance, small countries, characterised by a smaller population dispersed over a relatively large territory, by a higher dependency on agriculture and resource exploitation, and by a limited amount of manufacturing activity (Nelson, 1993a), all share the same basic features in terms of their techno-economic activity, which are consistent with our more synthetic treatment: that is, a basic-oriented R&D, mainly applied to the primary sector and, only to a limited and international extent, also to the industrial level; a greater pressure imposed by 'critical-mass' problems towards innovative specialisation; relatively thinner innovative sectors, that is, dependent on few firms and few technologies (see, for example, Freeman and Lundvall, 1988).

Table 4.2   Sectoral disaggregation

1	Food, beverages and tobacco
2	Textile industry, apparel and leather
3	Wood products and furniture
4	Paper, paper products, printing and publishing
5	Chemical industry, drugs and medicines
6	Energy products
7	Rubber and plastic products
8	Non-metallic mineral products
9	Ferrous and non-ferrous metals
10	Metal products
11	Non-electric machinery, office & computing, electric appliances, radio TV and communication
12	Shipbuilding and repairing
13	Motor vehicles and other transport
14	Professional goods
15	Other manufacturing

In the light of these and similar connections, we hope to benefit from the integration of already available knowledge on systems performance with our more compact and concise methodology. Accordingly, in the following we will present a separate analysis of the two indicators, each one complemented by a discussion of more traditional, pertinent indicators. The two indicators will then be drawn together in order to highlight the most important evidence and the full meaning of our analysis.

4.2.1 The Internal Connection Indicator

At the outset, clear clusters emerge from the analysis of the internal connection indicator (Figure 4.2): three countries (Japan, Germany and France) are characterised by values more or less higher than 0.3, with Japan steadily above 0.6. The rest of the countries have values around 0.1. Let us also observe that, in general, the connectivity of the TS is increasing over time, with the notable exception of the Netherlands. Interesting parallels emerge by interpreting the previous results in the light of knowledge already available on the corresponding systems of innovation: crossing data sources can actually improve the explanatory power of both.

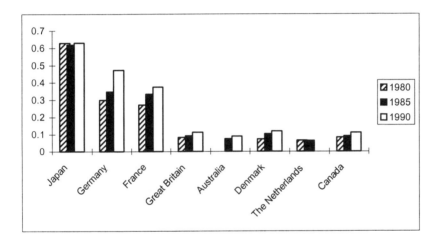

Figure 4.2   The internal connection indicator

First of all, this holds true with respect to Japan. Indeed, the outsider characteristics of the Japanese innovative performance are a widely recognised fact, at least from the early 1980s onward. It is in fact confirmed both by input and output innovation statistics (Odagiri and Goto, 1993). However, our results seem to supply also a quantitative confirmation of some recent qualitative studies on structural and techno-economic characteristics: the pervasive role of MITI and the diffused participation, either direct or indirect, in major economic and technology policy issues (Fransman, 1995);[4] the recent debate on the different models of capitalism (Dore, 1992); the predominance of diffusion-oriented innovative projects with respect to the mission-oriented ones (Freeman, 1988); the characteristics of dynamic versus myopic systems (Patel and Pavitt, 1991).

Also for France and Germany it is possible to relate our results to structural and institutional characteristics. Several more qualitative contributions point out, for instance, the wide participation base of the Rhenish model of capitalism (Albert, 1991) and the highly pervasive characteristics of their most competitive sectors (Dosi *et al.*, 1990).

It must be noted at this point that the high degree of internal connection in Germany seems to be the result of its superior ability at encouraging innovative intersectoral virtuous circles, rather than the result of its conspicuous R&D involvement (see, for example, Leoncini *et al.*, 1996 and Schnabl, 1995). Indeed, if we consider R&D expenditure as a percentage of GDP (Table 4.3), Germany would rank at least as high as Japan (indeed ahead in the early 1980s), but our internal connection indicator does not reflect this.

Table 4.3   Techno-economic characteristics of the dataset (1988)

	Japan	France	Germany	Great Britain	Denmark	Canada	Australia	The Netherl.*
GDP/per capita (1988 PPP)	14,228	13,603	14,161	13,428	13,555	18,446	13,412	11,860
Population (000)	122,613	55,873	61,451	57,065	5,130	25,950	16,538	14,700
Manufacturing output/GDP (%)	29	27	44	27	25	23	18	—
Manufacturing exports/GDP (%)	9	13	24	17	19	16	5	—
Literacy rate (%)	>95	>95	>95	>95	>95	>95	>95	>95
Secondary-level Enrolment rate (%)	96	92	94	83	107	104	98	103
Third-level Enrolment rate (%)	28	31	30	22	30	58	29	34
Scientists and Technicians (per 1,000 people 1986-90)	110	83	86	90	85	174	48	92
R&D/GNP (%)	2.9	2.3	2.9	2.3	1.3	1.5	1.4	2.3
Business R&D/ total R&D (%)	66.0	58.9	72.2	67.0	55.6	55.0	37.4	60.0

Note: * GDP/capita (1987); population (mid-1987); enrolment rates (1990).
Source: Nelson (1993); UNDP (1994); OECD (various years).

Moving to the second cluster of countries, it is interesting to note that a large country, such as Great Britain, exhibits unambiguously a trajectories-based configuration. Several qualitative arguments can be put forward also for this result: the Anglo-Saxon model of capitalism is notably not very effective at spurring industrial and social cohesion (Albert, 1991); the majority of the innovative projects are mainly mission oriented (Ergas, 1987); moreover, Great Britain is one of the most 'multinationalised' countries of the OECD area (both inward and outward, Patel, 1995), and this fact tends to stimulate intra-sectoral relationships with partner countries rather than intersectoral relationships within the country (Walker, 1993). Once more, as in the case of Germany, these structural and institutional characteristics are not caught by a performance analysis, according to which Great Britain is among the most innovative countries (Table 4.3).

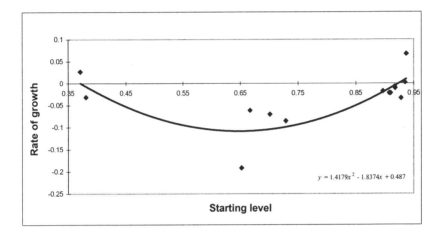

Figure 4.3   A non-linear model of convergence

The remaining countries of the sample show similar positions that can be traced, as we already pointed out, to their homogeneous structural characteristics as smaller countries.[5]

Interesting results finally emerge when the variations in the TS^*_{IN} indicator are considered in relative terms, that is, with respect to the value assumed by the internal indicator at the beginning of each period. By simply scattering these variations it is possible to show some peculiar features of their patterns of growth. Indeed, they seem to grow according to a non-linear pattern (Figure 4.3): only really backward countries and countries on the 'frontier' of systems' complexity (in terms of internal connectivity) exhibit a negative correlation between starting level and rate of growth, while the same relationship does not hold for systems that are positioned in-between. Such an interpretation certainly deserves a more rigorous analysis, but it is at least suggestive.

4.2.2   The External Connection Indicator

Also by looking at the external connection indicator (Figure 4.4) a clustering of Japan and Canada emerges, characterised by highly polarised revealed comparative advantages. Denmark, instead, shifts over time, from this cluster to another that comprises the rest of the countries.

A further integration with the statistics collected in Table 4.3 indicates that the present analysis is consistent with the common argument according to which dynamic small and medium-sized countries, for different reasons, exhibit a larger international involvement (Freeman and Lundvall, 1988). In some cases, small countries might not find their internal market large enough to repay a considerable investment in innovation, so that they need to pick highly selected sectors and exploit their results in international markets. This is the most suitable argument for the case of the Netherlands, whose R&D intensity is quite similar to that of the larger investors (Table 4.3), and whose international patenting activity is remarkably biased towards nationally controlled foreign subsidiaries (Table 4.4).

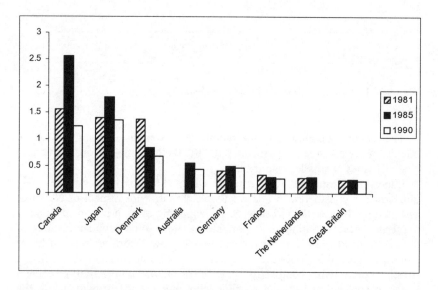

Figure 4.4   The external connection indicator

In contrast, in some other cases, a major degree of openness might be due to a massive injection of foreign capital which comes to control the new technologies, while more traditional sectors get innovated at a local level quite independently (again spurring a trajectories-based configuration). This seems to be the case with Denmark, whose inward foreign investments and new technology transfers are among the highest in the world (Mowery and Oxley, 1995), while the local agro-industrial complex gradually assumes the features of an independent development block (Edquist and Lundvall, 1993). A similar dependency account can be given for the Australian case: its origin as high-income colonial state has made the development of local technological capabilities a quite recent and still maturing need, while it has also implied a certain bias towards the key sectors of the colonisers, mainly Great Britain (Gregory, 1993).

Table 4.4   International patenting activity

	National source of USA patenting for large firms: 1981-86 (% of total patents granted by the USA patent office) (a)		Source of patent applications registered in each country: 1990 (% of total local patents applications)# (b)	
	Nationally controlled	Other	Domestic patents	Foreign patents
Japan	62.5	36.3	88.46	11.54
Germany*	44.8	44.2	32.62	67.38
France	36.8	53.2	16.15	83.85
Great Britain	32.0	49.0	21.46	78.54
The Netherlands	51.9	39.4	5.32	94.68
Denmark	n.a.	n.a.	6.82	93.18
Australia	n.a.	n.a.	24.63	75.37
Canada	11.0	72.1	6.76	93.24

Note: * West Germany for the first indicator; # Differences among patent systems are not taken into account.
Source: (a) Patel and Pavitt (1991); (b) OECD (1992).

Quite surprisingly, the same argument does not hold for the remaining small country in the sample (indeed the smallest of the 'large' OECD economies), that is, Canada, whose dominance of international linkages over domestic ones has been largely recognised by different sources (see, for example, Niosi and Bellon, 1996). Paquet's (1996) analyses of local Canadian economies seems to shed some light on this apparent contradiction, by suggesting that the balance between domestic oriented, natural resource based technological systems (energy, metallurgy, forestry, agriculture) and internationally oriented, human resource based ones (aeronautics, telecommunications, information technology), is not actually in favour of the latter, as has been documented by other more aggregated statistics (McFetridge, 1993). However, it seems more plausible that a truer explanation comes from the very 'local' (that is, national) nature of its internationalisation process, determined by the almost exclusive links (and therefore comparative advantages) with respect to the USA: most American subsidiaries operating in Canadian high-tech sectors only deal with parent companies and vice versa (OECD, 1992, p. 220). The most active development blocks (especially the motor vehicle sector[6]) are completely integrated with, rather than exclusively dependent on, the American ones, and human capital is mainly educated and trained in the USA rather than 'imported' through the American multinationals (McFetridge, 1993).

As far as the larger countries of the sample are concerned, we observe that there is a clear distinction between Japan and the three large European countries. To be sure, these latter are also differentiated: Germany shows higher and growing values (almost double those of Great Britain), and France has slightly higher values, though converging, than Great Britain. Again, it is possible to trace these differences to structural characteristics. In the case of Great Britain, for example, the absence of sound and virtuous relationships between users and suppliers and between public basic and private applied R&D (Walker, 1993) spurs firms, mainly large multinational corporations, to develop their research activities and protect their results abroad (Table 4.4).[7]

4.2.3   The Configurations of the TS

Finally, a taxonomy of different configurations can be composed for each of the investigated periods by combining the results of the internal and external connection indicators: some of the comments presented above separately can thus be put together here (Figures 4.5, 4.6, 4.7).

The first thing to notice is that very different patterns emerge even though the group of countries analysed is more or less homogeneous and of comparable levels of development. This methodology seems in fact to be quite powerful in detecting structural differences and similarities among countries undergoing very similar techno-economic processes, and which are barely distinguishable if more traditional approaches are adopted instead. Secondly, it enables us to classify TS through an exhaustive taxonomy encompassing two important dimensions of a TS: the degree of coherence among its internal building blocks, and the structure of its relationships with the outer environment.

As far as the main specific results are concerned, clear clusters of TS are easily detected. In the early 1980s, Japan is steadily in the top-right area, and is thus clearly identifiable as the most inward-oriented and pervasive TS. Canada and Denmark, in the bottom-right area, can be defined as national trajectories-based TS (that is, inward-oriented and segmented). The rest of the countries are characterised by an outward-oriented configuration, with Great Britain and the Netherlands defined as segmented, and France and Germany as pervasive.

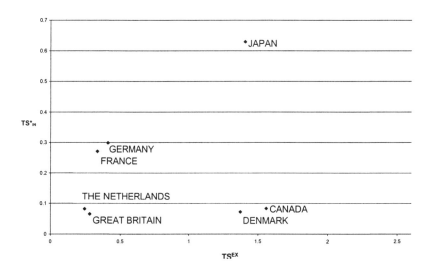

Figure 4.5   The technological system configurations, early 1980s

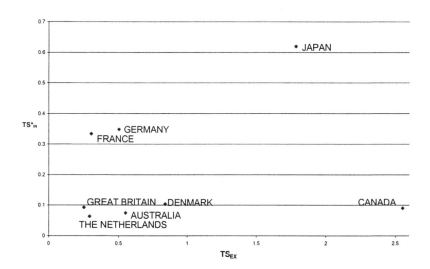

Figure 4.6   The technological system configurations, mid 1980s

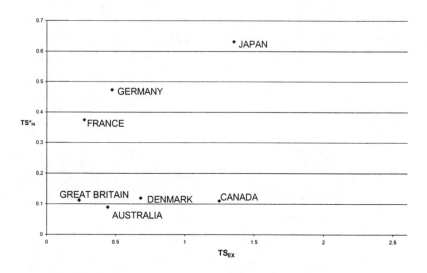

Figure 4.7   The technological system configurations, early 1990s

The whole picture is confirmed if the subsequent periods of time are taken into account, thus suggesting the structural nature of the indicators. The only two relevant dynamic patterns are that of Denmark, and those of France and Germany. Denmark shifts from one cluster (inward-oriented and segmented) to another (outward-oriented and segmented), joining Great Britain, the Netherlands, and also Australia (for which data on early 1980s were not available). France and Germany move upwards, and thus confirm their vocation of outward-oriented TS.

An important feature of the identified clusters is that within the same configuration different 'types' of countries have very different dynamics, and these dynamics seem to be diverging over time. Hence, similar clustering does not imply similar dynamic patterns. France and Germany, for example, are both characterised by a high level of internal coherence, coupled with a strong degree of internationalisation. In this case, it seems likely that their internal structure is particularly suited to exploiting the benefits arising from intense international linkages. For instance, as far as the German case is concerned, its systemic characteristics actually guarantee a certain degree of self-sufficiency.[8] A similar argument holds for France, whose intermediate position between Germany and Great Britain is confirmed by the analysis of external patents (Table 4.4).

A different story holds for Great Britain and the Netherlands, two cases of an apparent 'dualistic configuration', that is, with infrequent internal interaction and a high outward attitude. Australia and Denmark, instead, are the countries closest to the national trajectories-based configuration, of which Denmark was actually part in the early 1980s.

Finally, that internal coherence can allow one TS to be self-sufficient appears to be demonstrated by Japan, the most 'systemic' and simultaneously the most inward-oriented (that is, national).[9] However, if inward and outward innovative efforts are considered separately, as in Table 4.4, the importance of a coherent internal environment for the international exploitation of nationally developed technological capabilities emerges also in the case of Japan. The configurations of the Netherlands and Great Britain contrast with this interpretation and reveal that the same condition is necessary, but not sufficient.

4.3   CONCLUSIONS

In this chapter we have put forward an approach dealing with two crucial levels for the analysis of the TS, particularly suited to their empirical study: the degree of internal and external connection of their partitions (sectors). On this basis we have derived a taxonomy and identified four possible configurations for the TS.

We have also carried out an empirical application of this scheme of analysis, from which we have derived interesting results, both in terms of the classification of different TS, and in terms of their changes over time.

The need for crossing data sources has been repeatedly highlighted in order to complement qualitative studies with our more compact and concise approach. In spite of the limited extension of the application, the proposed taxonomy is able to provide some insights into possible patterns of change between countries over time. In particular, Japan turns out to be the only country whose configuration can be reasonably, and permanently, considered to be that of 'national system of innovation' (indeed, an inward-oriented pervasive TS), while Canada appears to be the only persistent 'national trajectory' (that is, an inward-oriented and segmented TS). The other countries can be classified as international (that is, open-oriented) configurations, although with very different characteristics. Indeed, France and Germany might be reasonably characterised as 'international systems' (as they are pervasive TS), while Great Britain, Australia and the Netherlands can be associated with 'international trajectories' (as they are segmented TS). The only exception is that of Denmark, for which it is possible to register a structural change of configuration, from an inward to an outward-oriented trajectory (that is, segmented TS).

NOTES

1.   Given the normalisation procedure, total flows by sector sum to 1.

2.   In the case of maximum polarisation the $\mathbf{F}^{E,Rel}$ matrix is composed of n values equal to l (one for each column). All the remaining elements are nil. However, only $(n-1)n$ of them, that is, all except those on the principal diagonal, are considered in their deviation from those values of f_{ij} that are different from zero and equal to $1/(n-1)$. It follows that the value of the internal connection indicator is in this case given by

$$TS_{IN} = n\left(1 - \frac{1}{n-1}\right)^2 + (n^2 - 2n)\left(-\frac{1}{n-1}\right)^2 = \frac{n(n-2)}{n-1}.$$

3.   A few words are due with respect to the choice of focusing on international trade flows. While for the internal connection indicator the technological dimension is explicit (R&D expenditure) and the economic dimension is implicit (intersectoral structure), the reverse holds for the external indicator, where the economic side is explicit (commercial exchange) and the technological one is implicit (embodied in the transferred goods). The techno-economic focus, which is here the only one compatible with the definition of systems' boundaries, will be relaxed in the following chapters, where the analysis will be concerned with the degree and type of internal connections among the system's components (its building blocks, or sub-systems). As we will see, from both a methodological and an empirical point of view, explicit technological indicators are necessary. For a first exploration in this direction, see Leoncini *et al.* (1996).

4.   For a more historically oriented account of the role of MITI, see also Brown (1980).

5.   In the most comprehensive collection of case-studies available at the moment (Nelson, 1993a), Denmark, Canada and Australia actually occupy (along with Sweden) a separate section of the book (Section II) under the heading of Smaller High-Income Countries.

6.   In fact, the motor vehicle sector is quite a significant case in which the USA-Canada integration has been supported institutionally through the so-called 'Auto Pact' (McFetridge, 1993).

7.   The high percentage of external patents obtained from foreign subsidiaries mainly follows from the attempt of the superior-order centres (for instance, Germany and the USA) to tap into the areas in which British expertise is greater (for example, chemicals and pharmaceuticals), rather than to extend those business activities they focus on in their home base (Cantwell, 1995).

8.   Table 4.2 confirms that its foreign participation is not among the highest, although Germany is the most important foreign location for the largest international firms (Patel, 1995).

9.   The national Japanese response to economic globalisation is a well-known story (Fransman, 1995).

5. Exploring the technological system

In the previous chapter we have shown that the different configurations of a TS depend on both its inward/outward orientation, and on the degree of pervasiveness/polarisation of its internal relationships. Of course, the latter, and the specific partitions (in our case sectors) among which they occur, are also extremely important in characterising a certain TS. For this reason, we now move, in this and the next chapter, from the systemic configuration to the analytical exploration of a TS. We will thus examine the maps designed by innovation flows of different magnitudes, the location of the core and terminal sectors (or groups of sectors) of a TS and the pervasive or dependent nature of its partitions.

Following the transformations suggested in Section 3.4, we look at embodied intersectoral innovation flows matrices as 'valued networks', whose nodes and edges are constituted, respectively, by the relevant sectors and intersectoral flows. As already pointed out, this makes it possible to apply some standard network analysis indicators with very significant interpretative power, and to better visualise what is going on inside a TS.

In this chapter, as in the previous one, we will limit our analysis to the relationships which occur within what we could call the 'private business core' (PBC): an important, but still limited part of the inner mechanisms that drive the complex functioning of a TS, based on the techno-economic relationships among the firms which populate it. The analysis will be made more complete by integrating the other constituent sub-systems, in Chapter 6, in which the role of the institutional set-up and the foreign sub-system will be addressed.

Stressing once more the complementarity between ours and other system approaches to technological change, we will follow up the practice of the previous chapter in crossing data sources and in paralleling the results with those obtained by other studies. Among these, the configuration analysis of the previous chapter plays a crucial role. Similar system configurations can in fact underlie different kind of internal networks, making the integration of the two procedures extremely important.

At first (Section 5.1), we will thus examine, from a methodological point of view, the network analysis rationale and indicators used, stressing their interpretative power in exploring the complex structure of TS. Section 5.2 will then present the discussion of the empirical results obtained. And finally, Section 5.3 contains the main conclusions.

5.1   NETWORK ANALYSIS

Among the several indicators and techniques of network analysis,[1] four are particularly helpful in investigating the internal structure of a TS: density, centralisation, centrality and oriented graphs. More precisely, the density and the centralisation of the relevant network may provide information about the degree of connectivity of a TS, while the degree centrality of the network nodes and the corresponding oriented graphs allow us to map innovative flows of a certain magnitude within a TS. Let us consider each of them in turn.

5.1.1   Density

The density of a valued network composed by n nodes (that is, a network represented according to a binary transformation such as (3.18)), is defined as a simple ratio between the actual number of edges surviving its dichotomisation with respect to a certain cut-off k, that is, s, and the maximum number of its directed edges, that is, $n(n-1)$:

$$DEN(k) = \frac{s}{n(n-1)}, \ 0 < DEN(k) < 1 \qquad (5.1)$$

It is straightforward that greater values of (5.1) indicate denser networks. The density of the network corresponding to a TS can thus be assumed to measure its degree of internal cohesion. That is, the higher is the density of the network, the more connected is the TS, and vice versa.

As the choice of an exogenous, usually arbitrary, threshold value for k is one of the main limitations of this indicator, in comparing say z different TS it is convenient to refer to a series of dichotomised matrices. In other words, it is preferable to use a set of cut-off vectors, $[\mathbf{k}_1, \mathbf{k}_2, \dots \mathbf{k}_j \dots, \mathbf{k}_z]$, each one made up of the ordered distribution of the values of $\mathbf{F}^{E,Rel}$ for a certain country j (as we will see, in our dataset $z = 8$), rather than a 'simple' scalar, k. In order to compare density distributions across different countries, it is helpful to jointly consider their diagrammatic representations. In so doing, it is necessary to refer to one country j^* and to work out the density distributions of all the other TS of the dataset with respect to $\mathbf{k}_{j^*}$. In this way, country j^* is used as a sort of *numeraire* to measure the relative distances between the density distributions of the various countries. The choice of country j^* is therefore not crucial for the final result, because the relative distances between countries do not change by changing the reference $\mathbf{k}_{j^*}$ vector.

5.1.2 Centrality, Centralisation and Oriented Graphs

While density is a characteristic of the whole network, centrality is instead proper to each of its nodes. Indeed, it measures how central a node of a valued network is (the reference is still to a dichotomic matrix such as (3.18)) through the number of its connections to and from the other nodes (Freeman, 1979).[2] Formally, the inward (*in*) and the outward (*out*) degree centralities of a certain node *j* are in general defined as follows:

$$G_{in}^j = \sum i_{in} \; ; \; G_{out}^j = \sum i_{out} \qquad (5.2)$$

where i_{in} and i_{out} indicate one of the edges coming, respectively, in and out of node *j*. It is immediate that the domain of $G_{(\cdot)}^j$ is defined as $0 < G_{(\cdot)}^j < n - 1$, and that the greater is $G_{(\cdot)}^j$, the more central is node *j*: either with respect to the incoming edges (G_{in}^j), or to the outcoming ones (G_{out}^j), or with respect to both.[3]

Also the centrality indicator assumes a particular meaning when the network considered is a TS. In fact, since the inward and the outward edges stand now for intersectoral innovative acquisitions and diffusions, respectively, the two measures of centrality help in determining whether a sector is pervasive or dependent.

Obviously, as the notation of (5.2) reveals, in order to perform this analytical examination of the sectoral nodes of a TS it is necessary to extract one or more selected cut-off values *k* from the $\mathbf{k}_z$ vectors described above. Thus, (5.2) is evaluated for the innovative acquisitions and diffusions which 'survive' the dichotomisation with respect to a certain *k*. As already said, the choice of the cut-off value is not free of a certain degree of arbitrariness. However, as will be clearer in the following, the analysis of the density distributions can be of help in attenuating this problem.

Although it is to be referred to a single sector, degree centrality can also be used to analyse the nature of the whole TS, at least in two ways.

First of all, centrality indices can be combined to work out the inward and the outward degree centralisation of one network, defined, respectively, as follows:

$$H_{in}(k) = \frac{\sum_j (G_{in}^{j^*} - G_{in}^j)}{(n-1)(n-2)}; \; H_{out}(k) = \frac{\sum_j (G_{out}^{j^*} - G_{out}^j)}{(n-1)(n-2)} \qquad (5.3)$$

where G^{j^*} is the centrality value of the most central node, j^*, either outward or inward.

According to (5.3), centralisation measures the relative 'centrality-gap' between each node and the most central one, with respect to the maximum level of centrality of a network composed by *n* nodes (that is, $(n-1)(n-2)$).

In general, therefore, a high index of centralisation identifies a network with wide gaps between the (centrality) positions of the nodes, while a low value identifies a network with similar (centrality) positions. In the present case, this corresponds to TS whose sectoral partitions can be deemed, respectively, 'hierarchic' (with high degree centralisation) and 'parithetic' (with low degree centralisation). As intuition suggests, the former case might be less conducive to interactive innovative relationships than the latter.

A second systemwide application of the centrality indices can be obtained by examining their sectoral distribution. In this way it is possible, for example, to identify the composition of a TS in terms of innovative cores and terminals. Intuitively, we define cores as those sectors, or clusters of sectors, that 'count' relatively more in terms of the number of sectors to which they transfer innovation flows (dominance of outward relationships). The contrary holds for the terminals, that is, the number of sectors from which innovations are acquired (dominance of inward relationships).

The numerical balance between cores and terminals is an important element in comparing the structure of different TS and in relating this to their 'connectivity degree', in turn proxied by their density and centralisation. However, it is as important to analyse how the cores map into the terminals, determining which sectors are innovated by which. This would actually further specify the analysis from a qualitative point of view.

In this last respect, it is convenient to integrate the analysis of centrality with that of the directed graphs which correspond to each of the selected dichotomised matrices: indeed, there is a 'bijection' between the set of matrices and the set of directed graphs. Although the concept of oriented graph and its varieties are defined in rigorous mathematical terms,[4] in what follows we are only interested in distinguishing different kinds of graphs in qualitative terms. In this respect, it should be noted that, as the present analysis is based on vertically integrated sectors, direct and indirect relationships are revealed jointly by a unique innovative flow. For this reason, the directed graph that is associated with a certain dichotomised matrix has to be interpreted as an ensemble of 'innovative couples' (univocal and biunivocal) and (possibly) 'development blocks' (DeBresson *et al.*, 1996, pp. 167-168). On the contrary, standard or non-standard 'trees' and 'cycles', or more simple 'technological complexes' do not apply to the same networks which can be read at most as particular 'cliques' (DeBresson *et al.*, 1996, pp. 169-171). Although this consideration introduces *a fortiori* a certain structural homogeneity, relevant differences can however be highlighted across different TS, just by comparing the sectoral composition of the 'innovative couples' and the sectoral location of the eventual 'development blocks'.

5.2   THE EMPIRICAL INVESTIGATION

The empirical investigation performed in this chapter refers to the same set of OECD countries, sectors, and to the same temporal spans of the previous chapter (Tables 4.1 and 4.2).

The analysis of the density distributions of Section 5.2.1 is performed with respect to the cut-off value vector of Canada (that is, k_{Canada}), and thus this distribution is the only one to be 'linear', while those of the remaining countries are distributed around it. Canada has been chosen simply because it allows for a better visualisation of the evolution of the density ranking among the TS in moving from large to small innovative flows.

For obvious scope constraints, given the relatively large number of countries and periods investigated, the analysis of centrality-centralisation and of the directed graphs (Section 5.2.2) is carried out with respect to only one cut-off value ($k = 0.005$).[5]

5.2.1   Density of the Relative Flows Matrices

As far as the density distribution analysis is concerned, the main results emerging from the inspection of Figures 5.1, 5.2, and 5.3 (referring to early 1980s, mid 1980s and early 1990s, respectively) can be summarised as follows:

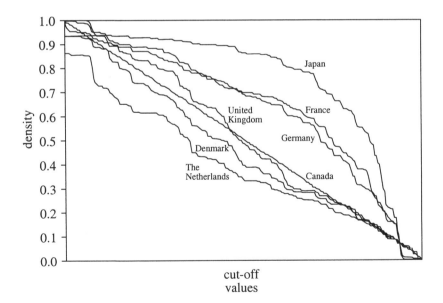

Figure 5.1   Density of innovation flows matrices, early 1980s

1. In the first period (Figure 5.1), Japan, Germany and France cluster as the densest TS along the whole distribution of cut-off values, hinting at their opportunity to exploit more synergetic benefits from closer relationships. The Japanese system, in turn, shows greater density values than the others, confirming its 'relatively' idiosyncratic nature. A cluster of intermediate density values also emerges, made up of Great Britain and Canada, with a lower degree of connectivity. Finally, Denmark and the Netherlands (the smallest countries among those considered) have the least dense distributions, suggesting how problems of innovative 'critical mass' might hinder extended interactions.[6]

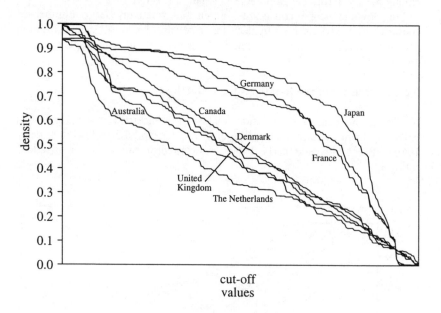

Figure 5.2   Density of innovation flows matrices, mid 1980s

2. The picture for the mid 1980s (Figure 5.2) resembles that for the early 1980s, as far as the densest distributions are concerned, although the gap between Japan, France and Germany narrows. The club of the most connected TS shrinks during the globalisation phase in which systems come to interact more intensively and extensively. This seems to have clear consequences for the sustainability of their internal innovative networks. With the exception of the Netherlands, still lagging behind in terms of density, the less connected TS also become more closely aligned. Only with respect to a limited range of intermediate cut-off values, Australia, another

small country, lies apart from the group of 'the others', which now appears more homogeneous following the substantial gain of Denmark.

3. In the early 1990s (Figure 5.3), with the exception of the most and the least dense distributions, the alignment between the investigated TS becomes even more apparent, hinting at how globalisation tends to reduce diversities among countries in terms of techno-economic relationships. Relevant changes occur also at the extremes. On the one hand, Japan loses its prominent position to the advantage of Germany, although only for intermediate cut-off values, while France remains apart. On the other hand, the range of cut-off values for which Australia lags behind is narrower than in the previous period.

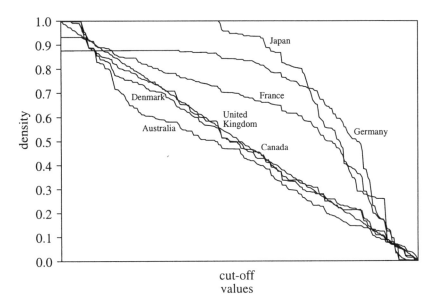

Figure 5.3   Density of innovation flows matrices, early 1990s

In general terms, the analysis of density distributions shows two main facts. First of all, the clustering of the investigated TS is highly affected by structural elements, such as, for example, the relevant model of capitalism and the country size. Secondly, the eight countries investigated show a rather evident process of 'convergence' in density values over time. To be sure, the convergence does not appear to be absolute. Although the three densest TS are more similar in their structure in the 1990s then they are in the 1980s, and the same holds (to a lesser extent) for Great Britain, Canada and Australia,[7] a clear lag persists between the two groups. Therefore, it seems possible to interpret this evidence as a process of 'conditional' convergence, that is, a process of intra-club rather than one of inter-club convergence.[8]

5.2.2   Centrality and Centralisation of Degree

Although limited to relatively few large innovative flows (as already said, the chosen cut-off value is 0.005), the sectoral analysis of centrality (Tables 5.1 to 5.3) confirms, to a different extent in different TS and periods,[9] some 'stylised facts' and some intuitions that one can draw on the particular focus of this study. For instance, the most traditional sectors – food, beverages and tobacco (Sector 1), textiles and leather (Sector 2), wood and furniture (Sector 3) and paper and printing (Sector 4) – are all dependent, as the indegree values are higher than the corresponding outdegree ones. In particular, with the sole exception of Japan (and of the German paper sector in the first two periods), the same sectors are 'totally' dependent, as the outdegree values are nil: the 'supplier dominated' nature of these branches appears therefore confirmed (Pavitt, 1984). Another general result concerns the most pervasive sectors of each TS. With a few exceptions – notably that of Japan[10] – these are a 'specialised supplier' sector – metal products (Sector 10) – and a 'science-based' sector – chemical products (Sector 5) – whose technology has a dominant 'material' nature and which are therefore prominent when 'embodied' innovative flows are considered. This interpretation obviously better fits the former sector that, unlike the latter, is totally pervasive (with a nil indegree, still apart from Japan and from Germany in the last period). The same kind of argument also holds for those sectors – such as shipbuilding and repairing (Sector 12) and motor vehicles (Sector 13) – whose 'large scale' (Pavitt, 1984) naturally calls for consistent intermediate and capital material inputs. With some relevant exceptions (notably that of German motor vehicles), these sectors are dependent, and to the maximum extent (apart from French motor vehicles and the Japanese shipbuilding sector). A general total dependent nature is also shown by the professional goods sector (Sector 14), although its innovative acquisitions are also substantially 'disembodied'.

The nature of the remaining sectors is more specific, as emerges when the sectoral distributions of centrality are considered along with the centralisation index. At the outset, this kind of analysis shows that in all periods two clusters of TS can be identified (Tables 5.1 to 5.3). The former, with a core constituted of two main pervasive sectors (Sector 10 and Sector 5), at most encompassing a few other slightly pervasive branches, and with a quite 'hierarchic' structure (high outdegree centralisation), is made up of Australia, Canada, Denmark, the Netherlands and Great Britain. Another cluster, whose core of pervasive sectors extends more substantially also to other sectors (in addition to Sectors 5 and 10), and whose structure is relatively more 'parithetic' (low outdegree centralisation) comprehends France, Germany and Japan. This partition resembles the taxonomy

Table 5.1   Freeman's degree centrality, early 1980s

Sectors	Canada Out	In	Denmark Out	In	Great Britain Out	In	The Netherl. Out	In	France Out	In	Germany Out	In	Japan Out	In
1	0	1	0	1	0	1	0	1	0	5	0	7	0	8
2	0	2	0	2	0	2	0	2	0	5	0	5	2	7
3	0	1	0	1	0	1	0	1	0	4	0	5	2	9
4	0	3	0	2	0	2	0	2	0	6	1	5	5	7
5	6	2	4	1	4	1	5	1	13	2	13	2	14	3
6	2	2	0	1	0	1	0	2	5	3	0	3	14	5
7	0	2	0	2	0	2	0	2	9	3	4	3	12	5
8	0	2	0	1	0	2	0	2	1	6	1	4	14	6
9	0	1	0	1	0	1	0	1	3	3	1	3	12	5
10	14	0	14	0	14	0	14	0	14	0	14	0	12	6
11	0	1	0	1	2	1	4	1	10	3	13	2	10	6
12	0	1	0	1	0	2	0	2	0	4	0	3	0	8
13	0	1	0	1	0	2	0	2	2	4	5	3	0	7
14	0	1	0	1	0	1	0	2	0	4	0	3	1	6
15	0	2	0	2	0	1	0	2	0	5	0	4	0	10
Descriptive statistics														
Mean	1.5	1.5	1.2	1.2	1.3	1.3	1.5	1.5	3.8	3.8	3.5	3.5	6.5	6.5
Std Dev	3.7	0.7	3.6	0.5	3.5	0.6	3.7	0.6	5.0	1.5	5.1	1.6	5.9	1.7
Sum	22	22	18	18	20	20	23	23	57	57	52	52	98	98
Var	13.6	0.5	12.7	0.3	12.6	0.36	13.5	0.4	24.6	2.3	26.5	2.5	34.2	2.9
Euc Nor	15.4	6.3	14.6	5.1	14.7	5.7	15.4	6.4	24.2	15.8	24.0	14.8	34.0	26.1
Min	0	0	0	0	0	0	0	0	0	0	0	0	0	3
Max	14	3	14	2	14	2	14	2	14	6	14	7	14	10
Network centralisation H_{out} and H_{in}														
%	103	12	105	6	104	5	103	4	84	18	87	29	61	29

presented in the previous chapter, and others that, mainly focusing on purely innovative and atomistic questions, split the same group of countries with respect to their size, their R&D intensities, patents scores, educational levels, and so on (see, for example, Nelson, 1993a). However, as the present analysis is carried out according to techno-economic and relational aspects, it is not fully consistent with them. Indeed, once TS, rather than countries, are considered, the 'myopic' way in which Great Britain organises the innovative process (Patel and Pavitt, 1994) actually becomes more decisive and makes it more similar to the less structured, 'small' systems of innovation. However, the two clusters are neither homogeneous nor completely stable over time, so

Empirical analysis: the macro perspective

Table 5.2   Freeman's degree centrality, mid 1980s

Sectors	Australia		Canada		Denmark		Great Britain		The Netherl.		France		Germany		Japan	
	Out	In	Out	In	Out	In	Out	In	Out	In	Out	In	Out	In	Out	In
1	0	1	0	1	0	1	0	1	0	1	0	6	0	8	0	8
2	0	2	0	2	0	4	0	3	0	2	0	5	0	5	2	8
3	0	1	0	1	0	2	0	2	0	2	0	5	0	6	2	10
4	0	2	0	2	0	3	0	3	0	2	0	7	1	5	6	7
5	6	1	6	1	8	1	8	1	6	1	13	3	13	2	14	2
6	0	2	0	2	0	3	0	2	0	2	5	3	1	3	11	5
7	0	2	0	2	0	2	0	2	0	2	9	3	4	4	11	6
8	0	2	0	2	0	3	0	3	0	2	3	6	3	4	14	6
9	0	1	0	2	0	2	0	3	0	1	5	3	1	4	13	3
10	14	0	14	0	14	0	14	0	14	0	14	0	14	0	12	7
11	0	1	3	1	6	1	7	1	4	1	13	3	13	2	9	5
12	0	1	0	2	0	1	0	2	0	2	0	4	0	3	0	7
13	0	1	0	1	0	2	0	2	0	2	2	5	6	3	0	6
14	0	2	0	2	0	2	0	2	0	2	0	6	0	3	0	6
15	0	1	0	2	1	2	0	2	0	2	0	5	0	4	2	10
Descriptive statistics																
Mean	1.3	1.3	10	1.5	1.9	1.9	1.9	1.9	1.6	1.6	4.3	4.3	3.7	3.7	6.4	6.4
Std Dev	3.7	0.6	3.7	0.6	4.0	1.0	4.1	0.8	3.7	0.6	5.2	1.7	5.1	1.8	5.5	2.1
Sum	20	20	23	23	29	29	29	29	24	24	64	64	56	56	96	96
Var	14	0.4	14	0.4	16	1.0	17	0.7	14	0.4	27	3.0	26	3.3	31	4.5
Euc Nor	15	5.7	15	6.4	17	8.4	18	8.2	16	6.6	26	18	24	16	33	26
Min	0	0	0	0	0	0	0	0	0	0	0	0	0	0	0	2
Max	14	2	14	2	14	4	14	3	14	2	14	7	14	8	14	10
Network centralisation H_{out} and H_{in}																
%	104	5	4	4	99	17	99	9	102	3	80	22	85	35	63	30

that a more detailed examination is necessary.

1. In the first period (Table 5.1), the group of 'simple-core' TS is clearly exemplified by the case of Denmark, with only two pervasive sectors (Sectors 5 and 10) whose outward centrality is quite different (greater for Sector 10) and whose interconnections are not mutual. The Netherlands and Great Britain appear instead slightly more 'connected', as they extend the simple core, still unbalanced towards Sector 10, to the machinery sector (Sector 11), a fact that could hint at the importance of their specialisation in the non-electrical division of the same sector. Issues related to the use and

Table 5.3   Freeman's degree centrality, early 1990s

Sectors	Canada Out	In	Denmark Out	In	Great Britain Out	In	The Netherl. Out	In	France Out	In	Germany Out	In	Japan Out	In
1	0	1	0	1	0	2	0	2	0	6	0	4	0	8
2	0	2	0	2	0	3	0	2	0	5	0	4	2	8
3	0	1	0	1	0	2	0	2	0	5	0	4	2	10
4	0	2	0	2	0	3	0	3	0	7	0	4	6	7
5	6	1	6	1	11	1	13	1	13	2	14	3	14	2
6	0	2	0	2	0	3	0	2	4	4	0	4	9	4
7	0	2	0	2	0	3	0	2	11	3	0	4	12	4
8	0	1	0	2	0	3	0	3	3	6	0	4	14	7
9	0	2	0	1	0	3	0	3	6	3	0	4	13	3
10	14	0	14	0	14	0	14	0	14	0	14	3	8	7
11	0	1	2	1	9	1	6	2	13	4	14	3	11	5
12	0	1	0	2	0	2	0	3	0	5	0	4	0	8
13	0	1	0	1	0	3	0	3	2	5	14	3	0	6
14	0	2	0	2	0	3	0	3	0	6	0	4	1	5
15	0	1	0	2	0	2	0	2	0	5	0	4	2	10
Descriptive statistics														
Mean	1.3	1.3	1.5	1.5	2.3	2.3	2.2	2.2	4.4	4.4	3.7	3.7	6.3	6.3
Std Dev	3.7	0.6	3.7	0.6	4.6	0.9	4.7	0.8	5.3	1.7	6.2	0.4	5.7	2.3
Sum	20	20	22	22	34	34	33	33	66	66	56	56	94	94
Var	13.7	0.4	13.6	0.4	21.4	0.9	21.9	0.7	28.6	3.0	38.3	0.2	28.7	5.4
Euc Nor	15.2	5.7	15.4	6.2	19.9	9.5	20.0	9.1	26.8	18.3	28.0	14.6	31.9	25.9
Min	0	0	0	0	0	0	0	0	0	0	0	3	0	2
Max	14	2	14	2	14	3	14	3	14	7	14	4	14	10
Network centralisation H_{out} and H_{in}														
%	104	5	103	4	97	6	97	7	84	21	85	2	64	31

availability of natural resources may instead have a role in explaining the Canadian core extension to the coal and petroleum sector (Sector 6). On the other hand, in both cases the extension (in terms of outward centrality) is not very appreciable, so that the corresponding outward centralisation is nearly the same.

As far as the cluster of 'dense' TS is concerned, France and Germany appear once again quite similar, as shown by their outward centralisation indices. The metal-chemical innovative core for these two TS is wider, but also more balanced towards maximum outward centrality values. The machinery sector (Sector 11) is almost as pervasive as Sectors 10 and 5. The 'resource-intensive' sectors (Sectors 6-9) are in the same case non-totally dependent, or even slightly pervasive (for example, the rubber and plastic products (Sector 7)). Centralisation indices are substantially lower than those regarding the previous cluster. A further peculiar feature is identified by the motor vehicles sector (Sector 13), nearly pervasive in France and highly pervasive in Germany. In this regard specialisation still identifies a potential explanatory factor.

A confirmation of other more qualitative studies comes from the highly idiosyncratic nature of Japan. Although metal products (Sector 10) are not as pervasive as in France and Germany, the pervasive core is the widest, as it spans from Sector 5 to Sector 11, with nearly maximum values. Furthermore, those which can be considered as terminal sectors – traditional sectors such as Sectors 1 to 4 – are less dependent than elsewhere, with the consequence that the (outward) centralisation index is lower than in the TS we have considered before.

2. In the second period (Table 5.2), Australia, a small and quite isolated system of innovation (Gregory, 1993), joins the cluster of 'dispersed' TS. In the same period, the dual core (Sectors 5 and 10) of Denmark becomes more balanced and extends, although to a lesser extent, to machinery (Sector 11). This seems to hint at the fact that the 'systemic evolution' of the Danish system (like the Swedish one) benefited from an active specialised supplier core, although with a consistent foreign penetration (Edquist and Lundvall, 1993). In this last respect, Denmark 'overtakes' Canada, whose core just substitutes 'energy' (Sector 6) for 'machinery' (Sector 11), and the Netherlands, 'catching up' with Great Britain, where the pervasiveness of machinery (Sector 10) and chemicals (Sector 5) also increases. Let us remember that a certain structural change has been identified for Denmark also in the previous chapter.

The centralisation level of the group of 'dense' TS is still quite distant from that of the 'dispersed' TS, in turn quite stable. The only relevant variation is actually the centralisation increase for France, in turn due to the outward centrality increase of machinery (Sector 11) and non-finished metals (Sector 9). In spite of this change, and of the slight decrease and increase of, respectively, Japan and Germany, in the centrality indices within the 'resource-intensive' partition (Sectors 6-9), the dichotomy between Japan, on the one hand, and France and Germany, on the other, still persists, somehow confirming the configuration gap shown before.

3. In the third period (Table 5.3), Australia is still the most centralised TS, revealing a configuration that appears structurally polarised around no more than two pervasive sectors, while the remaining sectors are totally dependent. Within the same 'simple-core' cluster, the Danish TS shows a further increase in the pervasiveness level of chemical products (Sector 5) and machinery (Sector 11), the latter switching from the least to the most centralised position. Once again, this seems to be a case of conditional catching up, induced by a structural change towards more synergetic

interrelationships. A similar pattern can be identified for Great Britain, whose two-sector pervasive core becomes more balanced too. A 'dynamic' sub-cluster, made up of Denmark and Great Britain, seems therefore identifiable within the cluster of 'dispersed' TS, as opposed to a 'structurally myopic' cluster, made up of Australia and Canada.

The most remarkable changes of the period are however in the second, more 'connected' cluster. Although the centralisation is unchanged, Germany radically changes the distribution of its pervasive core, which narrows to chemicals (Sector 5), metal products (Sector 10), machinery (Sector 11) and motor vehicles (Sector 13), but now with maximum (or nearly maximum) values of outward degree centrality. The remaining sectors become totally dependent, and this seems to point to an intensive, rather than an extensive structural change, focusing on and exploiting the externalities of the main sectoral specialisations. A different argument holds for France, whose core composition remains basically the same, but where the inward and the outward centrality degrees change in such a way as to make the system less centralised and more interconnected. The change of Japan, although less relevant, is instead in the opposite direction. In spite of the increase in the outward centrality of Sectors 14 and 15, the combined effect of a lower pervasiveness in metals (Sector 10) and energy products (Sector 6), and of a higher pervasiveness in machinery (Sector 11) and rubber and plastic products (Sector 7) determines a slight loss of connectivity (higher outward centralisation).

5.2.3   Oriented Graphs

At the outset, let us observe how the oriented graphs of the dichotomised matrices (Figures 5.4 to 5.6) make the two clusters of TS discussed above immediately apparent. On the one hand, we have Australia, Canada, Denmark, the Netherlands and Great Britain, with a set of relatively few 'innovative couples', exclusively (or nearly exclusively) univocal, and mainly (or solely) based on Sectors 5 (chemicals) and 10 (metal products). On the other hand, we have France, Germany and Japan, with more innovative couples, more frequently biunivocal (but just in relative terms), and also based on sectors other than Sectors 5 and 10. As suggested by the centrality analysis, the relationship between pervasive and dependent sectors is quite dichotomic so that within the latter, more systemic, cluster of TS it is not possible to identify 'development blocks' or similarly articulated structures (DeBresson *et al.*, 1996).

In general terms the two groups of TS show quite distinct sectoral specifications.

In all the TS of the former group the metal products sector (Sector 10) extends its innovative diffusions over all the remaining ones. Conversely, the chemical sector (Sector 5) innovates only some of them, namely traditional (for instance, Sectors 2, 3 and 4) and resource-intensive (for instance, Sectors

6, 7, 8 and 9) sectors which are technologically closer to it. The diffusions towards the sectors with a more immaterial technology are instead relatively less frequent and specific to certain countries and periods. The machinery sector (Sector 11), when it comes to integrate the previous core, follows a quite different pattern. Indeed, its diffusions generally reach only the scale-intensive sectors of the classification (that is, Sectors 12 and 13) and the residual branches (Sector 15). The traditional and/or resource-intensive sectors are affected only in some cases. The sectoral partitions which refer to Sectors 5 and 11 are quite separated (that is, the relative sectors overlap only slightly) and the same pivotal sectors do not communicate, although they are both innovated by Sector 10. Therefore, two distinct groups of sector areas emerge. They are based, respectively, on material and immaterial technologies. Extra-core diffusions are very limited, or even absent.

Within the second group of countries, the chemical sector (Sector 5) becomes as pervasive as the metal products one (Sector 10), which in turn has a maximum outward centrality. The exception is Japan, for which Sector 5, and not Sector 10, becomes more pervasive. A similar change applies to the machinery sector (Sector 11), which always innovates at least 70% of the remaining sectors. Although the three sectoral partitions now overlap to a greater extent, *a fortiori*, the pivotal sectors still do not generally communicate. The importance of the resource-intensive sectors (Sectors 6-9) increases. Indeed, sometimes they join Sector 5 (and eventually 10 and/or 11) in a sort of supercore, while in some other cases they constitute a sort of peripheral core. Extra-core diffusion is less exceptional, if not actually normal (as in the case of Japan).

A more precise specification of these regularities, and of their temporal evolution, obviously calls for a period-by-period analysis.

1. In the early 1980s (Figure 5.4), and within the first cluster, the Netherlands and Great Britain, unlike Canada and Denmark, show a core which marginally extends also to the machinery sector (Sector 11), as it pervades only the most adjacent branches, those related to transport equipment (Sectors 12 and 13).[11] The diffusions of the chemical sector (Sector 5) towards the resource-intensive partition encompass energy products (Sector 6) only in the most energy-endowed TS (Canada and the Netherlands). Moreover, in Canada Sector 13 also innovate Sector 12, identifying a characteristic biunivocal innovative couple.

Within the second cluster, Japan clearly stands out as the TS with the largest core. This is in turn made up of a mostly pervasive supercore, centred on basic materials and on their chemical transformation (Sectors 5, 6 and 8), and a peripheral core, made up of synthetic and intermediate metallic products (Sectors 7 and 9), and of finished metal products (Sector 10) and machinery (Sector 11). However, the former (Sectors 7 and 9) are neither linked between them nor with other nodes, while the latter (Sectors 10 and 11) exceptionally do not innovate the chemicals (Sector 5) and some other

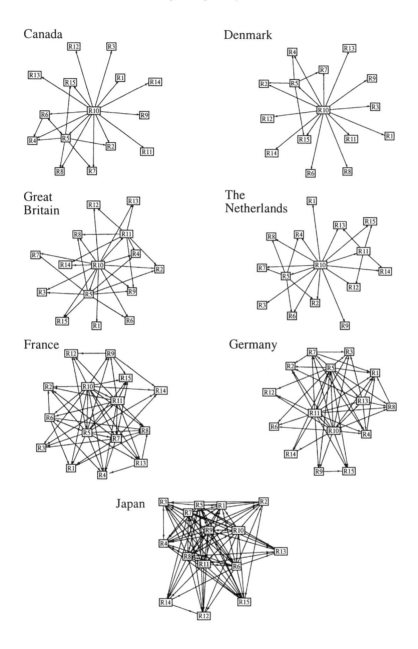

Figure 5.4   Oriented graphs, early 1980s (k = 0.005)

traditional and resource-intensive sectors. In France and in Germany the supercore is limited to Sectors 5, 10 and 11, still non-entirely interlinked, while the resource-intensive sectors are much less pervasive than in Japan. Energy products (Sector 6) and rubber and plastics (Sector 7), especially in France, are the only remarkably pervasive sectors, concentrating diffusions towards both traditional and other resource-intensive sectors. Exceptionally, some of the Japanese traditional sectors (for example, Sectors 2 and 3, Sectors 3 and 4) constitute biunivocal innovative couples and also reach the residual sector (Sector 15). Another relevant extra-core diffusion is that of the German motor vehicles (Sector 13), affecting, in addition to Sectors 4 and 8, as in France, also traditional sectors, such as Sector 1, 2 and 3.

2. Coming to the second period (Figure 5.5), the three-node pervasive core (Sectors 5, 10 and 11) becomes dominant in the first group of TS, as Australia is the only one exclusively based on Sectors 5 and 10. The chemical diffusions become wider, as they now systematically reach also the energy sector (Sector 6) and all the traditional sectors, except for food and beverages (Sector 1).[12] A similar trend can be observed for machinery (Sector 11), in particular in the British and in the Danish TS, where it innovates also some 'upper' sectors (that is, Sectors 2, 4, 6 and 8), showing how the traditional and the resource-intensive sectors here benefit from virtuous backward linkages. In the Netherlands the same linkages are instead limited to the 'lower' sectors (that is, Sectors 12, 13, 14 and 15).[13]

The structure of the TS within the second group of countries is identical to the previous period, but its specification is slightly different. The Japanese energy products sector (Sector 6) switches from the supercore to the periphery, losing its diffusions to Sectors 11, 13 and 14. The reverse holds for ferrous and non-ferrous metals (Sector 9), which becomes peripherally pervasive in Japan, where it does not affect the chemical (and some traditional and resource-intensive sectors). The machinery sector (Sector 11) is mostly pervasive in France and in Germany. Out of the resource-intensive sectors, instead, the pervasiveness of rubbers and plastics (Sector 7) decreases in Japan, getting disconnected from Sectors 5, 8, 9, 10 and 11, while it increases in France and in Germany. The same holds for the French energy products (Sector 6), while the German sector only innovates Sector 1. A similar dichotomy holds for the ferrous and non-ferrous metal products (Sector 9), the diffusions of which are in Germany limited to the residual sector (Sector 15), while in France the same sector is connected to the peripheral core, mainly innovating Sectors 12, 13, 14 and 15. As far as the extra-core diffusions are concerned, the traditional, biunivocal, innovative couples of Japan, and the univocal, motor vehicles-based, innovative couples of France and, especially, of Germany are still the most representative.

3. In the early 1990s (Figure 5.6), the first cluster confirms the dichotomy between Australia and the remaining TS. Among the latter, in turn, Canada is clearly distinct from Great Britain and Denmark, at least in two respects. On the one hand, their chemical sector (Sector 5) gets closer to the role it has in

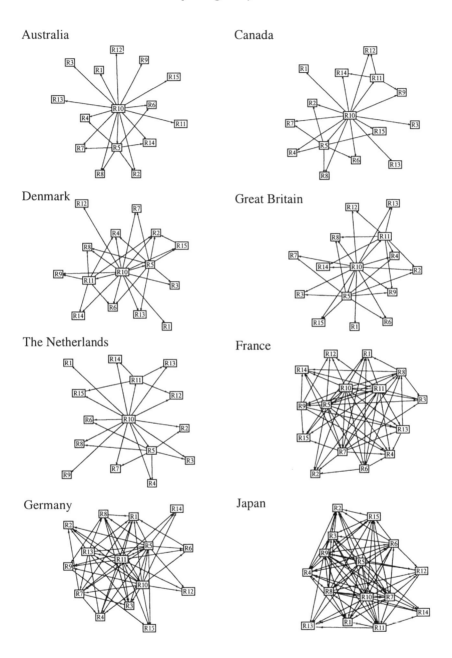

Figure 5.5   Oriented graphs, mid 1980s (k = 0.005)

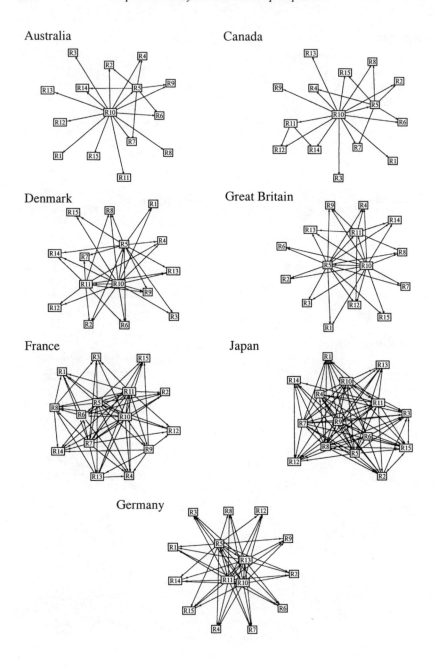

Figure 5.6   Oriented graphs, early 1990s (k = 0.005)

the large countries cluster (it innovates the most immaterial technology-based sectors (that is, Sectors 13, 14, 15, and, in Great Britain, also Sectors 11 and 12). On the other hand, a similar argument holds for machinery (Sector 11) which also reaches some traditional and resource-intensive sectors (Sectors 4, 8, 9, and, in Great Britain, also Sectors 2, 6, and 7). The combined effect of these two patterns implies a clear reduction in the dichotomy between the terminal sectors that are innovated, quite evident in the previous periods, especially in the early 1980s. In this period, therefore, Denmark and Great Britain seem to converge towards the structure of the second cluster.

Here also, important changes are observable. The most relevant is, as we have already said, that of Germany, whose TS degenerates in an enlarged supercore of mostly pervasive and interlocked sectors, made up of chemicals (Sector 5), metal products (Sector 10), machinery (Sector 11) and motor vehicles (Sector 13). Also France enlarges the 'standard' 5-10-11-Sector core, with the addition of rubbers and plastics (Sector 7). The peripheral core of the resource-intensive sectors generally reduces its outdegree centrality. Finally, Japan maintains its idiosyncratic structure, and also the sectoral specification of both the supercore and the peripheral core (except for the diminishing pervasive role of rubbers and plastics). Small changes only occur in the extra-core diffusions: paper and printing increases its innovative weight, diffusing, in addition to all the other traditional sectors, also Sectors 8, 10 and 15. Moreover, relevant diffusions also emerge in the lower part of the classification, particularly those from professional goods (Sector 14) to shipbuilding (Sector 12).

5.3   CONCLUSIONS

As we wanted to investigate the innovative flows that constitute the skeleton of the TS, we have opted for an instrument, network analysis, which proves to be particularly appropriate for the examination of complex techno-economic interrelationships. By applying some of its most standard indicators to the same group of countries, and to the same temporal span as the previous chapter, interesting results have emerged.

The density analysis, performed to measure the connectivity of the TS, shows that separate clusters emerge according to structural kinds of elements, such as size, technological intensity, models of capitalism, and institutional arrangements. Furthermore, the eight TS investigated show a process of 'conditional convergence', hinting that the globalisation phase they entered in the last decade may have also attenuated differences of structural nature, but only in relative terms. In this last respect, several analogies with the analysis of the previous chapter have been emphasised.

The centrality analysis mainly confirms other standard sectoral taxonomies. However, the exclusive reference to embodied innovative flows ends up emphasising the role of specialised suppliers sectors and of those sectors whose technology is basically material.

The centrality distributions and the centralisation analyses also point to quite separate, although not completely homogeneous and stable, groupings. A first cluster, with a quite hierarchic structure, is made up of Australia, Canada, Denmark, the Netherlands and Great Britain. A second one, whose structure is relatively more evenly distributed, includes France, Germany and Japan.

The analysis of the oriented graphs, mapping the sectoral origins and destinations of the innovative flows, further refines the differences. In all the TS of the first cluster, the chemical sector innovates only some of the traditional and resource-intensive sectors, while the diffusions towards the immaterial technology sectors are instead relatively less frequent. Within the second cluster, the chemical sector becomes generally as pervasive as the metal products one, with a maximum outward centrality. The same holds for machinery. Unlike the first cluster, the resource-intensive sectors gain remarkable importance, and significant innovative couples, sometimes even biunivocal, can be identified in the more traditional sectors (Japan) and in motor vehicles (Germany).

Although these characteristics are more or less persistent over the three periods, two major structural changes can however be identified. The more evident is that of Germany, which by the early 1990s radically changes the sectoral distribution of its pervasive core which narrows to four (chemicals, metal products, machinery and motor vehicles), with maximum (or nearly maximum) outward centrality. The remaining sectors become totally dependent, and this seems to point to an intensive, rather than to an extensive, structural change, possibly due to the strategy of addressing and exploiting the externalities of the main sectoral specialisations. The second substantial change is that of Denmark (and to a lesser extent that of Great Britain) which, in the second, and especially in the third period, gets closer to the structure of the cluster comprising Japan, France and Germany. This change, mainly due to the pervasive role acquired by the machinery sector, which becomes more vertically integrated with the others, appears even more significant when it is coupled with the structural configuration jump detected in the previous chapter for Denmark.

NOTES

1. In this section, we will limit ourselves to a very brief presentation of the indicators that are used in the following analysis. It is obviously not this section's function to be either exhaustive or systematic in argument. A deeper discussion can be found, for example, in Freeman (1979), Knoke and Kuklinski (1982), Scott (1991), Faust and Wasserman (1995).

2.   This is what is called degree centrality. Centrality can also be referred to closeness, measuring the distance between two nodes in terms of the number of intermediate edges, and to betweenness, measuring the frequency with which a node falls between other nodes (Mitchell, 1969). These versions of centrality are however not relevant in the present context.

3.   If auto-cycles are also considered, the maximum centrality is of course n instead of $(n - 1)$. In the present analysis, focused on relational aspects, auto-cycles, which represent intra-sectoral innovative flows, are not relevant and will not be considered. It should also be pointed out that, while coincident in symmetric networks, in asymmetric networks, such as the present ones, inward and outward centrality measures are different.

4.   For a formal treatment of the subject see, for example, Harary (1969, Ch. II).

5.   Although the choice of this cut-off value is completely arbitrary, a preliminary sensitivity analysis has allowed us to establish two facts with respect to it. First of all, given that extreme cut-off values determine, respectively, either almost completely connected or nearly totally disconnected networks, the chosen value is an intermediate one: indeed, it allows for the detection of peculiarities in the structure of the TS investigated. Secondly, the structure singled out is quite stable for reasonably large variations in the cut-off value.

6.   The results of this and the following analysis seem to suggest the existence of a clusterization of countries which parallels that put forward by other, more qualitative types of analysis related to the so-called 'models of capitalism' (Albert, 1991). Although we put this forward as a tentative conjecture which should be backed up by further investigation, it is worth stressing also a certain parallelism between these results and those of the system configuration (Chapter 4).

7.   It must however be noted that the process seems to be more evident also because of the absence of data regarding the Netherlands for the third period (early 1990s).

8.   Let us remember that a special kind of convergence had been identified also in terms of system configurations in the previous chapter.

9.   The sectoral analysis will be limited to some general regularities, while differences will be examined in dealing with oriented graphs.

10.   The specificity of the Japanese system, already evident on the basis of the density analysis, will be investigated in depth later on.

11.   To be sure, the relevant innovation flows also from machinery to professional goods (Sector 14) – in the Netherlands – and to the residual sector (Sector 15) – in Great Britain.

12.   The chemical sector also systematically innovates the residual sector (Sector 15), while in Denmark and Great Britain it extends, respectively, to Sectors 9 and 13.

13.   Upper and lower refer to the order of the relative sectoral classification.

6. The complete technological system: a comparative analysis of core and extra-core relationships

The analysis presented in the previous chapters has allowed us to identify and compare the skeleton of different TS: that is, what we termed the private business core (PBC) of a TS. Within this chapter we will try to consider the whole set of processes and relationships a TS is made up of. As we will show, this amounts to 'unfolding' the TS. Indeed, opening the black box hidden within each TS turns out to be crucial in order to make their comparative investigation more specific.

The aim of this chapter is therefore that of presenting and applying a methodology which can be useful in moving towards such a kind of complete (unfolded) analysis of the TS. In fact, we will elaborate a more sophisticated version of the R&D expenditure-based methodology of the previous chapters that will allow us to analyse the whole set of relationships established within a TS by its constituent building blocks. More precisely, we will be able to separately investigate the relationships among the private business core (PBC), the institutional set-up and the foreign market. In order to do this, rather than referring to R&D expenditure, we use *R&D financing flows* as a proxy for the techno-economic relationships of a TS.

This chapter is organised as follows. In Section 6.1, the rationale of this new methodology is first of all presented, discussed and related to that of the more general intersectoral analysis of the TS it draws on. Such a rationale is then translated into new kinds of intersectoral matrices (R&D financing flows matrices), to which standard and more complex network analysis indicators are then applied. In Section 6.2, such a methodology is applied to compare five technological systems (France, Germany, Great Britain, Japan and Italy) for the mid 1980s (1985). The ensuing results are there discussed and related to those of previous analyses of the same set of countries. Some conclusive remarks are finally drawn in Section 6.3.

6.1   THE INSTITUTIONAL SET-UP AND THE FOREIGN MARKET: DIRECT VS. INDIRECT ANALYSES

6.1.1   Unfolding the TS: R&D Expenditure and R&D Financing Intersectoral Flows

In the previous chapters, the main relationships which constitute the TS have been proxied (with some relevant *caveats*) by the flows of R&D expenditure which are made by each economic sector of a TS, and diffused to the others through the exchange of intermediate commodities in which they are embodied. To be sure, such flows *directly* account only for the relationships which constitute what we have termed the 'private business core' (PBC) of a TS. Such a PBC is in fact made up of firms which invest in innovation, obtain new products and processes, and spread their innovative results to other firms (mainly their suppliers and their users) and to the final demand, both in the form of spillovers and through some form of technology transfer.[1] However, the same flows also account, although *indirectly*, for the relationships which occur between the PBC and the other two building blocks of the TS (the institutional set-up and the foreign market). Indeed, not only is the embodied R&D expenditure funded by private enterprises, but its volume and its sectoral structure are also affected by public and foreign financing. Given that making funds available for innovation is one of the most important channels, although not the sole one, through which the institutional set-up and the foreign market interact with the PBC, the analysis of R&D-embodied flows has allowed us to refer somehow to the TS as a whole. Accordingly, by mapping these flows by means of intersectoral matrices, we have been able to work out measures of density and centralisation of the TS as a whole, as well as measures of centrality of its constituent sectors and the direction of the corresponding techno-economic flows.

The previous analysis provides us with a picture which is the result of the co-evolution of different sub-systems, where it is impossible to disentangle the contributions of each one. However, appreciating the weight and the role that the different constituent sub-systems play in co-determining these aggregate results is also important, for at least two reasons. First of all, the core and the peripheral partitions of a TS can be identified more precisely, distinguishing those which more directly refer to the private business sector from those which instead pertain to the public and/or to the foreign sub-system. Secondly, and consequently, policy recommendations can be put forward more accurately.

Unfortunately, as we have shown in a previous work (Leoncini *et al.*, 1996), unfolding the TS with respect to its sub-systems by keeping using R&D expenditure as such is not straightforward. In particular, in order to retain R&D expenditure intersectoral flows also in the analysis of the complete TS, it is necessary to make use of heterogeneous proxies for the

PBC and for the other sub-systems, thus making the analysis not entirely satisfactory.

Looking for a more consistent approach, in this chapter we put forward a methodology which, although different from the previous one, remains logically connected to it. More precisely, rather than referring to *R&D expenditure flows*, we suggest looking at *R&D financing flows*, in addressing both the techno-economic relationships within the PBC – proxied by privately funded R&D flows – and those between the PBC and, respectively, the public sub-system – proxied by government-funded R&D flows – and the foreign sub-system – proxied by foreign-funded R&D flows.

Apparently, by resorting to R&D financing rather than R&D expenditure we make our innovation proxy less accurate than before. Indeed, the proportion of a certain financial project transformed into actual innovations is presumably less than the corresponding actual expenditure: in a sense, the input nature of our innovative proxy has been elevated to the square. Furthermore, financial relationships, of which intersectoral R&D financing flows can be deemed a reliable proxy, have to be considered along with, let us say, 'arm's length financing', for which the allocation and the destination of innovative funds are not directly observable (Bergemann and Hege, 2001). In addition to these conceptual problems there are other methodological issues that, as we will see in the next section, make the present methodology not completely satisfactory.[2] On the other hand, the new approach that we put forward seems to us the (second) best solution to the trade-off between data availability and methodological accuracy that we had to face in looking for a methodology to unfold the TS in a coherent way.

6.1.2 R&D Financing Flows Matrices: 'Edged' Matrices and Network Analysis

In the previous chapter we have assumed that innovations, proxied by R&D expenditure, diffuse among sectors in an embodied way. More precisely, the embodiment process, as described by equation (3.15), is assumed to occur with respect to all the resources through which sectoral R&D expenditure is financed. The latter can be, in principle, of three kinds: private, that is originating from the firms themselves, public, that is from universities, research institutes and other public institutions, and foreign, that is from firms (in general multinational subsidiaries) and other public and private organisations based abroad.

In addressing the connectivity of a TS as a whole, the assumption of such a 'full' embodiment process is quite helpful. Indeed, the PBC, the institutional set-up and the foreign market can be simultaneously retained, either explicitly or implicitly. The analysis is thus carried out with respect to standard, square intersectoral matrices, to which different kinds of analytical tools (mainly network analysis) are then applied.

However, when one wants to separately disentangle the role of the different sub-systems of a TS, this assumption is no longer suitable. Indeed, it is more realistic to assume that, while the embodiment channel is relevant for the innovations a certain sector gets from the PBC, the flows coming from the public and the foreign sub-systems have a more disembodied nature. For example, public subsidies to R&D and international technology transfers are typically explicit and direct flows, rather than implicit and indirect.

On the basis of this argument, although both channels of innovative diffusion are at work with respect to both the PBC and the other two sub-systems, we can assume, as a first approximation, that privately funded R&D expenditure circulates within the PBC only through the embodied mechanism that we have previously analysed. Accordingly, such flows can be proxied by a matrix $\mathbf{F}^E{}_{Pr}(n \times n)$ defined as:

$$\mathbf{F}^E_{Pr}(n \times n) = \hat{\mathbf{r}}_{Pr}\left[(\hat{\mathbf{x}})^{-1}\mathbf{B}\hat{\mathbf{d}}\right] \tag{6.1}$$

where $\hat{\mathbf{r}}_{Pr}$ $(n \times n)$ is the diagonal matrix of the sectoral R&D expenditure which is privately funded. *Mutatis mutandis*, the meaning of each cell of (6.1) is equivalent to that defined in equation (3.15).

Still as an approximation, we can then assume that the relationships between the public and the foreign sub-systems, on the one hand, and the economic sectors of the PBC, on the other hand, are exclusively of a disembodied nature. Accordingly, these relationships can be proxied by the shares of R&D expenditure made by each of the n sectors which are financed by, respectively, public (*Pub*) and foreign sources (*For*), shares that we can order in the two row vectors $\mathbf{r}_{Pub}(1 \times n)$ and $\mathbf{r}_{For}(1 \times n)$, respectively.

Finally, in order to represent the whole set of flows which occur between all the sub-systems of a TS, we can 'edge' the $\mathbf{F}^E{}_{Pr}$ matrix, which accounts for the intersectoral flows of the PBC, with two extra rows and two extra columns: the two rows ($\mathbf{r}_{Pub}$ and $\mathbf{r}_{For}$) measure the innovative diffusions from the public and from the foreign sub-systems to the economic sectors of the PBC; the two columns are instead two nil vectors which are introduced to transform the matrix into a square matrix.[3] This operation gives us back an 'edged' matrix, $\mathbf{F}_{Pr,Pub,For}((n + 2) \times (n + 2))$, which provides us with a full account of all the intersectoral flows of a TS, and that can be represented as follows:

$$\mathbf{F}_{Pr,Pub,For} = \begin{bmatrix} F_{Pr,11}^E & \cdots & F_{Pr,1j}^E & \cdots & F_{Pr,1n}^E & 0 & 0 \\ \vdots & \vdots & \vdots & \vdots & \vdots & \vdots & \vdots \\ F_{Pr,i1}^E & \cdots & F_{Pr,ij}^E & & F_{Pr,in}^E & 0 & 0 \\ \vdots & \vdots & \vdots & \vdots & \vdots & \vdots & \vdots \\ F_{Pr,n1}^E & \cdots & F_{Pr,nj}^E & \cdots & F_{Pr,nn}^E & 0 & 0 \\ r_{Pub,1} & \cdots & r_{Pub,j} & \cdots & r_{Pub,n} & 0 & 0 \\ r_{For,1} & \cdots & r_{For,j} & \cdots & r_{For,n} & 0 & 0 \end{bmatrix} \qquad (6.2)$$

Although the structure of a TS appears in this way more explicit, matrix (6.2) is however made up of heterogeneous, non-comparable flows. In order to get rid of this problem, we must, first of all, relate each intersectoral and inter-sub-system R&D financial flow to the relative total sectoral R&D financing: that is, the sum of the private R&D financing that a certain sector acquires indirectly from the other sectors of the PBC, and of the public and foreign R&D financing it acquires directly from the other two sub-systems. In other words, the absolute values matrix of (6.2) must be transformed into a new matrix, $\mathbf{F}_{Pr,Pub,For}^{Rel}$, defined as:

$$\mathbf{F}_{Pr,Pub,For}^{Rel} = \mathbf{F}_{Pr,Pub,For}(\hat{s})^{-1} \qquad (6.3)$$

where $\hat{s}$ is the diagonal matrix of total sectoral R&D financing acquisitions:

$$s_{ij} = \sum_i F_{Pr,Pub,For,ij} \qquad (6.4)$$

By means of this transformation we get rid of scale effects. Furthermore, and above all, we are able to reshape the edged matrix $\mathbf{F}_{Pr,Pub,For}$, in which the core matrix $\mathbf{F}_{Pr}$ and the edging vectors ($\mathbf{r}_{Pub}$ and $\mathbf{r}_{For}$) are simply 'juxtaposed', into an internally consistent matrix whose cells all refer to a system variable for the whole matrix: the total by sector of R&D financing.

However, in spite of this transformation, the intersectoral flows of $F_{Pr,Pub,For}^{Rel}$ still have a different nature. Those of the inter-industrial partition in fact measure the incidence of private R&D financing indirect acquisitions as a proportion of the total acquisitions of each sector. Those of the last two row vectors, instead, measure the incidence as a proportion of the total of direct public and foreign R&D acquisitions.

Because of this heterogeneity, the density and the centralisation analyses we have performed elsewhere with respect to total R&D expenditure flows cannot be applied directly to (6.3). However, we can still compute the density of each single sub-system (the PBC, the institutional set-up and the foreign market), by working out, as usual, the ratio between the number of edges, $s_{(.)}$, greater than a selected threshold, k, and the total number of potential edges:

$$DEN_{PBC}(k) = \frac{s_{Pr}}{n \times (n-1)} \; ; \; DEN_{Pub}(k) = \frac{s_{Pub}}{n} \; ; \; DEN_{For}(k) = \frac{s_{For}}{n} \qquad (6.5)$$

Each indicator in (6.5) lies between 0 and 1, and is the greater the more connected is the corresponding sub-system. Moreover, indicators cannot be compared with the density values of the whole TS (DEN) as calculated in (5.1). Therefore, rather than comparing them, we will instead compute the degree of correlation between their rankings. In this way, we can partly overcome the problems entailed by flows heterogeneity. Furthermore, we can get at least some hints about the mutual relationships between the different sub-systems, and between them and the TS as a whole.

By adopting the Spearman correlation index,[4] for example, we can first of all control to what extent a higher position in terms of density of the PBC gets reflected in a similar position with respect to the TS as a whole.

Secondly, the correlation between the TS ranked according to $DEN_{PBC}(k)$, $DEN_{Pub}(k)$ and $DEN_{For}(k)$, will give evidence of the way in which a higher/lower density of the PBC is complemented/substituted for (in the case of positive/negative correlation) by a higher/lower density of the institutional set-up and of the foreign sub-system. Indeed, depending on the sign and the intensity of the correlation, we might infer that a certain TS compensates the low connectivity of its PBC with highly connected public and foreign sub-systems, or vice versa. Alternatively, we might infer that the low (high) connectivity of the PBC of a certain TS negatively (positively) affects the connectivity of the other two sub-systems. Similar interpretations can be put forward by working out the ranking correlation of the TS according to $DEN_{Pub}(k)$ and $DEN_{For}(k)$.

While the density analysis has to be amended as above, that of the centrality of the different nodes, and of the direction of the edges of the corresponding oriented graphs, can be carried out in the same way as for the R&D expenditure flows. Let us observe that, in this way, the embodied and disembodied flows that overcome a certain cut-off value are not added up, but rather mapped and examined separately. More precisely, the relative weight that the institutional set-up and the foreign sub-system have within a TS can be estimated by working out the outdegree centrality of the corresponding nodes, in the same way as we have done for all the other sectors of the PBC through (5.2), that is:[5]

$$G_{Out}^{Pub} = \sum i_{out}^{Pub} ; G_{Out}^{For} = \sum i_{out}^{For} \; \text{with} \; 0 < G_{Out}^{(.)} < n-2 \qquad (6.6)$$

where i_{Out}^{Pub} and i_{Out}^{For} indicate one of the relevant edges (that is greater than a certain cut-off value) coming out from, respectively, the public and the foreign sector. Conversely, in order to evaluate the degree of dependence of a certain economic sector of the PBC, to a standard indegree centrality indicator (G_{In}^{PBC}) we add two dual indegree indicators capturing its dependence on (values equal to 1) or independence from (values equal to 0), respectively, the public (G_{In}^{Pub}) and the foreign sub-system (G_{In}^{For}).

As in (5.3), on the basis of the previous PBC centrality indicators, we can work out a centralisation indicator of system-wide connectivity:

$$H_{Out}^{PBC} = \frac{\sum_i \left(G_{Out}^{PBC^*} - G_{Out}^{PBC} \right)}{(n-1)(n-2)} \tag{6.7}$$

where G_{Out}^{PBC} is the outdegree centrality of sector i out of the n of the PBC, while $G_{Out}^{PBC^*}$ is the outdegree centrality of the most central node. *Mutatis mutandis*, its meaning is equivalent to that of (5.3).

Finally, in order to identify the sectoral partitions of the PBC which are more affected by the two sub-systems it is necessary to convert the relative edged matrix $\mathbf{F}_{Pr,Pub,For}^{Rel}$ into oriented graphs and to look at the direction of the edges which come out from the public and the foreign sub-system.

6.2   A CROSS-SECTION ANALYSIS OF FIVE TS

In this section we will compare five TS (France, Germany, Great Britain, Japan and Italy) with respect to sixteen manufacturing sectors (see Table 6.1) for the mid 1980s. This empirical application is much more limited in scope than those we have carried out in the previous chapters. This is due to the fact that data on R&D disaggregated by economic sector and source of financing, which have to be both comparable and consistent with input-output tables, are very scant. This forced on us the following trade-off. On the one hand, had we chosen to extend our analysis over time, the comparison would have comprised very few TS. On the other hand, we could have enlarged the set of countries, but only at the price of an exclusively cross-section analysis. Since our methodology appears to be particularly suitable for comparative investigations, we have decided to focus on the latter. Accordingly, to the set of countries of the previous chapters, we have added a TS (Italy), for which comparable input-output data are available for one single year only (1985), and that was in fact excluded in the corresponding temporal analysis.

Table 6.1   Sectoral disaggregation

1	Food, beverages & tobacco
2	Textiles, apparel & leather
3	Wood, cork and furniture
4	Paper, paper products & printing
5	Chemical products (incl. Pharmaceuticals)
6	Rubber & plastic products
7	Non-metallic mineral products
8	Basic metals, ferrous (iron and steel)
9	Basic metals, non ferrous
10	Fabricated metal products
11	Non electrical machinery (incl. Office & computing)
12	Electrical machinery (incl. Radio, TV & communication equip)
13	Instruments
14	Motor vehicles
15	Aerospace
16	Other manufacturing n.e.c.

Because of the flows heterogeneity between the PBC and the other two sub-systems, we will not analyse the density distributions of the TS, but we will rather refer to two cut-off values: $k = 0.005$ and $k = 0.05$. As in the previous chapters, these cut-off values have been selected on the basis of heuristic criteria, by solving the trade-off between non-elementary (that is, significant) and not too complex (that is, observable) structures. Let us observe that while one cut-off value ($k = 0.005$) is the same as for our previous applications on a larger set of TS, to which we will therefore refer, the other ($k = 0.05$) has been added in order to take into account relatively large innovative flows.

6.2.1   Density Analysis

Small and large innovative flows: $k = 0.005$
In looking at the density of the three sub-systems of the investigated TS, interesting relationships can be identified. First of all, let us observe that by keeping both small and large (relative) innovation flows ($k = 0.005$) a parallel can be drawn, in terms of ranking, between the density values calculated on the basis of R&D private financing flows and those calculated in the previous chapter on the basis of R&D expenditure flows (Table 6.2).

The densest PBC is that of the most connected TS (Japan), and also Germany ranks among the most connected in both respects. As for the least connected TS, Italy, whose national innovation system is described by more qualitative analyses as scarcely coherent (Malerba, 1993), it has also the least systemic PBC. Great Britain, on the contrary, represents a relevant exception: quantitative and qualitative evidence about a weakly consistent TS actually clashes with a PBC which is connected as much as Germany and France. Apart from this exception, on which we will focus later, it seems however that the connectivity of the core actually exerts a sort of system-wide effect which makes the corresponding TS relatively more connected. Such a qualitative observation can be more rigorously confirmed by computing the Spearman correlation between the TS ranked according to the two density values: the correlation (0.4) is in fact positive and also appreciable.

Table 6.2   Density analysis, mid 1980s (k = 0.005 and k = 0.05)

		k = 0.005		k = 0.05	
		Density	Rank	Density	Rank
TS*	France	0.30	2	0.11	1
	Germany	0.27	3	0.10	3
	Great Britain	0.14	4	0.07	4
	Japan	0.46	1	0.11	1
PBC	France	0.39	4	0.08	4
	Germany	0.41	2	0.08	4
	Great Britain	0.40	3	0.10	2
	Japan	0.45	1	0.11	1
	Italy	0.37	5	0.10	2
Public sub-system	France	0.94	2	0.44	4
	Germany	0.94	2	0.69	1
	Great Britain	1.00	1	0.56	2
	Japan	0.50	5	0.06	5
	Italy	0.94	2	0.50	3
Foreign sub-system	France	0.63	2	0.31	2
	Germany	0.25	4	0.06	4
	Great Britain	1.00	1	0.63	1
	Japan	0.06	5	0.00	5
	Italy	0.44	3	0.25	3

Note: * The density ranking for the TS as a whole has been obtained on the basis of the results of the previous chapter.

A second interesting relationship concerns the parallel one can establish between the density of the PBC and of the innovative flows pertaining to the public sub-system. Although by retaining both small and large flows nearly all the TS have very dense public sub-systems, the least connected Japanese public sub-system contrasts its highest density ranking in terms of PBC, and determines a Spearman correlation (−0.05), which is quite low but still negative. A substitutability relationship, according to which weakly (highly) connected PBC call for (do not require) a highly connected public interface cannot therefore be put forward in general, but rather holds for the Japanese case only, a point we will come back to later.

A third, and stronger relationship can be finally identified by crossing the density ranking of the TS according to the PBC with that according to the innovative flows of the foreign sub-system. Indeed, in this case the Spearman correlation (–0.6) is negative and quite high so that a substitutability relationship appears more pertinent. In other words, it seems that, on the one hand, the foreign market works as a compensation channel for the low connectivity of the PBC (such as in the case of Great Britain) while, on the other hand, highly connected PBC make the dependence of the TS on the foreign market less stringent (such as in the case of Japan and Germany). Let us also observe that the Spearman correlation across the TS according to the public and the foreign sub-system is positive and very high (0.55) thus suggesting a complementarity relationship between these two sub-systems.

Large innovative flows: $k = 0.05$
The set of relationships we have identified above changes slightly when the reference is to innovative flows larger than 5% of the total intersectoral acquisitions. First of all, there is a substantial reshuffling in the ranking with respect to the previous cut-off (the British and the Italian PBC are now denser than the French and the German ones). However, this change is accompanied by a certain reshuffling in the ranking according to the density of the TS as a whole. Because of this parallel movement, the Spearman correlation remains unchanged (0.4), so that the 'system-wide' effect of the PBC appears robust with respect to the dimension of the innovative flows.

As far as the relationship between the density of the PBC and of the public sub-system is concerned, the reliance on consistent public funds now makes the TS more differentiated among them. For this reason, to the most evident clash of the Japanese TS (first and last in the two corresponding rankings) we have now to add other less evident asymmetries which make the substitutability interpretation more plausible than before: the Spearman correlation index is in fact still negative but double (-0.1) that with the previous cut-off.

Finally, looking at the foreign sub-system, in spite of the appreciable changes in the density values, the ranking remains substantially the same as before. However, given the parallel change in the ranking according to the PBC, the correlation now becomes basically absent (the Spearman index is equal to 0.00). The substitutability interpretation with respect to the foreign sub-system seems therefore to hold only when small and medium flows are also considered, while it is not appreciable when we consider consistent forms of reliance on the same sub-system. In other words, the PBC and the foreign sub-system appear 'weak' substitutes.[6]

6.2.2   Centrality Analysis and Oriented Graphs

As already said, density is a typical system-wide indicator which might hide further differences across the TS in terms of centrality of the constituent sectors, both inward and outward. This is particularly true for the BPC, which might be, for example, equally connected in different TS but with different underlying sectoral structures.

The density of the other sub-systems is instead nothing but a *relative* measure of their *absolute* outdegree centrality. In spite of this equivalence, while their density (or relative centrality) has just been related to that of the PBC and of the TS as a whole, their absolute centrality will here be analysed separately in order to evaluate their relative weight within different TS.

Also this analysis will be carried out by retaining, first, both large and small flows (k = 0.005), and, then, consistent innovative acquisitions only (k = 0.05). In the light of the system-wide effect of the PBC, and given our prevailing interest in the public and the foreign sub-system, the centrality of the economic sectors of the PBC will just be quickly sketched, mainly by looking for the most significant differences with respect to our previous analyses of the TS as a whole.

Small and large innovative flows: $k = 0.005$
Starting from the PBC, let us observe that for flows higher than 0.5% of the total innovative acquisitions, the average centrality of its sixteen sectors is still quite high and homogeneous across the investigated TS (Table 6.2): in each of them, the 'mean sector' innovates and gets innovated by nearly half of the others (around seven sectors). In spite of this homogeneity, the average sectoral centrality ranges from the minimum of Italy (6.56) to the maximum of Japan (7.69), with France, Great Britain and Germany subsequently in-between, thus suggesting and confirming the evidence of the different scale of their innovative (financial) operations.

Further confirmations with respect to a more institutional kind of literature can be obtained by looking at the average outdegree centrality gap with respect to the most central sector. Indeed, the outdegree network centralisation (H_{Out}^{PBC}) for Japan and Great Britain in fact shows, respectively, the least ($H_{Out}^{PBC} = 63.3\%$) and the second most ($H_{Out}^{PBC} = 68.1\%$) asymmetric (systemic) sectoral structures. On the other hand, by referring to financial flows the centrality gap is lower for Italy than for France and Germany, suggesting that the structure of the PBC does not necessarily overlap with that of the corresponding TS.

In spite of this important *caveat*, the identity of the most and of the least central sectors is not dissimilar from that we have found in dealing with total R&D expenditure flows: in general, the most pervasive is again a science-based sector of material nature, that is, the 'broad' chemical sector (Sector 5), while the most dependent is, apart from some exceptions, a traditional one, that is, the 'broad' wood sector (Sector 3). However, the direct reference to private financing implies some important changes with respect to our previous analyses. First of all, the 'broad' (that is, extended to electronics) electrical machinery sector (Sector 12), an immaterial technology-based

Table 6.3 Freeman's degree centrality, mid 1980s: PBC, public and foreign sub-system (k = 0.005)

PBC	Great Britain				France				Germany				Japan				Italy			
	G_{Out}^{PBC}	G_{In}^{PBC}	G_{In}^{Pub}	G_{In}^{For}	G_{Out}^{PBC}	G_{In}^{PBC}	G_{In}^{Pub}	G_{In}^{For}	G_{Out}^{PBC}	G_{In}^{PBC}	G_{In}^{Pub}	G_{In}^{For}	G_{Out}^{PBC}	G_{In}^{PBC}	G_{In}^{Pub}	G_{In}^{For}	G_{Out}^{PBC}	G_{In}^{PBC}	G_{In}^{Pub}	G_{In}^{For}
1	2.00	10.00	1.00	1.00	2.00	10.00	1.00	1.00	1.00	9.00	1.00	0.00	1.00	8.00	0.00	0.00	1.00	9.00	1.00	0.00
2	2.00	9.00	1.00	1.00	3.00	9.00	1.00	0.00	2.00	8.00	1.00	0.00	3.00	8.00	1.00	0.00	1.00	7.00	1.00	0.00
3	1.00	12.00	1.00	1.00	1.00	9.00	1.00	0.00	2.00	10.00	1.00	0.00	3.00	12.00	0.00	0.00	1.00	9.00	1.00	0.00
4	8.00	7.00	1.00	1.00	4.00	8.00	1.00	0.00	5.00	8.00	1.00	0.00	10.00	8.00	1.00	0.00	1.00	8.00	1.00	0.00
5	16.00	1.00	1.00	1.00	15.00	4.00	1.00	1.00	16.00	3.00	1.00	0.00	16.00	4.00	1.00	1.00	15.00	3.00	1.00	1.00
6	9.00	8.00	1.00	1.00	15.00	4.00	1.00	1.00	11.00	6.00	1.00	0.00	13.00	6.00	0.00	0.00	14.00	4.00	1.00	1.00
7	8.00	8.00	1.00	1.00	9.00	6.00	1.00	1.00	9.00	9.00	1.00	0.00	16.00	5.00	1.00	0.00	5.00	9.00	1.00	0.00
8	10.00	8.00	1.00	1.00	7.00	8.00	1.00	1.00	7.00	6.00	1.00	0.00	14.00	4.00	1.00	0.00	7.00	8.00	1.00	0.00
9	5.00	7.00	1.00	1.00	8.00	5.00	1.00	1.00	4.00	4.00	1.00	1.00	12.00	3.00	1.00	0.00	13.00	4.00	1.00	0.00
10	10.00	10.00	1.00	1.00	9.00	7.00	1.00	1.00	11.00	8.00	1.00	0.00	13.00	8.00	0.00	0.00	14.00	7.00	1.00	1.00
11	15.00	5.00	1.00	1.00	12.00	7.00	1.00	1.00	15.00	7.00	1.00	0.00	6.00	9.00	1.00	0.00	12.00	6.00	1.00	1.00
12	15.00	3.00	1.00	1.00	16.00	3.00	1.00	1.00	16.00	4.00	1.00	1.00	8.00	8.00	0.00	0.00	15.00	6.00	1.00	1.00
13	1.00	5.00	1.00	1.00	1.00	8.00	1.00	1.00	2.00	8.00	1.00	0.00	3.00	9.00	0.00	0.00	2.00	7.00	1.00	0.00
14	9.00	7.00	1.00	1.00	6.00	8.00	1.00	0.00	12.00	8.00	1.00	0.00	1.00	9.00	0.00	0.00	2.00	7.00	1.00	0.00
15	1.00	4.00	1.00	1.00	1.00	2.00	1.00	1.00	1.00	4.00	0.00	0.00	1.00	11.00	0.00	0.00	1.00	1.00	1.00	1.00
16	1.00	9.00	1.00	1.00	1.00	12.00	1.00	0.00	1.00	13.00	1.00	1.00	3.00	11.00	0.00	0.00	1.00	9.00	1.00	0.00
Mean	7.06	7.06	1.00	1.00	6.88	6.88	0.94	0.63	7.19	7.19	0.94	0.25	7.69	7.69	0.50	0.06	6.56	6.56	0.94	0.44
SD	5.21	2.77	0.00	0.00	5.23	2.62	0.25	0.50	5.49	2.53	0.25	0.45	5.50	2.57	0.52	0.25	5.88	2.32	0.25	0.51
Sum	113.00	113.00	16.00	16.00	110.00	110.00	15.00	10.00	115.00	115.00	15.00	4.00	123.00	123.00	8.00	1.00	105.00	105.00	15.00	7.00
Var	27.18	7.68	0.00	0.00	27.36	6.86	0.06	0.25	30.15	6.40	0.06	0.20	30.21	6.59	0.27	0.06	34.62	5.37	0.06	0.26
NE	35.11	30.35			34.55	29.43			36.18	30.48			37.80	32.42			35.26	27.84		
Min	1.00	1.00	1.00	1.00	1.00	2.00	0.00	0.00	1.00	3.00	0.00	0.00	1.00	3.00	0.00	0.00	1.00	1.00	0.00	0.00
Max	16.00	12.00	1.00	1.00	16.00	12.00	1.00	1.00	16.00	13.00	1.00	1.00	16.00	12.00	1.00	1.00	15.00	9.00	1.00	1.00
H_{Out}^{PBC}	68.1%	37.6%			69.5%	39.1%			67.1%	44.3%			63.3%	32.9%			64.3%	18.6%		
G_{Out}^{Pub}	16.00				15.00				15.00				8.00				15.00			
G_{Out}^{For}	16.00				10.00				4.00				1.00				7.00			

Table 6.3 (continued)   Freeman's degree centrality, mid 1980s: PBC, public and foreign sub-system (k = 0.05)

PBC	Great Britain G_{Out}^{PBC}	G_{In}^{PBC}	G_{In}^{Pub}	G_{In}^{For}	France G_{Out}^{PBC}	G_{In}^{PBC}	G_{In}^{Pub}	G_{In}^{For}	Germany G_{Out}^{PBC}	G_{In}^{PBC}	G_{In}^{Pub}	G_{In}^{For}	Japan G_{Out}^{PBC}	G_{In}^{PBC}	G_{In}^{Pub}	G_{In}^{For}	Italy G_{Out}^{PBC}	G_{In}^{PBC}	G_{In}^{Pub}	G_{In}^{For}
1	1.00	2.00	0.00	1.00	1.00	3.00	0.00	1.00	1.00	3.00	0.00	0.00	1.00	3.00	0.00	0.00	1.00	3.00	0.00	0.00
2	1.00	3.00	1.00	0.00	1.00	4.00	0.00	0.00	1.00	2.00	1.00	0.00	1.00	2.00	0.00	0.00	1.00	3.00	0.00	0.00
3	1.00	5.00	0.00	0.00	1.00	3.00	1.00	0.00	1.00	3.00	1.00	0.00	1.00	5.00	0.00	0.00	1.00	4.00	0.00	0.00
4	1.00	4.00	1.00	0.00	1.00	2.00	0.00	0.00	1.00	3.00	0.00	0.00	1.00	2.00	0.00	0.00	0.00	1.00	1.00	1.00
5	11.00	1.00	0.00	1.00	10.00	1.00	1.00	0.00	11.00	1.00	1.00	0.00	14.00	1.00	0.00	0.00	12.00	2.00	1.00	1.00
6	2.00	2.00	0.00	1.00	5.00	2.00	0.00	0.00	1.00	2.00	1.00	0.00	3.00	2.00	0.00	0.00	5.00	4.00	0.00	0.00
7	1.00	3.00	0.00	0.00	1.00	2.00	0.00	1.00	1.00	2.00	1.00	0.00	4.00	2.00	0.00	0.00	1.00	1.00	0.00	0.00
8	2.00	4.00	1.00	1.00	2.00	3.00	0.00	0.00	3.00	1.00	1.00	0.00	4.00	2.00	0.00	0.00	1.00	4.00	0.00	0.00
9	1.00	2.00	1.00	1.00	2.00	1.00	0.00	0.00	2.00	2.00	1.00	0.00	3.00	1.00	1.00	0.00	4.00	2.00	1.00	1.00
10	1.00	5.00	0.00	1.00	1.00	4.00	0.00	0.00	2.00	3.00	1.00	0.00	2.00	4.00	0.00	0.00	3.00	4.00	1.00	0.00
11	7.00	2.00	1.00	1.00	2.00	2.00	1.00	1.00	2.00	2.00	1.00	0.00	1.00	4.00	0.00	0.00	2.00	2.00	1.00	0.00
12	8.00	1.00	1.00	1.00	4.00	1.00	1.00	0.00	8.00	1.00	1.00	0.00	5.00	2.00	0.00	0.00	6.00	1.00	1.00	0.00
13	1.00	2.00	1.00	1.00	1.00	1.00	1.00	1.00	1.00	3.00	1.00	0.00	1.00	2.00	0.00	0.00	1.00	2.00	1.00	0.00
14	1.00	2.00	0.00	0.00	1.00	1.00	0.00	0.00	1.00	2.00	0.00	0.00	1.00	3.00	0.00	0.00	1.00	1.00	1.00	0.00
15	1.00	1.00	1.00	1.00	1.00	1.00	1.00	1.00	1.00	1.00	0.00	1.00	1.00	6.00	1.00	1.00	1.00	1.00	1.00	1.00
16	1.00	2.00	1.00	0.00	1.00	4.00	0.00	0.00	1.00	7.00	0.00	0.00	1.00	3.00	0.00	0.00	1.00	6.00	0.00	0.00
Mean	2.56	2.56	0.56	0.63	2.19	2.19	0.44	0.31	2.38	2.38	0.69	0.06	2.75	2.75	0.06	0.00	2.56	2.56	0.50	0.25
SD	3.04	1.27	0.51	0.50	2.32	1.13	0.51	0.48	2.80	1.41	0.48	0.25	3.19	1.35	0.25	0.00	2.94	1.46	0.52	0.45
Sum	41.00	41.00	9.00	10.00	35.00	35.00	7.00	5.00	38.00	38.00	11.00	1.00	44.00	44.00	1.00	0.00	41.00	41.00	8.00	4.00
Var	9.25	1.62	0.26	0.25	5.40	1.28	0.26	0.23	7.86	1.98	0.23	0.06	10.19	1.81	0.06	0.00	8.62	2.12	0.27	0.20
NE	15.91	11.45			12.77	9.85			14.70	11.05			16.85	12.25			15.59	11.79		
Min	1.00	1.00	0.00	0.00	1.00	1.00	0.00	0.00	1.00	1.00	0.00	0.00	1.00	1.00	0.00	0.00	0.00	1.00	0.00	0.00
Max	11.00	5.00	1.00	1.00	10.00	4.00	1.00	1.00	11.00	7.00	1.00	1.00	14.00	6.00	1.00	0.00	12.00	6.00	1.00	1.00
H_{Out}^{PBC}	64.3%	18.6%			59.5%	13.8%			65.7%	35.2%			85.7%	24.8%			71.9%	26.2%		
G_{Out}^{Pub}	9.00				7.00				11.00				1.00				8.00			
G_{Out}^{For}	10.00				5.00				1.00				0.00				4.00			

industry which in the analysis of R&D expenditure was only moderately pervasive, is now the most (or nearly the most) central: indeed, its outdegree centrality overtakes that of such sectors as non-electrical machinery (Sector 11) and fabricated metal products (Sector 10), which were previously among the most pervasive.[7] Therefore, it seems that the reference to R&D financing, rather than to R&D expenditure, weakens to a certain extent the bias towards material technologies which is implicit in our embodied diffusion hypothesis. In this last respect, let us observe that two previously pervasive sectors – scientific instruments (Sector 13) and aerospace (Sector 15) – now become structurally dependent. Although these sectors are typically science based when we refer to the limited amount of R&D expenditure implemented by other sectors from which they benefit, their higher involvement in the technological projects financed by the other sectors makes them acquire the nature of 'supplier dominated' sectors.[8]

A second important difference between the analysis of R&D expenditure and that of R&D financing flows concerns the most resource-based sectors of the disaggregation. Indeed, according to a sort of Heckscher-Ohlin-Samuelson interpretation, the intensity of natural resources seems to be the unique sectoral feature for which there emerge substantial differences across the TS.

Apart from the differences in the most resource-intensive industries, the only other sector which turns out to be significantly differentiated also with respect to both small and large flows is that of motor vehicles (Sector 14). Indeed, although its acquisitions are large in all the TS, the number of diffusions is quite variable. Accordingly, the sector ranges from highly dependent, in Italy and Japan, to nearly neutral, in France, to slightly pervasive, in Germany and Great Britain. Also in this last respect, it seems thus that the reference to the private financial system introduces into the analysis some strategic and institutional kinds of elements which attenuate the structural features of the motor vehicles sector emerging when R&D expenditure is considered in aggregate terms.

Coming now to the other two sub-systems, let us preliminarily observe that by considering both small and large flows the relative weight of the institutional set-up is very high in all the European TS (Table 6.2). That the innovative performances of the group of TS are typically stimulated through public funds, rather than through structural interventions on the functioning of the system itself, is therefore at least suggested. This holds true, in particular, for Great Britain, where all the economic sectors of the PBC have a relevant public interface, and in France and Italy, where it is only the residual sector which is not significantly affected by public funds.[9] For these TS, therefore, two interpretations can be put forward. On the one hand, the applied and instrumental kind of research that is presumably carried out in their economic sectors by using private resources always needs to be integrated, at least to a minimum extent, by a more basic and general

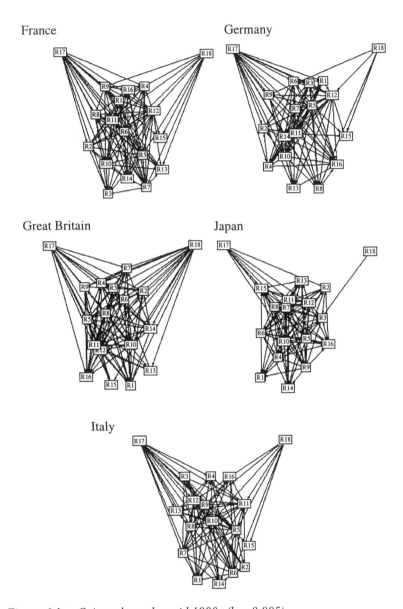

Figure 6.1   Oriented graphs, mid 1980s (k = 0.005)

oriented kind of research which is typically publicly financed: the standard 'labour division' of the innovative process seems therefore at work here.[10]

On the other hand, looking at the same result from another perspective, all the economic sectors of the European TS are able to overcome the selective process of institutional interactions which leads to the provision of public funds.

Still looking at both small and large flows, we can see that the public sub-system appears to play quite a different role in the Japanese TS. Indeed, while the innovative acquisitions from the PBC sectors (both in terms of private financing and R&D expenditure) are relatively higher and more diffused than in the other TS, the interface between the PBC and the institutional set-up is limited to half of the relevant sectors. Two interpretations can be put forward just by looking at their centrality. On the one hand, the high degree of public involvement that the literature on national systems of innovation identifies in the case of Japan (Odagiri and Goto, 1993) is apparently institutional and systemic rather than economic/financial and sectoral, as in the European TS. On the other hand, the higher R&D intensity of the Japanese firms seems able to make private financing more conducive to a basic kind of research, thus making less necessary the standard labour division of the innovative process.

The previous interpretations can be further refined by looking at the corresponding oriented graphs (Figure 6.1).[11] In the Japanese TS public funds reach a minimum threshold level (0.5% of the total intersectoral acquisitions) neither in the most traditional sectors (though with the relevant exception of textiles (Sector 2)), nor in the majority of the scale-intensive ones (fabricated metal products and motor vehicles). The public (finance) interface is instead active with respect to nearly all the resource-based sectors (both ferrous and non-ferrous basic metals) and with respect to the high-tech sectors of the disaggregation (chemical products and electrical machinery). These results are extremely interesting as they suggest that the high connectivity degree of the Japanese PBC allows for the institutional set-up to be more selective, in a sort of compensating relationship. Indeed, it focuses on those sectors which either need more support, such as for those intensive in resources with which Japan is not well endowed, or are more able to induce international competitiveness: the presence of textiles along with the most high-tech sectors can in fact be read in this light.

Moving to the analysis of the foreign sub-system (Table 6.2), the most evident result is that, even by considering small flows, its relative weight is quite different in different TS. As we expected, the relationships of a certain TS with the rest of the world are not as necessary and structural as the institutional ones which are associated with public funds, but more dependent on their inner characteristics. The maximum degree of openness of Great Britain (with an outdegree centrality of 16), for example, clashes with the minimum one of Japan (with an outdegree centrality of 1). Both these results can be integrated by taking into account the evidence on the foreign orientation of the two TS, especially in terms of FDI, suggested by several international studies.[12] Indeed, Great Britain is pointed out as a highly multinational system, both in outward and, especially, in inward terms, while the international technological activities of Japan are very much outward

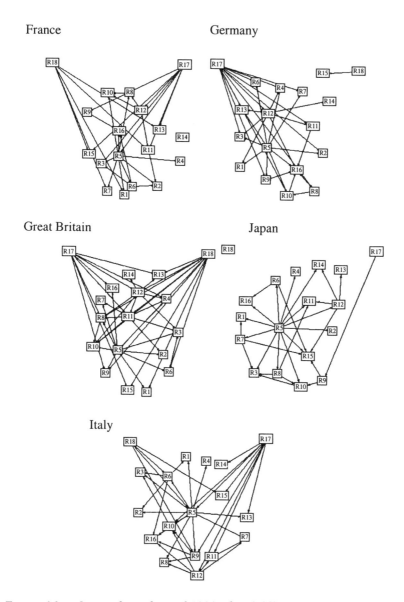

Figure 6.2   Oriented graphs, mid 1980s (k = 0.05)

unbalanced. As we said in dealing with density, to this evidence we should also add a more system kind of interpretation which relates their international orientation to their internal connectivity in a sort of substitutability relationship.

In supporting our interpretation of the higher differentiating role of the foreign sub-system with respect to the public one, let us observe that the Japan-Great Britain clash is not, unlike for the latter, the only remarkable element of diversity. On the contrary, also in-between the Japanese and the British extremes the centrality of the foreign sub-system turns out to be quite differentiated. This appears particularly true by comparing two TS (Germany and France) that are usually grouped together under the Rhenish capitalism model heading. Indeed, when the functioning of the whole TS is broken down into that of its sub-systems, we discover that the foreign sub-system contribution to their similar connectivity is definitely higher in France than in Germany.

Once again, the investigation of the foreign sub-system can be enriched by looking at the corresponding oriented graphs (Figure 6.2). Let us observe that all the TS, in spite of some relevant exceptions, get funds from abroad to finance the innovative projects of the most high-tech sectors – chemicals (Sector 5), electrical machinery (Sector 12), and aerospace (Sector 15).[13] In these sectors, therefore, having a foreign interface, at least of a minimum scale, appears necessary unless one TS identifies the corresponding world-wide frontier. Indeed, as we have already mentioned, this is the case of Germany, in the chemical sector (Sector 5), and of Japan, in electrical machinery (Sector 12) and aerospace (Sector 15), whose indegree centrality with respect to the foreign sub-system (G_{In}^{For}) is actually nil (Table 6.2). In this last respect we should keep in mind that these are industries in which the innovation diffusion channel based on FDI, presumably at work also in the other sectors of the disaggregation, is reinforced by numerous high-tech collaboration initiatives and partnerships on a world-wide scale (Hagedoorn and Schakenraad, 1993).

In interpreting the role of the foreign sub-system, international and technological competitiveness are relevant too. We can in fact argue that the comparative advantages that some European TS (in particular, France and Italy) have in such scale-intensive sectors as rubber and plastic (Sector 6), fabricated metal products (Sector 10) and non-electrical machinery (Sector 11),[14] also benefit from the significant foreign support they show in this analysis. Apart from the sectoral features described above, which apply to both the least and the most foreign oriented of the TS, let us observe that the higher involvement of the French TS abroad[15] is due to industries of different nature. Although to a lesser extent than in Great Britain, where all the sectors receive significant financial funds from abroad, France's heterogeneity suggests an international kind of openness, which is extensive rather than intensive.

Large innovative flows: k = 0.05
By considering large innovative flows, the centrality of the 16 sectors of the PBC reduces substantially (Table 6.2), and the corresponding structures

become less significant: indeed, in all the TS, the 'mean sector' innovates and gets innovated by no more than three of the others.[16] Furthermore, the PBC now becomes more homogeneous across the TS in terms of average centrality: more precisely, Japan and Italy now become more aligned, while it is only France which lags somehow behind. Also when we look at private financial flows, therefore, it seems that the reference to technological initiatives of a remarkable scale make all the PBC collapse in a sort of common super-core of few active sectors. In other words, the investigated TS differ more with respect to the intersectoral diffusion of 'secondary' (possibly incremental) rather than 'primary' (possibly radical) private innovation projects.

The previous argument is also relevant in interpreting the results of the outdegree network centralisation analysis which are substantially different from the previous cut-off. Indeed, it is the Japanese TS which now has the most asymmetric PBC ($H_{Out}^{PBC} = 85.7\%$), while that of Great Britain is among the most 'systemic' ($H_{Out}^{PBC} = 64.3\%$). This evidence, along with the relative ranking of the other TS, clashes with the results of the institutional studies on the corresponding innovation systems, which have instead been confirmed, at least to a certain extent, by the analysis of the previous cut-off. Once more, it seems that by cutting out small and intermediate flows we are in fact referring to the connectivity of super-cores which do not perfectly overlap with the corresponding PBC and, *a fortiori*, with the TS within which they operate.

In spite of the structural homogeneity of the super-core of the TS, relevant differences however still emerge, both with respect to the pervasive[17] and the dependent[18] sectors. As a consequence of these variations, the reference to large innovative flows reintegrates, within the PBC, the standard distinction between science-based and supplier-dominated sectors. Finally, while relevant elements of differentiation across the TS can still be found, as for the previous cut-off, by referring to the most resource-intensive sectors of the disaggregation, further differences can also be traced to their capabilities and/or their institutional/strategic features.[19]

Coming to the other two sub-systems, the picture that we get is much more differentiated than for the previous cut-off (Table 6.2). Indeed, it emerges that drawing on large public funds for innovation is more an institutional, rather than a structural feature of the TS. In other words, while up to a certain level the intervention of the public sub-system appears unavoidable, after a certain minimal threshold the degree of interaction with the public interface becomes more dependent on the specificity of the TS itself and, possibly, more strategic. Indeed, with the exception of the minimal incidence that the public sub-system shows in Japan,[20] the other four TS appear now more clearly and differently ranked. First of all, let us observe that nearly half of the public innovative diffusions of the British TS do not reach the 5% of the corresponding total intersectoral acquisitions, while this happens for only four of the German public diffusions. Accordingly, the German TS, possibly in relation to its larger average firm size, shows the most pervasive public interface, while that of the British TS appears more extensive than intensive. Retaining only large innovative flows, the Italian TS gets more public finance than the French one, thus suggesting two symmetrical interpretations: on the one hand, the diffuse involvement of the Italian public sub-system in quite large innovative projects; on the other hand, the higher degree of selection existing in France (Ergas, 1987).

This differentiation emerges also when the sectoral orientation of the public interface is taken into consideration. Indeed, only two elements of communality can be identified across the five investigated TS. First, the only sector which receives significant public funds in *all* of them is non-ferrous metals (Sector 9): a result that, while somehow unexpected, should be read by retaining the crucial role that this sector plays in conveying important raw materials to other more technology-intensive sectors. Secondly, the only sector whose indegree centrality with respect to the public sub-system (G_{In}^{Pub}) is nil in *all* the investigated TS is food, beverages and tobacco (Sector 1). In none of the TS, therefore, at least in the investigated period (1985), this sector has reached such a state of technological development as to justify a significant degree of public intervention as for other traditional sectors.

In addition to the previous general results, another aspect which can be traced in the majority of the investigated TS is their consistent public financing of some of the most high-tech sectors, that is: non-electrical (Sector 11) and electrical machinery (Sector 12), precision instruments (Sector 13), and aerospace (Sector 15). Let us observe that these are sectors that the foreign sub-system had already selected by considering both small and large innovative flows, that is, for the previous cut-off. As we expected, therefore, we can conclude that the public sub-system, which insulates them only by retaining consistent innovation flows, seems to be less selective than the foreign one: indeed, it replicates its dynamics only at a higher dimensional level. Furthermore, also from a qualitative point of view, the public interface with respect to the high-tech sectors appears different from the foreign one, and in several respects. First of all, non-electrical machinery (Sector 12) replaces chemicals (Sector 5) within this group of core sectors, given that the G_{in}^{Pub} of the latter is in general nil, except for France and Italy. This would suggest that the non-electrical machinery sector is possibly more idiosyncratic than the chemical one, that is, characterised by specific needs which its public sub-system can detect more promptly than the foreign one: accordingly, it would also be less sensible than for the chemical sector for it to be fuelled from standard innovative projects which are carried out on a word-wide scale. A second difference concerns the set of TS with respect to which the public selection process operates even *within* the core of the high-tech sectors. In particular, this is the case of Great Britain, where consistent public funds only reach the aerospace sector (Sector 15), while non-electrical machinery (Sector 11), electrical machinery (Sector 12) and precision instruments (Sector 13) have a nil G_{In}^{Pub}.[21] Quite significantly, therefore, the *extensive* kind of dependence of the British high-tech sectors on the foreign sub-system is reflected in an *intensive* kind of dependence on the public one: indeed, the remarkable value of G_{Out}^{Pub} in Great Britain is rather due to its public intervention in more traditional and resource-intensive sectors, in which it is arguably less competitive, such as textiles (Sector 2), paper and printing (Sector 4) and ferrous metals (Sector 8).

As far as the other TS are concerned, let us observe that the analysis of the oriented graphs confirms how the remarkable position of the Italian TS in terms of G_{Out}^{Pub} derives also from an exceptionally consistent public involvement (mainly through subsidies) in the innovative initiatives of its motor vehicles sector (Sector 14), and of one of its main supplier sectors, that is fabricated metal products (Sector 10).

Moving to the analysis of the foreign sub-system, that drawing resources from abroad is less a structural need than obtaining them from public institutions is confirmed by retaining only large innovative flows. Indeed, with the sole exception of the British TS, the relative weight of the foreign sub-system is now definitely lower than that of the corresponding public sub-system. Furthermore, unlike for the public diffusions, moving from small/large to large innovative flows *does not* change the ranking of the openness degree of the investigated TS. However, retaining only large flows entails appreciable changes in the relative distance among the TS themselves. First of all, the German TS is now much closer to the Japanese TS as a nearly 'autonomous' system: the evidence of a consistent gap between, respectively, an international and a highly national TS that we got by looking at a more aggregate openness indicator has therefore to be qualified with respect to the size of the relevant flows. Secondly, the same kind of gap between France and Italy, on the one hand, and the most foreign dependent TS (Great Britain), on the other, gets substantially narrower, especially between Great Britain and Italy, for which the difference in terms of outdegree centrality passes from nine to six nodes. Also with respect to foreign funds, therefore, it appears that the Italian TS becomes the more dependent on the extra PBC sub-systems, the larger is the size of flows through which the relative interface is established. In this last respect, the evidence of a TS with a small-scale core, thus only capable of incremental and process innovations, which has to be 'inflated' from the outside to be able to implement more important paradigmatic jumps, appears relevant and highly suggestive (Malerba, 1993).

Also for large innovative flows, the role of the foreign sub-system can be further qualified through graph analysis. In this last respect, the most remarkable result is that large financial flows are nearly systematically associated only with the aerospace sector (Sector 15). Indeed, this appears to be the only sector in which all the TS have consistent foreign relationships: once more, this result should be read by considering that the sector itself is one of the more 'intensive' of international partnerships and innovative collaborations, and one in which the internationalisation process has recently been quite strong (McGuire, 1999).[22] Equally remarkable is the fact that as many as three out of the four traditional sectors of the disaggregation – textiles, apparel and leather (Sector 2), wood, cork and furniture (Sector 3) and paper, paper products and printing (Sector 4) – together with the residual sector (Sector 16) and, especially, with motor vehicles (Sector 14), are systematically insulated from large foreign flows.[23] Following our previous interpretation, we can conclude that for innovative operations of large size the foreign sub-system becomes extremely selective, not only with respect to traditional kinds of sectors, but also with respect to some key, strategic industries, such as motor vehicles (Sector 14). Indeed, in addition to Japan, this selection process becomes nearly complete also in Germany, where the aerospace sector is in fact the only one with a non-nil G_{In}^{For}.

As far as the other TS are concerned, the intermediate position of the French TS in terms of G_{Out}^{For} is substantially due to the exclusive (or nearly exclusive) foreign contributions it receives in such sectors as non-metallic mineral products (Sector 7), non-electrical machinery (Sector 12) and precision instruments (Sector 13). In the case of Italy, instead, foreign acquisitions are significant for chemical products (Sector 5), rubber and plastic (Sector 6), and non-ferrous metals (Sector 9). In spite of the similar weight the foreign sub-system has in these two TS, its sectoral profile appears therefore differentiated, with the latter being more oriented towards material kinds of technology than the former. To a certain extent, this distinction is consistent with the different structure of their manufacturing systems.

Finally, let us observe that the British TS gets its primacy in terms of foreign sub-system ($G_{Out}^{For} = 11$) through the consistent funds it acquires abroad to finance innovation in such mid and high-tech sectors as ferrous metals (Sector 8), fabricated metal products (Sector 10), and electrical machinery (Sector 11). Quite significantly, therefore, the British TS is the only case in which an extensive foreign involvement, such as we had detected by also retaining small flows ($G_{Out}^{For} = 16$), reduces, by leaving them out, to a quasi-complete kind of dependence which excludes only traditional sectors. The international profile of the British TS we had shown in previous chapters is in this way further confirmed.

6.3   CONCLUSIONS

In this chapter we have put forward an intersectoral methodology that, with some *caveats*, allows us to unfold the TS with respect to its main constituent sub-systems: the PBC, the institutional set-up and the foreign market. By combining input-output tables with sectoral R&D data by source of financing, we have been able to measure and map embodied flows of private R&D, mainly circulating within the business core, along with disembodied flows coming from public sources and from abroad.

By building up consistent enlarged matrices of intersectoral R&D financing flows for a set of five TS (France, Germany, Italy, Japan and Great Britain), and by applying to them some simple network analysis indicators, we have obtained, for 1985, interesting results, both general and TS specific.

As far as the general results are concerned, first of all, we have found that a relatively denser PBC is usually associated with a relatively more connected TS. In other words, the density of the PBC seems to exert a sort of 'system-wide effect' which makes the corresponding TS relatively more internally integrated: what is more, this 'system-wide' effect appears robust with respect to the dimension of the innovative flows we have considered. On the basis of this result we can reasonably maintain that, in spite of the methodological differences, the results of the present study are substantially aligned with those of other previous, more aggregated, studies based on total R&D expenditure. However, interesting differences emerge when comparing the centrality of the economic sectors of the PBC in terms of R&D financing with that in terms of R&D expenditure flows. First of all, for both small and large flows, the resort to private innovation funding reduces the typical bias towards 'material' technologies shown by the embodied methodology. Furthermore, with respect to the analysis of R&D expenditure, the reference to financial flows seems to increase the relative weight of TS specific (that is, institutional) considerations over the sector-specific (that is, structural) ones: this appears particularly evident for chemicals and motor vehicles. Finally, the same change of proxy makes the resource-intensive sectors of the retained disaggregation pivotal, that is, the most differentiated sectors of the investigated TS.[24]

A second general result concerns the substitutability relationship that we have detected, in terms of density, both between the PBC and the public sub-system, and between the PBC and the foreign sub-system. With respect to the former, it seems that weakly (highly) connected PBC call for (do not require) a highly connected public interface. As for the latter, the foreign market works as a compensation channel for the low connectivity of the PBC while, on the other hand, highly connected PBC make the dependence of the TS on the foreign market less stringent. Although quite interesting, these two relationships are very much dependent on the size of the considered innovation flows: indeed, while the former holds only for large innovative flows, the latter can be found only when both small and large flows are considered.

A third general result has to do with the different nature that the public and the foreign sub-systems have in the investigated TS: the former being more structural and homogeneous across the TS, the latter more institutional and differentiated across them. This difference is also reflected in the selection that the two sub-systems operate, through their financing activity, with respect to the economic sectors of the PBC. As we expected, the public interface turns out to be less selective than the foreign one, both in quantitative and qualitative terms. Indeed, in quantitative terms, the public sub-system replicates the selection process of the foreign sub-system in favour of the high-tech sectors, but only with respect to larger innovative flows. In qualitative terms, as suggested by the analysis of the oriented graphs, the selection process of the foreign sub-system leaves out more strategic, science and technology intensive sectors (such as motor vehicles) than the public sub-system.

In addition to these general results, interesting aspects also emerge with respect to some specific TS. First of all, when both small and large flows are considered, the nature of the public intervention turns out to be quite different in the European TS, where it is apparently based on direct financing (subsidies), and in Japan, where it is possibly more structural and systemic. Furthermore, as is shown by graph analysis, the higher connectivity of the Japanese TS allows it to be more selective towards crucial sectors, such as the resource based and the most internationally competitive ones.

Secondly, by comparing the results of the two selected cut-offs, the British TS shows a public interface which is quite 'intensive', that is, concentrated on few sectors when small flows are left out, and a foreign interface which is instead structurally extensive. Indeed, the British case is the only one in which complete foreign involvement, that the TS shows for both small and large flows, turns into a quasi-complete kind of dependence (with the exclusion of traditional sectors only), when only large flows are retained.

Finally, a third TS specific result concerns Italy. Apart from other institutional peculiarities which emerge in analysing the nature of the PBC sectors (in particular with respect to the motor-vehicles sector), quite interestingly, the Italian TS becomes relatively more dependent on the extra PBC sub-systems (both public and foreign), the larger the size of flows through which the relative interface is established. As we said, the stylised fact provided by the institutional literature of a TS whose small-scale core needs to be substantially supported from the outside to reach significantly consistent performances, is in this way somehow confirmed.

NOTES

1.   Referring to the basic elements of our notion of TS (Chapter 2), the PBC is identified by the techno-economic flows which occur among the innovative core, the productive sub-system and the internal market sub-system.
2.   First of all, this analysis cannot be formally linked to the previous one: interesting relationships between the two can however be established at least from a qualitative point of view. Secondly, data on R&D disaggregated by source of financing are very scant, covering a very limited set of countries and

of periods. Interesting results can however be obtained just by re-examining some of the TS we have previously compared in terms of R&D expenditure.

3. Innovation diffusions from the PBC to the institutional set-up and the foreign sub-system, as well as those between the two sub-systems themselves, are not immediately open to interpretation.

4. This is a correlation index between two rankings which is defined over the domain [-1;+1]. The closer the index is to +1 (-1), the more the two rankings are similar (dissimilar), that is, the first position of the first ranking is closer to the first (last) position of the second ranking, and so on.

5. For the sake of clarity, the outdegree centrality of each sector of the PBC with respect to the others will be here denoted as G_{Out}^{PBC}.

6. Once again, it seems that there is a complementarity relationship between the public and the foreign sub-systems.

7. This result does not hold for Japan, where the electrical-electronic sector (Sector 12) has only average diffusions and acquisitions. As we will see, this is only one of several anomalies that the Japanese TS reveals in terms of sectoral centralities with respect to the other investigated TS.

8. This is particularly evident in the case of Japan, where the aerospace sector (Sector 15) is one of the most dependent sectors of the disaggregation.

9. A slightly different case is that of Germany, where the only PBC-disconnected sector is not residual, but rather an important node of the relative TS, that is, aerospace (Sector 15).

10. To be sure, such a conclusion should be based on R&D private and public expenditure, rather than private and public financing. However, lacking sectoral data about the former, we refer to the latter to provide at least an attempt at interpretation.

11. In the oriented graphs the PBC sectors are numbered from 1 to 16 according to Appendix 1, while the public and the foreign sub-system are denoted as, respectively, Sector 17 and Sector 18.

12. Among others, see Cantwell (1995).

13. To these sectors we have also to add non-ferrous basic metals (Sector 9), in which all the TS, apart from Japan, receive significant funds from abroad.

14. This is evidence reported by several studies on the topic (see, for example, Amendola *et al.*, 1992).

15. Let us observe that the French foreign sub-system is the closest to Great Britain, with an outdegree centrality of 10 versus 16, while the other TS lag somewhere behind (Table 6.2).

16. In spite of its limited interpretative power with respect to the PBC, the present cut-off has been chosen on the basis of the structures that it entails for the other two sub-systems.

17. This is the case, for example, for the chemical sector (Sector 5), in which it thus seems that structural (sectoral) features dominate contextual (that is, TS specific) elements unless we consider large-scale technological flows. A similar argument applies to the second most pervasive sector, that is, electrical machinery (Sector 12), whose centrality gap with respect to the other sectors is now more differentiated than with the previous cut-off.

18. The traditional industries of the disaggregation (Sectors 1, 2 and 3) are now systematically the most dependent, while, unlike for the previous cut-off,

dependency is rarely a feature of some of the most high-tech sectors, such as precision instruments (Sector 13) and aerospace (Sector 15).

19. This is particularly true for non-electrical machinery (Sector 12), whose pervasiveness is in Great Britain substantially higher than elsewhere, and for aerospace (Sector 15), whose dependency is an idiosyncratic feature of the Japanese TS.

20. In interpreting the Japanese result, the 'structural' kinds of aspects we have pointed out for the previous cut-off are still relevant and lead to the extreme result of a single, consistent innovative diffusion.

21. The reverse holds for Germany and Japan, where the aerospace sector, unlike the other three, does not need substantial public interventions.

22. The only relevant exception is that of the Japanese TS, whose scarce international propensity gets further confirmed by a nil G_{Out}^{For}.

23. The other traditional sector, that is, food, beverages and tobacco (Sector 1), receives substantial foreign funds only in France and Great Britain.

24. As we have previously noticed, for large innovative flows the PBC of all the TS degenerates into a sort of super-core. This is more homogeneous than for the previous cut-off in terms of centrality, and is less aligned with the other analyses of the connectivity of the TS in terms of centralisation. As we said, the larger cut-off mainly helps to differentiate the TS with respect to the other two sub-systems.

PART THREE

Empirical Analysis: the Sectoral Perspective

7. The automobile technological system

As we have already argued in the Introduction, the boundaries of the notion of TS proposed in this book are not forced to overlap with those of a macro-economic system, be it national or international. On the contrary, the TS can also be interpreted at a sectoral level, providing such a level of analysis is meant in 'broad' terms, that is, by taking into account the actual degree of 'intersectoralisation' and 'internationalisation' of a certain industry. Indeed, the TS view we adhere to seems to be naturally capable of dealing with a two-fold process of sectoral integration. On the one hand, the volume of trade between countries has increased, and other channels, foremost among them foreign direct investments, have been established in the diffusion of goods, services, capital and knowledge around the world. This is true also with respect to technological change. The fact that innovation can be produced and appropriated in locations other than those where innovative firms reside, by exploiting a scientific knowledge base which spreads across countries, induces us to think in terms of 'techno-globalism'. On the other hand, the innovative relationships within and between different economic sectors, either in the form of deliberate investments (that is, technological transfers) or of positive side-effects (that is, spillovers) have largely increased.

These integration phenomena have put traditional industrial analysis in question and, in particular, have raised the problem of how to study the structure of a certain industry and its actual degree of 'intersectoralisation' and 'internationalisation'. In this chapter we argue that a sectoral interpretation of the concept of TS can be usefully adopted in pursuing this goal. Indeed, the spatial and inter-industrial extension of the techno-economic relationships that make up a TS are two key elements in evaluating the structure of an industry and the nature of the structural change it eventually undergoes over time.

The argument we put forward appears particularly relevant in the case of the two industries with respect to which we have, accordingly, chosen to carry out our sectoral empirical analysis: the automobile and the chemical industries.

As far as the former is concerned, in the next section we will show that the automobile industry is characterised by three stylised facts which make the TS sectoral perspective particularly useful in dealing with it. First, its degree of techno-economic 'intersectoralisation' appears quite high, a fact emerging once producer-user and producer-producer relationships are considered. Secondly, the role of institutional regulations, both as innovative constraints and as innovative incentives, is particularly evident, as well as that of the organisations with which the relative firms interact. Finally, the industry is one in which international relationships are so widespread as to identify a truly transnational, if not even a global kind of TS.

As far as the chemical industry is concerned, in the next chapter we will show that, as Walsh put it, '(t)he chemical industry is itself an entity with shifting boundaries' (1997, p. 119), both with respect to its 'functional' (that is, sectoral) and its 'geographical' boundaries. A standard industrial analysis might therefore be misleading, while a system approach once again seems more appropriate. Indeed, on the one hand, chemical downstream and upstream relationships draw on a wide spectrum of industries, both in terms of intermediate and capital good transactions, and in terms of diversification strategies. On the other hand, both the introduction and the exploitation of chemical innovations occur increasingly on a world-wide basis, and through different internationalisation channels.

In the light of the system nature of the two considered sectors, the aim of this and of the following chapter is that of defining empirically and evaluating the sectoral TS of the automobile and of the chemical industries with respect to the four largest European economies (France, Germany, Great Britain and Italy). The two selected sectors present in fact such strong European idiosyncrasies as to make it convenient to restrict the field of investigation of the previous chapters to these four countries only. Furthermore, as we will show, automobiles and chemicals represent, in the same four countries, two of the most internationally competitive sectors.

In the following, using data on production and innovation intersectoral flows, along with data on bilateral trade and foreign direct investments, we will try to map the most important relationships within the main building blocks constituting the automobile and the chemical TS. In so doing, we intend to furnish a novel viewpoint with which we will try to make a direct appreciation of the phenomena linked to (or determining) the evolution of the corresponding industries, such as, for instance, the degree of decentralisation in production, at both national and international level, and the relevant user-producer linkages.

7.1   THE EXTENSION OF A SECTORAL TS

A sectoral TS is constituted by the clustering of the techno-economic activities of the relevant actors (that is, not only firms), and is quite different in its extension from the sector itself. We are thus interested neither in a purely industrial nor in a typical organisational analysis of the relevant sectors, for which there is an abundance of literature.

Our viewpoint is that the domain of a sectoral TS is identified by referring to the extent to which the firms of a certain sector establish, enlarge (or narrow) and intensify (or weaken) industrial and innovative relationships with firms and organisations of the economic system outside the sector itself. Accordingly, we will draw on two related research lines. On the one hand, we will refer to that part of the literature on TS that refers to sectoral or industrial specification (for example, Carlsson and Stankiewicz, 1991). On the other hand, we will also refer to some other contributions which stress the importance of the clustering of techno-economic activities (for instance, DeBresson, 1996). Indeed, firms and other institutional actors are linked by different kinds of interactions (such as, for example, user-producer and input-output relations) and constitute networks which are reducible neither to the industry nor to the national level. Although both levels are liable to be appropriate dimensions for an industry whose actors are surely national champions (for example, motor vehicles and chemicals, as in the following), it is also true that they extend their field of action into other industries too, both inside and outside their own countries.

Our starting point is therefore the idea that there exists a 'sectoral' TS for a certain industry, with an 'inter-industrial' dimension which is bigger than the national one for some aspects, and smaller for some others.

The definition of the boundaries of a sectoral TS thus becomes a very important issue and cannot be resolved with an *ad hoc* definition.[1] Indeed, as it is crucial in identifying the domain within which the main institutional and techno-economic relationships occur, the question of the boundaries should be solved before starting any serious analysis of the nature of the relevant actors and of the kind of clustering they constitute. In this last respect, our approach to the issue is not yet entirely satisfactory, as we will still mainly proceed on a country-by-country basis. However, by looking at international trade and FDI flows that are exchanged by the sector of a certain country, we hope at least to catch how far the sector itself overlaps with the corresponding country and how far the national perspective that we adopt turns out to be appropriate.

The way in which we intend to determine the extension and the characteristics of a sectoral TS is partially different from, but still consistent with, that we have developed in the previous chapters.

First of all, the two parts of the analysis (the internal and the external) through which we have configured the TS are here preceded by a deep investigation of what we have called the industrial side (Section 7.2 for motor vehicles and Section 8.1 for chemicals). The sectoral perspective we are following naturally requires this extension. However, this analysis will be carried out by looking at the production structure of the motor vehicles and the chemical TS through the same kind of intersectoral perspective of the previous chapters.

Secondly, although still focused on intersectoral innovation flows, the analysis of the innovative side (Section 7.3 and Section 8.2, respectively) will be supplemented by specific indicators, also, but not only, based on the flows themselves, in order to catch the peculiar role (that is, dependent or pervasive) of the sectoral TS within broader macro TS.

Finally, the analysis of the international side (Section 7.4 and Section 8.3, respectively) will also be made a bit more sophisticated, by integrating the examination of the trade specialisation indicators (of the kind used in Chapter 2), in turn made more specific in geographical terms, with the same analysis of the relevant foreign direct investments. This kind of analysis is of course essential in analysing such internationalised sectoral TS as automobiles and chemicals.[2]

In synthesis, we will try to determine the extension and the characteristics of the automobile and the chemical TS for France, Germany, Great Britain and Italy, by looking at three interrelated aspects: the type and intensity of the industrial relationships, the nature and the map of the innovative interactions, and the structure and the direction of their international extension. Indeed, these are three important dimensions to understanding how different institutional arrangements among certain actors generate different techno-economic performances.

7.2   THE INDUSTRY SIDE

In this section we will first of all provide a very brief sketch of the automobile industrial structure in the European Union (Section 7.2.1) with a particular emphasis on the four countries that are the focus of the next two chapters (France, Germany, Great Britain and Italy). The picture we provide is deliberately not very detailed: on the one hand, we do not want to replicate the vast literature on the topic, and, on the other hand, our focus is on inter-industry relationships. More precisely, by means of input-output techniques, we intend to investigate the role of the surrounding industrial set-up for the material acquisitions and diffusions of the automobile sector (Section 7.2.2).

At the outset we have to point out that, as in the previous chapters, our analysis has been constrained by the availability of comparable input-output tables and innovation data for the four investigated countries. Some specific years and sectoral disaggregations had therefore to be chosen, both for this and the next chapter on the chemical TS. However, the structural nature of the data allows us to extend the relative results at least to a certain extent.

7.2.1   General Outlook

As already said, in this section we will analyse few overall data, in order to understand the main problems at stake in dealing with the kind of empirical analysis we intend to pursue.

This brief sketch will focus on 10 European producers (BMW, Fiat, Ford, General Motors, Mercedes, PSA, Renault, Saab, Volkswagen and Volvo), and concentrate only on their production in the European Union, leaving out production elsewhere. This is because we are interested in the patterns of production that the big manufacturers implement in their home country and in countries with comparable techno-economic conditions.

First of all, car production in the European Union has witnessed, over the 1990s, a considerable expansion in production. In 1998, 14.5 million cars were produced with a doubling of the annual rate of change, which reached 7.9% in 1997/98, from around nearly 3.5% in the preceding four years. Favourable elements have to be considered as mainly responsible for this increase, such as the well-known policies of State aid to consumers (via scrapping schemes).

Secondly, the four markets considered (France, Germany, Great Britain and Italy) are indeed the biggest European markets from the demand side, as they account for around three-quarters of the total registrations of new cars (1.9 million, 3.7 million, 2.2 million and 2.3 million, respectively, in 1998). The evolution over time is however quite different for the four countries. Germany and Great Britain seem to have recently gained a sort of comparative advantage, while Italy and France have experienced, at different times, State-funded scrapping schemes, which contributed to smooth the decline. Such a policy seems to have worked better in Italy (+38.8% in 1997) than in France (+10.4% in 1996), probably because of the older age of the car stock.[3]

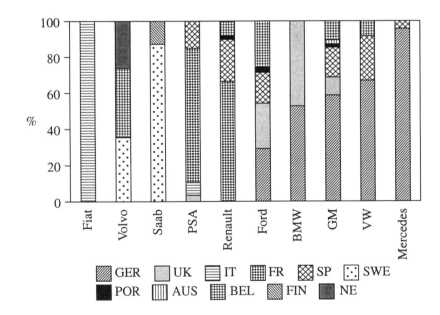

Figure 7.1   Car production by plant location, 1985

Thirdly, spatial concentration of European car producers is high. In 1995, Germany and France, with around 5 million and 2.5 million cars produced, respectively, concentrated nearly half of total European production (32.7% and 17.8% respectively). Italy and Great Britain both accounted for nearly 11% of the whole European market.[4]

Finally, geographical decentralisation of production is not that evident (Figure 7.1). In 1995, almost all car manufacturers privileged their home nation for production, with percentages higher than 50%. However, marked differences emerge. On the one hand, Fiat, Mercedes and Saab show the highest national concentration, with percentages above 80%. On the contrary, Ford appears to be the only truly multinational producer, with its European operations almost equally split between Germany and Great Britain.[5] An intermediate case is that of BMW, whose production is split almost equally between Germany and Great Britain, due to the acquisition of Rover.[6]

According to these preliminary figures, therefore, contrasting evidence emerges with respect to the role of globalisation in shaping the automobile sector. Hence, we will now dig a little deeper in order to better qualify the extension and main characteristics of the corresponding TS.

7.2.2   Backward and Forward Linkages

Consistently with the system perspective of the whole book, and with its emphasis on linkages, an important aspect to be dealt with for a deeper industrial analysis of the automobile TS is that of its intersectoral relationships. Although limited to intermediate domestic goods transactions, standard backward and forward linkages indicators are extremely helpful in this respect.[7] Indeed, they measure the role of a sector in the production activity of other sectors of the economy from both a demand (backward) and a supply (forward) perspective.

More precisely, the backward linkages indicators measure the importance of a certain sector in terms of what it acquires from the other sectors of the economy (that is, they describe the material transactions of a sector with the rest of the economy from an input perspective). Two backward linkages indicators are available: direct and total. The first one (DBL) accounts for the acquisitions made by sector j from the others to obtain its direct immediate inputs, and is given by: $DBL_j = \sum_i a_{ij}$, where a_{ij} is the generic element of the input coefficient matrix $\mathbf{A}$ (defined in eq. 3.3). Accordingly, $0 < DBL_j < 1$.

The total backward linkages indicator (TBL) instead refers to both the direct and indirect acquisitions (that is, in subsequent production rounds) of sector j from the others, and is given by: $TBL_j = \sum_i \alpha_{ij}$, where α_{ij} is the generic element of the standard Leontief inverse, $\mathbf{B}$ (equation 3.6).

Forward linkages indicators measure the role of a certain sector for the acquisitions of the others (that is, they indicate the importance of a sector for the rest of the economy from an output perspective). Similarly to the backward linkages indicators, forward linkages indicators can be either direct or total. The former, which still refer to the output that sector i directly provides to the others (DFL), is given by: $DFL_i = \sum_j a^*_{ij}$, where a^*_{ij} is the generic element of the 'output' coefficient matrix $\mathbf{A}^*$.[8] The total forward linkages indicator (TFL), which again measures the importance of a certain sector i in terms of the output that it provides to the others, both directly and indirectly, is given by: $TFL_i = \sum_j \alpha^*_{ij}$, where α^*_{ij} is the generic element of the 'output' Leontief inverse $\mathbf{B}^\#$.[9]

The backward and forward indicators defined above have been calculated for the automobile sector with respect to 29 other manufacturing sectors. In fact, since these indicators are built on the basis of industrial input-output tables only (without matching them with R&D data), the concordance of the latter tables for the selected countries and available years has returned a disaggregation of 30 sectors (see Table 7.1 for details).

Table 7.1 Sectoral disaggregation for backward and forward linkages

1	Agriculture, forestry & fishing	16	Electrical apparatus (incl. radio, TV)
2	Mining & quarrying	17	Shipbuilding & repair (incl. other)
3	Food, beverages & tobacco	18	Motor vehicles
4	Textiles, apparel & leather	19	Aircraft
5	Wood & furniture	20	Professional goods
6	Paper, paper products & printing	21	Other manufacturing n.e.c.
7	Chemical industry (incl. drugs)	22	Electricity, gas & water
8	Petroleum & coal products	23	Construction
9	Rubber & plastic products	24	Wholesale & retail trade
10	Non-metallic mineral products	25	Restaurants & hotels
11	Iron & steel	26	Transport & storage
12	Non-ferrous metals	27	Communication
13	Metal products	28	Finance & insurance
14	Non-electrical machinery	29	Community, social & personal serv.
15	Office & computing	30	Producers of government serv.

The results are presented in Table 7.2. First of all, since the automobile sector is typically 'scale intensive' (Pavitt, 1984), the backward linkages indicators are systematically higher than the forward linkages indicators, both direct and total. Furthermore, although the direct linkages indicators are in general much more similar between them than the total ones (given the way they have been constructed), the picture emerging is more homogeneous when forward linkages rather than backward linkages are considered. This fact suggests that the demand for intermediate automobile goods from the other sectors is a structural aspect. Indeed, the ratio between total and direct indicators is higher for the forward linkages than for the backward ones. This indicates that the automobile sector is characterised by downstream relationships which are more complex and pervasive than the upstream ones.

This difference is particularly relevant in the case of Italy (the 'backward ratio' is 4.04 while the forward one is 6.25), and also for Great Britain: in 1980, for example, the backward and the forward ratios are, respectively, 4.29 and 7.11, while, in Germany they are, respectively, 3.76 and 5.78.

In addition to these aspects, some other interesting facts emerge. First of all, Germany and France, two countries whose national TS have been shown in previous chapters to be the most connected of the four, are characterised by the highest values of the backward linkages indicators. This is particularly true when total backward linkages are considered: indeed, France and Germany have values above or close to 2. Hence, from an input perspective, the motor vehicle sector contributes with its direct and indirect production requisites to shape a more systemic environment.

Table 7.2   Motor vehicles national backward and forward linkages

		Direct		Total		Total/Direct	
		Backward	Forward	Backward	Forward	Backward	Forward
France	1972	0.54	0.20	2.04	1.28	3.78	6.40
	1977	0.52	0.18	1.96	1.24	3.77	6.89
	1980	0.51	0.18	1.92	1.23	3.76	6.83
	1985	0.50	0.18	1.88	1.23	3.76	6.83
	1990	0.48	0.18	1.85	1.23	3.85	6.83
Germany	1978	0.52	0.22	2.02	1.32	3.88	6.00
	1986	0.54	0.23	2.03	1.33	3.76	5.78
	1988	0.55	0.23	2.04	1.32	3.71	5.74
	1990	0.53	0.22	1.98	1.30	3.74	5.91
Great Britain	1968	0.66	0.31	0.11	1.49	0.17	4.81
	1979	0.42	0.18	1.80	1.28	4.29	7.11
	1984	0.40	0.20	1.69	1.30	4.23	6.50
	1990	0.43	0.23	1.78	1.38	4.14	6.00
Italy	1985	0.44	0.20	1.78	1.25	4.05	6.25

Secondly, the French automobile TS is characterised by the lowest total forward linkages (around 1.2 over the period considered). The other countries, and Germany above all, show values close to, or even higher than 1.3. Although, as we said, the differences in terms of output relationships are less apparent, this result suggests that the other sectors of the French TS rely on the automobile industry to a lesser extent, at least in terms of intermediate inputs.

As far as the temporal analysis is concerned, the trend in the linkages indicators over the last twenty years is in general quite steady, suggesting that we are investigating a structural aspect. Consistent jumps in moving from one sub-period to another can be found only in the case of Great Britain, with respect to total backward (from 2.42 in 1977 to 1.78 in 1990) and total forward linkages (from 1.49 in 1977 to 1.38 in 1990). Indeed, the British automobile TS is the only one showing what could be deemed a structural kind of change: the values of both types of indicators, in contrast to the other countries, tend to decrease over time. Different interpretations can of course be put forward to explain this evidence: the effect of an increase in the 'multinational' degree of the same sector over the period is quite plausible. The well-known and increasing role of foreign direct investments, in particular from Japan and Germany, might in fact have rendered the British automobile sector less pervasive in stimulating the demand of both domestic and imported intermediate inputs, as well as in providing for them a considerable inputs supply.

7.3   THE INNOVATIVE SIDE

We now move to the analysis of the innovative activity performed by the automobile TS, first of all, by looking at the usual indicators of innovative efforts: R&D expenditure and patenting activity. Subsequently, we will try to evaluate the techno-economic interrelationships by means of the intersectoral network analysis approach presented in Chapter 5.

7.3.1   R&D and Patents

R&D expenditure and patents are widely utilised as indicators of input and output of the innovative activity, although with some *caveats*. Accordingly, they allow us to track down how the different arrangements of each TS are reflected in its technological performance. As is well known, the level of R&D expenditure is likely to be correlated with the perceived market possibilities open to the various firms, while the level of patenting activity (for example, by patents count) is used to proxy how successful a firm is in translating its technological activity into innovation, and hence into effective techno-economic performances.

The weight of the automobile sector in terms of R&D expenditure has increased over the last three decades for all the countries considered, although with different patterns. On average, the four countries have experienced a compounded rate of growth of 11.6% between 1973 and 1992. Germany has the highest growth rate (13.7%), followed by Italy (11.3%), France (10.8%) and, with a certain gap, Great Britain (9.7%). After a first substantial increase from 1973 to 1980[10] a substantial stand-by has followed in the first half of the 1980s. From then on, R&D has shown a further substantial increase, with Germany and Great Britain as the best and worst performers.

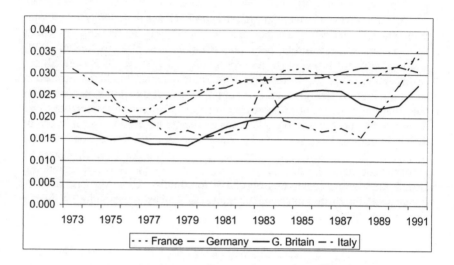

Figure 7.2   R&D intensity in the motor vehicles

The different patterns of the four countries' automobile R&D expenditure are only partially reflected in the temporal trends of R&D intensity (Figure 7.2). Indeed, the pattern shown by R&D intensity suggests how the expansion of the automobile industrial production has been accompanied by the implementation of R&D innovative efforts to a different extent in the four countries.

Indeed, while Germany and France show almost coinciding and relatively steady patterns, Great Britain and Italy are characterised by lower values with more pronounced cyclical variations. At the outset, this could be due to a less structural attention to the automobile sector. More particularly, Great Britain shows a worsening of its innovative intensity starting from the mid 1980s. This could be related to the fact that the British car industry is owned by foreign groups that relocated R&D functions abroad. Italy shows a very pronounced increase in the final years of the period, when the relative incidence of R&D increases to catch up with that of France.

The analysis of patents is based on the computation of a Revealed Technological Advantages index (δ_{ic}). This is nothing but a specialisation Balassa index based on patent counts.[11] For sector i of country c, the indicator is thus defined as follows:

$$\delta_{ic} = \frac{PAT_{ic} / \sum_c PAT_{ic}}{\sum_i PAT_{ic} / \sum_i \sum_c PAT_{ic}} \qquad (7.1)$$

where PAT_{ic} denotes the patents granted to country c in sector i. This indicator has the usual meaning. In fact, it indicates a certain degree of technological specialisation in sector i of country c if it is greater than one, and technological despecialisation with respect to total manufacturing if it is less than one. Having no upper limit, this indicator can be normalised in a simple way:

$$\delta_{ic}^n = \frac{\delta_{ic} - 1}{\delta_{ic} + 1} \qquad (7.2)$$

Accordingly, country c turns is despecialised in sector i if $-1 < \delta_{ic}^n < 0$, while it is specialised if $0 < \delta_{ic}^n < 1$.

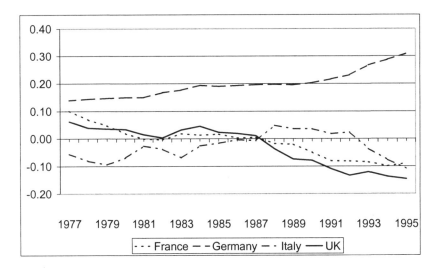

Figure 7.3   *Normalised revealed technological advantages for motor vehicles (five year moving average)*

The analysis of Figure 7.3 shows a rather evident diverging trend in patenting, suggesting an increasing level of polarisation in the innovative results of the different TS.[12] Germany is in fact the only country with positive and increasing values of the δ_{ic}^n for the whole period examined. On the opposite, the rest of the countries experience a decline in their relative technological advantages, though with different intensity.

Three main types of evidence emerge. First, there is the steady increase of the motor vehicles technological comparative advantage of Germany, which therefore seems to have been an explicit target of its technological activity. Secondly, we see the irregular, but still apparent increase in the automobile despecialisation of France and Great Britain, which suggests a possible shift in their sectoral technological priorities. Finally, there is the performance of Great Britain and Italy, which appears to be more contrasted and in need of a more complete kind of analysis in order to exhaust the whole spectrum of possible causes.

7.3.2　Innovative Pervasiveness and Dependency

As in the case of the industry side, also for the innovative side a deeper analysis is carried out with respect to interactive aspects.

A first preliminary indicator of the techno-economic interrelationships within the automobile TS is related to the innovative pervasiveness or dependency of the corresponding economic sector. Indeed, similarly to the backward and forward linkages indicators, the pervasiveness/dependency indicators identify the role of a certain sector within a certain web of interactions, but this time in innovative terms (that is, by looking at intersectoral innovation rather than production flows).

Once again, the reference can be to either direct or total innovation flows, and the latter can in turn be measured in different ways (Montresor, 1998). Consistently with the previous analysis, the same indicators will be built up on the basis of the intersectoral embodied innovation flows matrix $\mathbf{F^E}$ (as defined in equation 3.15).

As each element of $\mathbf{F^E}$, f_{ij}^E, measures the innovation produced by sector i and embodied in the final production of sector j, an absolute index of pervasiveness/dependency (APD) can be defined as the ratio between net intersectoral innovative diffusions and acquisitions (Marengo and Sterlacchini, 1990). For sector k such an index can thus be defined as:

$$APD_k = \frac{D_k - I_k}{A_k - I_k} = \frac{\sum_j f_{kj}^E - f_{kk}^E}{\sum_i f_{ik}^E - f_{kk}^E} \tag{7.3}$$

where D_k are the innovative diffusions of sector k (that is, the row total of the innovation flows matrix, $\mathbf{F^E}$, for the sector), A_k the innovative acquisitions (that is, the column total of $\mathbf{F^E}$ for the sector), while I_k stands for the intra-sectoral diffusions of the sector itself, as from the corresponding cell on the principal diagonal. Since we are interested in inter-sectoral relationships, intra-sectoral ones will be left out, so that the numerator and the denominator denote net diffusions and net acquisitions.

The meaning of the indicator is quite straightforward. If $APD_k > 1$, sector k is said to be pervasive, that is, its intersectoral innovative acquisitions are less than its diffusions. The reverse holds if $0 < APD_k < 1$, as sector k, in this case, depends to a greater extent on the rest of the economic sectors for its innovative inputs than the others depend on it.

The previous index has no upper ceiling, thus can be normalised as follows:

$$NPD_k = \frac{APD_k - 1}{APD_k + 1}. \qquad (7.4)$$

The normalisation produces an index which is symmetric with respect to a zero mean. Thus, deviations from the mean can be directly compared. Accordingly, sector k will turn out to be dependent if $-1 < NPD_k < 0$, while it will be pervasive if $0 < NPD_k < 1$.

The two indices are shown in Table 7.4 for those years that are comparable with the linkages indicators we have calculated before, although with respect to a different sectoral classification (Table 7.3).[13]

Table 7.3   Sectoral disaggregation for pervasiveness/dependency and network indicators

1	Food, beverages & tobacco	11	Metal products
2	Textiles, apparel & leather	12	Non-electrical machinery
3	Wood & furniture	13	Office & computing machinery
4	Paper, paper products & printing	14	Electrical apparatus (incl. radio, TV)
5	Chemical industry (incl. drugs)	15	Shipbuilding & repair (incl. other)
6	Petroleum & coal products	16	Motor vehicles
7	Rubber & plastic products	17	Aircraft
8	Non-metallic mineral products	18	Professional goods
9	Iron & steel	19	Other manufacturing n.e.c.
10	Non-ferrous metals		

In part reflecting the industrial analysis on which, to a certain extent, the innovative one is based,[14] the data show that the automobile sector is quite dependent for its technological acquisitions on the rest of the economic sectors. In absolute terms, its innovative diffusions are generally less than 10% of the corresponding acquisitions.[15]

By looking at the normalised values of the indicator it emerges that France has the lowest and most stable values of the four countries, so that its motor vehicles sector turns out to be the most structurally dependent out of the four countries. The well-known strength of the French automobile industry therefore seems to rely on a substantial contribution from other sectors, to whose identification we will turn in the next section.

Table 7.4   Motor vehicles innovative pervasiveness and dependency

		Absolute	Normalised
France	1977	0.026	-0.950
	1980	0.022	-0.956
	1985	0.024	-0.953
	1990	0.026	-0.949
Germany	1978	0.070	-0.870
	1986	0.074	-0.862
	1988	0.072	-0.865
	1990	0.078	-0.855
Great Britain	1979	0.049	-0.906
	1984	0.095	-0.827
	1990	0.157	-0.728
Italy	1985	0.052	-0.901

For Germany also the normalised indicator shows a remarkable degree of stability over time, but at higher values than France, contributing to explain the greater connectivity of the corresponding national TS. As far as Italy is concerned, the very dependent nature of the automobile sector seems to confirm the well-known backward innovative linkages relating the Italian monopolist of the sector and a dense network of specialised suppliers.

Finally, a very interesting pattern emerges for Great Britain, showing an appreciable increase over time of the normalised indicator. The sustained process of internationalisation which has characterised the sector over the 1980s seems therefore to have also made it more internally pervasive, at least in innovative terms.

In concluding this section, we should remember that the pervasiveness/ dependency indicator measures the role of a certain sector in innovation relationships, rather than the relationships themselves. Hence, a more detailed picture can be obtained by mapping the innovation flows throughout network analysis in a way similar to that of Chapters 5 and 6.

7.3.3   Network Analysis

Network analysis techniques and indicators can be helpful also in analysing the structure of a sectoral TS, once the relevant sector has been 'isolated' from the others. Accordingly, the set of techniques which continue to be of significance reduces to two: degree centrality and graph analysis. Once again, in order to get rid of scale effects, in the following we will refer to the normalised relative acquisition matrix, $\mathbf{F}^{E,Rel}$, as defined in (3.17). Furthermore, as in the earlier chapter, we also need to consider a dichotomised version of it, as in (3.18). In order to make our analysis less dependent on the arbitrariness of the threshold selection, two cut-off values have been chosen, referring to, respectively, almost all the flows (acquisitions larger than 0.1%, that is, $k = 0.001$), and to 'large' flows only (greater than 0.5%, that is, $k = 0.005$).

Table 7.5 shows the values of the indegree (G_{in}^{16}) and outdegree (G_{out}^{16}) centrality indicators (as defined in (5.2)) for both cut-off values utilised.[16]

Table 7.5   Motor vehicles Freeman's degree centrality

Cut-off		0.005		0.001	
		Out	In	Out	In
France	1977	1	7	10	11
	1980	1	6	9	11
	1985	1	7	9	12
	1990	1	7	10	11
Germany	1978	9	6	14	9
	1986	20	7	16	9
	1988	10	7	16	9
	1990	10	6	16	9
Great Britain	1979	6	7	12	14
	1984	6	7	12	12
	1990	10	8	17	13
Italy	1985	2	5	10	9

A first important observation is strictly related to those of the previous section. In general, the indegree centrality values are greater than the outdegree ones, thus confirming the dependent nature of the sector. However, this does not hold for Germany, where, for all the flows that we have retained, the outdegree centrality is higher, so that the sector is pervasive. To be sure, such switches, with respect to the aggregate analysis performed in the previous section, can also be found in other countries, but they are more limited. In the case of Great Britain, for example, the sector turns from dependent into pervasive, moving from the mid 1980s to the early 1990s, in particular with respect to large flows. The fact that the British automobile sector becomes less dependent, while being taken over by foreign companies, should not come as a surprise. Indeed, this being an indicator of internal pervasiveness, it shows that crucial functions related to the technological sphere are now performed abroad.

Italy, for which only one year (1985) is available, is shown to be pervasive only when small flows are concerned: for $k = 0.001$, in fact, G_{in}^{16} and G_{out}^{16}

are equal to 9 and 10 respectively. This seems to hint at the fact that if innovative interrelationships which possibly also involve small suppliers of both components and final products are considered, the nature of the sector changes quite substantially. A further important observation concerns the different importance (that is, centrality) that the automobile sector exhibits in the four countries in respect of flows of different magnitude.

As for the outdegree values, the German automobile sector is the most central with respect to both cut-off values and, what is more, with relatively fewer 'drops' in cutting out small and medium innovative acquisitions, that is, in moving from 0.001 to 0.005. If the British automobile sector is the second most central for all the cut-off values, the changes we observe in France and Italy by increasing the magnitude of the relevant threshold are more appreciable than in Great Britain.

Substantially different results emerge from the analysis of the indegree centrality. With some exception, the differences between the four countries are less evident than for the outdegree values. The 'homogenising' effect of their input-output structures (caught by the columns) seems therefore to weigh more than the 'differentiating' effect entailed by their R&D system (captured by the rows). Also the differences we observe in moving between the cut-off values appear generally less substantial than for the outdegree values. Acquisitions seem therefore more homogeneous than diffusions for the present cut-off values, as their critical thresholds are possibly higher. Finally, the ranking of the countries is also substantially different. Though with some exceptions, the acquisitions of the British automobile sector count more than in the other countries, although in retaining large flows acquisitions reduce substantially. What we have previously observed in aggregate terms, therefore, finds confirmation only for a limited subset of innovation flows. This is even truer for Italy, as the dependent nature of its automobile sector appears evident only when flows of a certain magnitude are left out. The intermediate indegree centrality of the sector in France and Germany is instead more stable across the cut-off values.

As far as the temporal changes are concerned, they are, in general, not so relevant. However, because the outdegree centrality is slightly more variable than the indegree one, possibly, the incidence of R&D expenditure varies more than the input-output structures over time. However, the temporal changes are relatively more consistent when both small and large flows are considered, while the reference to large flows only entails a greater degree of stability.[17]

While the previous analysis just refers to the number of innovative diffusions and acquisitions by the automobile sector, more qualitative considerations about their destination and origin can be obtained by applying the other typical network analysis technique we have already used in previous chapters, that of oriented graphs.

Figures 7.4 and 7.5 report the edges of such oriented graphs for the selected cut-off values with respect to the mid 1980s only. These graphs visualise the linkages of the 'automobile network', a network that can be obtained by leaving out all those edges which do not originate from, or converge to, the motor vehicles sector. As far as the choice of the selected period is concerned, as we have seen in the previous centrality analysis, the most apparent changes occur in considering innovative flows of different magnitude, rather than the same kinds of flows with respect to different periods. Accordingly, the evaluation has been limited to the period with the most numerous observations.

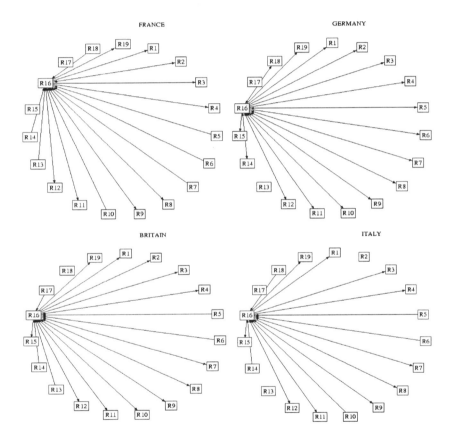

Figure 7.4   Oriented graphs, mid 1980s (k = 0.001)

When nearly all the innovative flows are considered ($k = 0.001$), the four graphs are quite similar (Figure 7.4). Indeed, the density of the automobile network – defined as the ratio between the number of 'actual' and 'potential' automobile-based innovative flows – is in the case of France and Italy only slightly lower than in Great Britain and Germany: that is, 0.061 and 0.055, versus 0.070 and 0.073.

As far as the flows direction is concerned, as expected, the automobile industry (Sector 16) is in general purely 'diffusive' only with respect to the most traditional sectors of the disaggregation (Sectors 1-4), and to the residual one (Sector 19).[18] As much expected is the fact that the automobile sector is purely 'acquisitive' with respect to the chemical (Sector 5) and the energy products (Sector 6) sectors. However, the underlying techno-economic relationships become biunivocal with respect to chemicals in Germany, thus providing us with a further confirmation of the more interconnected nature of its national TS. A similar 'acquisitive' argument, this time presumably for the external parts and the engines of the automobiles, also holds with respect to non-ferrous metals (Sector 10) and electrical equipment (Sector 14), which benefit from substantial motor vehicles innovations only in Germany and, for the former, also in Great Britain.

As far as the remaining sectors are concerned, the automobile industry establishes biunivocal innovative relationships with nearly all those sectors which supply to it physical kinds of artefacts (Sectors 7, 8, 9, 11 and 12).[19] The relationships with the suppliers of more 'sophisticated' components, typically in the office and computing machinery sector (Sector 13), are instead purely acquisitive in France and Great Britain, or even below the relative threshold, such as in Germany and in Italy.

Finally, and quite surprisingly, innovative relationships turn out to be in general quite rare with the other transport equipment sectors (Sectors 15 and 17), and with the professional goods one (Sector 18).

When only large innovation flows are considered ($k = 0.005$), a density gap between the German and the other automobile TS becomes apparent (Figure 7.5). The percentage of actual innovative linkages is, in the first case, nearly 5% of the total, while it is around 4% in Great Britain ($DEN(0.005)_{16} = 0.038$), and 2% in France and Italy ($DEN(0.005)_{16} = 0.023$ and $DEN(0.005)_{16} = 0.020$, respectively).

Paralleling what can be observed by looking at all the innovative interrelationships (see Chapter 4), the German automobile network is by far the densest. On the one hand, the only sectors which fall out of the network are the energy products (Sector 6) and the aircraft sector (Sector 17) as in the other countries, the professional goods sector (Sector 18) as in Great Britain and Italy, and the office and computing industry as in Italy. On the other hand, much of the suppliers of the relevant physical components receive substantial innovative flows from the automobile sector.

As far as the other countries are concerned, the only innovative flows that survive the dichotomisation in France and in Italy relate to some of the sectors in the central part of the disaggregation (Sectors 7, 9, 11), to which may be added the professional goods sector (Sector 18) in France. Furthermore, apart from the non-metallic mineral products (Sector 8), these relationships are all univocal and identify innovative transfers towards the motor vehicles sector. The same kind of univocal relationships can also be identified in Great Britain, where 'large' diffusions can however still be identified from the automobile sector to food and beverages (Sector 1) and to textiles (Sector 2).

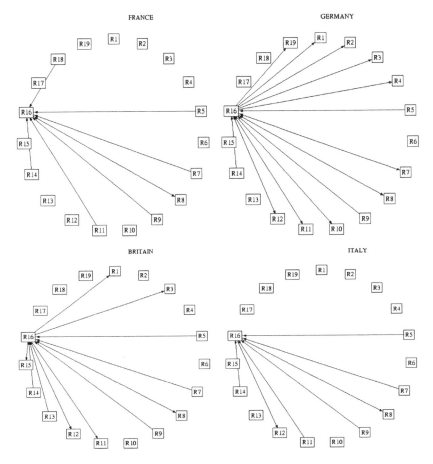

Figure 7.5   Oriented graphs, mid 1980s (k = 0.005)

In conclusion, it should be stressed that, although quite specific and very detailed, the results of the graph analysis allow us to accomplish two important tasks: to directly identify the crucial diffusion channels of automobiles-embodied innovation, both from and towards the rest of the system, and to evaluate their role with respect to innovative flows of different magnitude.

7.4   THE INTERNATIONAL SIDE

The relationships we have considered in the previous sections are exclusively domestic. In other words, we have focused our attention on those production and innovation interactions that the automobile TS establishes within the country where the relative companies reside. However, as we have said at the beginning of this chapter, a sectoral TS extends also outside their home-base country, and through different material and immaterial exchanges.

Among others, trade flows and foreign direct investments represent two channels whose analysis can be useful in disentangling the actual degree of internationalisation (trade) and transnationalisation (FDI) of the automobile TS. To these flows we now turn our attention.[20]

7.4.1   Bilateral Revealed Comparative Advantages

As we are interested in mapping the degree of specialisation/despecialisation with respect to specific countries/regions, in the following we work out a Bilateral Revealed Comparative Advantages indicator, β_{ic}^{j}, which is a geographical specification of that defined in (4.6):

$$\beta_{ic}^{j} = \frac{EX_{ic}^{j} / \sum_{c} EX_{ic}^{j}}{\sum_{i} EX_{ic}^{j} / \sum_{c} \sum_{i} EX_{ic}^{j}} \qquad (7.5)$$

where EX_{ic}^{j} denotes the export made by country c in sector i to country j. In other words, β_{ic}^{j} is nothing but the ratio between the sectoral and the total export shares of a certain origin country c to a destination country j.

As for the standard β_{ic}, the meaning of this indicator depends on its values being greater or lower than one. In the former case, it shows a revealed bilateral comparative advantage, that is, the exports of the automobile sector perform better than those of the rest of the industrial sectors with respect to a certain country. Hence, we have a relative specialisation in this sector, but with respect to a specific geographical area. The opposite holds for values less than one, which indicates a relative despecialisation in automobile manufacturing with respect to a certain area.

Therefore, the reference to bilateral, rather than to standard, comparative advantages allows us to map geographically the relative strength of a certain country in the automobile sector. We are thus able to compare the different spatial patterns of internationalisation that the relative TS has undergone, at least by allocating national production abroad. As far as the calculation is concerned, the reference years have been chosen in order to work out the BRCA indicator for the same periods of the previous indicators.[21] As for the destination countries, they have been chosen in order to give an account of the automobile international specialisation in the main world markets, both established, such as the EU,[22] USA and Japan, and emerging, such as South Eastern and South Western Asia (Singapore and China) and Latin America (Brazil). Of course, we are quite aware that this choice may lead to some distortions.

The results we have obtained with respect to the European market confirm our expectations, at least to a certain extent (Table 7.6).

France and Germany are the only countries with a persistent specialisation in this area. Furthermore, the recent expansion of the mergers and acquisitions of the German automobiles producers seems to be confirmed by

Table 7.6   Motor vehicles bilateral revealed comparative advantages

Destination: Origin:	EU	USA	Japan	Brazil	Czech Rep.	Singapore	China	OECD	Non-OECD
1975									
France	1.64	0.31	0.32	0.34	3.03	1.20	2.27	1.08	1.21
Germany	1.33	1.44	3.35	1.14	0.78	2.19	0.14	1.10	1.49
Great Britain	1.11	0.50	1.04	0.91	1.20	2.50	0.42	0.81	1.21
Italy	1.06	0.76	0.95	0.67	2.01	1.64	2.54	0.82	0.95
1980									
France	1.50	0.45	0.47	0.38	2.11	0.46	1.58	1.10	1.18
Germany	1.48	1.49	5.82	1.23	1.10	1.94	1.30	1.30	1.41
Great Britain	0.88	0.38	1.67	2.30	1.53	1.39	0.20	0.66	1.09
Italy	0.84	0.47	1.12	2.55	2.00	1.16	0.25	0.67	0.78
1985									
France	1.30	0.31	0.30	1.36	0.75	0.48	0.67	0.77	1.23
Germany	1.55	1.31	6.52	1.38	1.15	2.12	0.56	1.15	1.46
Great Britain	0.64	0.38	0.81	1.37	0.82	1.43	0.59	0.43	0.81
Italy	0.70	0.47	0.66	1.48	1.65	2.90	0.48	0.40	0.64
1990									
France	1.25	0.26	0.71	2.39	2.20	0.59	1.22	0.94	1.20
Germany	1.42	1.09	4.38	1.42	1.32	2.56	2.61	1.26	1.35
Great Britain	0.85	0.36	1.21	2.14	0.52	1.32	0.74	0.66	0.69
Italy	0.76	0.24	0.52	1.37	0.80	2.07	0.19	0.58	0.60
1993									
France	1.23	0.23	0.36	0.56	1.06	0.44	1.72	0.88	0.91
Germany	1.38	0.94	4.26	1.21	1.08	3.37	1.97	1.17	1.40
Great Britain	0.92	0.28	1.17	0.95	0.48	1.64	0.91	0.66	0.56
Italy	0.64	0.16	0.59	2.04	0.96	1.47	0.28	0.47	0.59

the shift we observe in the magnitude of the β_{ic}^{j} indexes from France to Germany. The pattern in the β_{ic}^{j} of Great Britain and Italy is decreasing, a result that might also be due to the penetration of other car producers in Europe (notably from the Far East). Moreover, it also emerges that Great Britain and Italy might have shifted their specialisation area, rather than competing with France and Germany in the same market. A suggestive example is given by the case of the Brazilian market, in which, from the early 1980s, both Italy and Great Britain have acquired a specialisation which is greater than, or at least comparable with, those of France and Germany.

As far as the other destination countries are concerned, Germany appears the only competitive car producer of the four in the USA, although with a decreasing trend, and, more evidently, in Japan. Furthermore, in the most recent period, it has overtaken the previously unique and consistent specialisation of France in the Chinese market.

For the Eastern market (here represented by the Czech Republic), a certain change emerges which confirms the increasing internationalisation of the German car producers. Until the early 1980s, France and Italy were the most competitive producers in that area. However, entering the globalisation phase, Italy has lost its comparative advantages, apparently at the expense of Germany, which has recently joined France as the only specialised country in the Czech Republic.

Although the conclusions we have drawn with respect to the selected target countries can't be extended too far, it suffices here to observe how the consideration of bilateral trade flows makes the standard analysis of specialisation more complete, providing important elements for evaluating the geographical extension of the specialisation pattern of the sector.

7.4.2   Foreign Direct Investments

As is widely held, one characteristic of the globalisation process is that the volume of foreign direct investments (FDI) has been increasing more than exports as a means of international integration (OECD, 1992, Ch. 10). Indeed, by establishing production and innovation units abroad, firms have changed from being purely international to transnational, if not even global.

This holds true, in particular, for the motor vehicles sector, for which the geographical dispersion of the subsidiaries of a certain parent company around the world is becoming so widespread that, in some cases, the actual nationality of an automobile transnational corporations (TNC) could not be determined on the basis of a purely territorial criterion. A certain confirmation of this fact can be obtained by looking at the largest TNC (abroad) and foreign affiliates (in the host economy) of the four countries analysed, in terms of sales (Table 7.7).[23]

Table 7.7   *Ranking of motor vehicle companies among the 10 largest TNC and among the largest foreign affiliates by sales (1988)*

	Company	Rank	Home economy	Sales (million US$)
Largest transanational corporations abroad				
France	Régie Nationale des Usines Renault S.A.	1		10313.7
	Peugeot S.A.	2		23242.3
Germany	Daimler Benz AG	1		41848.2
	Volkswagen AG	3		33720.5
	Bayerische Motorenwerke AG	10		13931.5
Great Britain	–			
Italy	Fiat S.p.a.	1		37812.1
Largest foreign affiliates in the host economy				
France	Fiat France	4	Italy	4237.6
Germany	Ford-Werke AG	1	USA	10959.3
	Adam Opel AG	2	USA	9942.9
Great Britain	Ford Motor Co. Ltd	1	USA	10559.1
	Vauxhall Motors Ltd.	7	USA	3477.6
Italy	–			

Source: UNCTAD (1993).

Firms operating in the motor vehicles sector are the biggest TNC in three out of the four countries examined, where these firms rank in the first three positions apart from one case only (Germany). Also the dimensions of the automobile foreign affiliates are quite large, with the sole exception of Italy, although the only non-US foreign affiliate (in France) is Italian.

A certain level of differentiation seems to emerge between two groups of countries. France and Germany seem to be characterised by a certain balance between the presence abroad and that at home of automobile TNC. Great Britain and Italy, instead, have very unbalanced, although opposite, characterisations (inward in one case, outward in the other). This seems to be a clear consequence, for Italy, of the monopolistic position of its only national producer, which makes the penetration of foreign producers more difficult, and for Great Britain, on the contrary, the result of the progressive loss of a 'true' national champion.

Similarly to the case of exports, also with respect to FDI, it is interesting to establish whether the motor vehicles sector is one in which a country reveals a comparative advantage or disadvantage. Just as for exports and patents, in order to see if a country c turns out to be specialised in sector i, a Balassa index of transnational activities (γ_{ic}) can be calculated:

$$\gamma_{ic} = \frac{FDI_{ic} \Big/ \sum_c FDI_{ic}}{\sum_i FDI_{ic} \Big/ \sum_i \sum_c FDI_{ic}} \tag{7.6}$$

For reasons that will appear clear in a while, it is convenient to rearrange the previous formula as the ratio between the sectoral FDI share of country c and that of the 'World' of reference:

$$\gamma_{ic}^* = \frac{FDI_{ic} \Big/ \sum_i FDI_{ic}}{\sum_c FDI_{ic} \Big/ \sum_i \sum_c FDI_{ic}} \tag{7.7}$$

The numerator of the previous equation is a first indicator of the 'absolute' importance of the automobile sector for the transnational activities of country c (Figure 7.6).[24]

As far as outward stocks are concerned, they appear to be very important in Italy in the early 1980s (about 10%) and in Germany in the early 1990s (about 5%). Furthermore, over the decade we observe a more general trend as the relative weight of the transnational activities of the automobile TS shows an overall decrease. This is possibly due to an increase in the shares of outward FDI stocks of other sectors (that is, to an enlargement of the internationalisation process beyond the automobile sector). Coming now to the inward FDI stocks, their incidence in manufacturing is the highest in Italy and Great Britain (around 8%) in the early 1980s, with a consistent gap with respect to Germany (about 4%). Following the decrease experienced by the sector also in inward terms, the ranking appears quite different in the early 1990s.[25]

As a result of these temporal changes, Italy, which experiences the biggest drop in both types of FDI, shows a structural kind of change, turning from a net exporter to a net recipient. The decrease is less consistent for the inward FDI of Germany, which appears to be the only country of the group that, although structurally a net exporter, successfully managed to remain 'palatable' to foreign investors. A positive balance is also shown by France, while Great Britain, in spite of the above-mentioned changes, remains a net recipient over the decade.

In order to obtain more significant results we need of course to normalise the previous indicator with respect to the relative weight of the world FDI outward stock in the motor vehicles sector, that is, the denominator of the previous equation. In so doing, a proper revealed transnational advantages/ disadvantages indicator can be obtained, whose meaning is the same as the previous one.

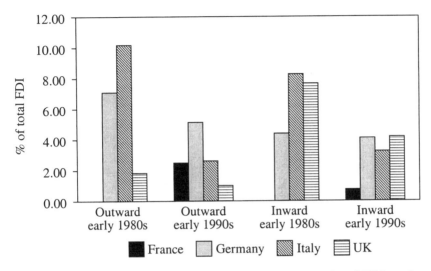

Figure 7.6   Stock of motor vehicles FDI as a proportion of total FDI stock

Unfortunately, the data for the denominator of γ^*_{ic} are difficult to obtain. In particular, as they are not available for all countries in the world and for the same periods, a 'second best' solution is to work out the specialisation/ despecialisation index with respect to a more circumscribed area (the OECD countries) and to use wide temporal references (such as the early 1980s and the early 1990s), encompassing years that, although not coincident, are close enough between them.[26]

The computation of γ^*_{ic} shows a more composite picture (Table 7.8) than the previous figures. In the first period, Italy is the most specialised country in the automobile sector. However, it experiences a very sharp drop in the early 1990s, when it is overtaken by Germany, for which, in turn, the indicator remains more or less stable, suggesting a persistent specialisation. To be sure, Italy is the only country for which, again, a structural change occurs, from specialised to slightly despecialised. This is certainly due to the very low level of the denominator of the γ^*_{ic} formula, and thus simply expresses the irrelevance of the rest of the economic sectors, with respect to the automobile one, in terms of FDI. Therefore, the large decrease of the indicator seems to be due more to the internationalisation of the Italian economy as a whole, rather than to an absolute weakening of the transnational activities of the automobile sector.

Finally, Great Britain, as expected, has the lowest values, and is the only despecialised country in the early 1980s. France, for which data are available for the last period only, is characterised by a despecialisation with values almost equal to those of Italy, but with a completely different underlying structure of FDI.

Table 7.8   Motor vehicles revealed transnational advantages

| | early 1980s | | early 1990s | |
	absolute	normalised	absolute	normalised
France	–	–	0.78	-0.12
Germany	1.74	0.27	1.61	0.23
Great Britain	0.46	-0.37	0.33	-0.51
Italy	2.52	0.43	0.81	-0.10

As in previous sections, this last set of results also provides complex insights about the sectoral and national domain of the automobile TS. An attempt at synthesising and interpreting all the various aspects which have emerged is therefore necessary. To this task we will turn in the last section.

7.5   CONCLUSIONS

The aspects we have addressed in this chapter are quite numerous and have been examined by using a set of heterogeneous analytical instruments. The results we have obtained are manifold and difficult to synthesise exhaustively. Some important conclusions can however be drawn.

The first set of conclusions relate to the importance of the sectoral TS as the unit of analysis. Indeed, fresh insights can be brought into the study of a very traditional industry such as the automobile industry.

At the outset, we have detected a very high degree of stability in the face of change. The various TS examined managed, more or less successfully, to maintain their stability by means of a high level of internal change. In fact, in front of an overall persistence of the usual industrial indicators, our different levels of analysis have detected a sustained process of change in the various elements of the automobile TS, all of which contributed to a relatively steady path of development.

Secondly, the TS dynamics are very much dependent on the co-evolution of its various elements, rather than on the performance of only one (or a few) of them. Therefore, an imbalance between the elements of the TS constitutes a problem to be solved for the TS dynamics. The various TS examined are in fact characterised by different structural relationships, and, in order to maintain their overall dynamics, a variety of different ways to overcome bottlenecks have been worked out.[27]

Thirdly, the TS dynamics we have observed are more varied than that characterising the single TS units. As we have noted, dynamic effects are very diversified. Different parts of the TS, with different relative dimensions and weights, have undergone substantial changes over time. These changes were different among the various TS, but also, when they were more or less similar, the result was never the same. Indeed, some of them were subject to structural change determined by the underlying process of diffused technological change; for others globalisation played an important role; for others it was rather institutional change that triggered the evolution of the TS. In all cases, the combination of these three elements was never the same.

Coming now to more detailed aspects, the following points are worth stressing again.

First of all, when internal techno-economic relationships are considered, the automobile industry shows some general sectoral properties (such as dominant backward linkages and innovative dependency) that hold in all the countries examined. However, the same characteristics apply to the four countries to a different extent, thus suggesting how the institutional set-up, within which a certain industry operates, might work as a differentiating element. Further differences emerge when the specific nature of the techno-economic flows is analysed in more detail, with the automobile sector turning into pervasive from dependent (for example, Italy), and with Germany emerging as the TS with the largest relative flows exchange.

Secondly, temporal aspects are also very relevant in analysing (internal) intersectoral relationships. Indeed, over the considered period apparent divergence phenomena can be found by looking at proper innovative indicators. Although cyclical factors also intervene in explaining these results, as is apparently shown by the irregular trends of the Italian TS, more structural kinds of changes can also be detected. A significant example is provided by British motor vehicles, with respect to which the well-known recent pattern of internationalisation has much to say.

Finally, as far as export flows are concerned, apart from the uncontested dominance of France and Germany in the European market, the countries considered reveal different patterns of specialisation in different geographical areas. A similar argument holds when foreign direct investments are considered. On the one hand, automobile companies are among the most multinationalised in all of our countries, both in terms of transnational subsidiaries abroad and of hosted foreign affiliates. On the other hand, inward FDI are more relevant than outward in some countries (such as Great Britain), while the reverse holds in some other countries (for example, Germany). Country-specific effects can also be identified by looking at the temporal changes in both inward and outward FDI, which are in general decreasing from the early 1980s to the early 1990s.

Many other important aspects have been left out of the analysis, which could therefore be integrated in several respects (in particular organisational). However, the results obtained suggest how the 'relational' and 'contextual' elements that are caught by the notion of TS are among the most important factors accounting for the different national performances of the European automobile industry. In other words, the automobile TS reveals properties that, although idiosyncratic, induce different innovative outcomes, depending on their matching with different institutional set-ups, which are sectoral but also, and especially, national. Different systemic approaches should therefore be considered as complementary, rather than as substitute or even contrasting.

NOTES

1. In Chapter 2 we have shown that these problems apply, though in a different way, also to macro TS.
2. Given the sectoral focus, this analysis is more easily implemented than in the case of a macro TS, especially because of the lack of data.
3. As far as the other European countries are concerned, Spain is the only other market to overcome the threshold of one million new cars registered, so that the presence of a certain level of industrial concentration in the European automobile sector can be at least inferred.
4. As for the other European countries, Spain has a share of 15%, with only one national producer (Seat, owned by Volkswagen), and Belgium is the first largest producer (8.5%) with no national car manufacturers.
5. This picture is further confirmed if Volvo, which has recently been acquired, is consolidated into the Ford figures.
6. At the time of writing, Rover was being sold by BMW, so that by now BMW will have joined the group of the most nation-based companies.
7. Being derived from domestic I-O tables, backward and forward linkages indicators are national.
8. This matrix is similar to $\mathbf{A}$, but refers to inter-industrial outputs, rather than inputs and is defined as $\mathbf{A}^* = (\hat{\mathbf{x}})^{-1}(\mathbf{X})$.
9. This is a Leontief inverse obtained on the basis of $\mathbf{A}^*$ as $\mathbf{B}^{\#} = (\mathbf{I} - \mathbf{A}^*)^{-1}$.
10. If 1973 is made equal to 100, in 1980 R&D expenditure was 275, with the highest and the lowest values for Germany (359) and for Italy (193), respectively.
11. In fact, it is equivalent to β_{ic}, defined with respect to trade flows in Chapter 4 (equation 4.6).
12. In order to overcome unavoidable institutional differences between different patent offices, we have based our analysis on the number of patents granted by the US Patents and Trademark Office during the period 1977-1995 (USPTO, OEIP/TAF Database, 1996).
13. The data on sectoral R&D (DSTI (STAN, Anberd), 1994) are not available on a comparable basis before 1973, thus the earlier years of the linkages and pervasiveness indicators do not coincide. The same holds for the relative sectoral disaggregation. Indeed, by matching input-output tables with R&D data we have now a less disaggregated classification of 19 sectors (see Table 7.4).
14. The innovative flows utilised to produce the APD indicators are embodied in intersectoral production flows.
15. This is particularly true for France, where they are stable at around 2%, while in Great Britain innovative diffusions reach and overtake 10% of corresponding acquisitions.
16. The relevant *j* sector in this case is, in fact, Sector 16 of Table 7.3.

17. The most consistent variations concern Great Britain, where the outdegree centrality of the automobile sector increases substantially for all the cut-off values, in particular from 1984 to 1990. Furthermore, apart from the large flows, its indegree centrality also progressively decreases over time.

18. The only exception is that of textiles (Sector 2), from which it receives innovative flows above the threshold in France.

19. The only exceptions are rubber and plastic (Sector 7), that in France turn out to be only diffusive, and non-metallic mineral products (Sector 8), that in Italy is only acquisitive.

20. An important point has to be stressed here. Similarly to the analysis carried out in Chapter 4, the data utilised in this section have a different nature with respect to those of the preceding section. Indeed, these data do not relate very easily to technological flows. However, as it is impossible to find indicators more developed in this regard, we reckon it is worth introducing a further approximation in order to perform a more complete analysis.

21. The data on trade flows between countries are taken from the OECD STAN database on Bilateral Trade (DSTI (STAN, Bilateral Trade Database), 1997).

22. Although the extension of the EU area has changed over the period, the relative nature of the specialisation indicator we have used makes temporal comparisons possible anyway.

23. Data have been taken from what is, at the time of this writing, the latest available UNCTAD World Investment Directory (UNCTAD, 1993) which do not extend beyond 1988: the most recent mergers and acquisitions are thus not caught.

24. The data to build up such an indicator with respect to the motor vehicles sector are available for all of our countries for the early 1980s and the early 1990s, although the reference years are not the same. More precisely, the data for France refer to 1982 and 1989, those for Germany and Italy to 1980 and 1990, and those for Great Britain to 1981 and 1987 (UNCTAD, 1993).

25. In fact, with the exception of France (where it has a very low weight, less than 1%), Italy and Great Britain are joined by Germany with a share of around 3-4% of all the manufacturing inward stocks.

26. To be sure, the reference-point for our calculations is a subset of the OECD countries. However, the countries for which data are not available are presumably not very important in terms of outward FDI.

27. In this regard the notion of 'reverse salient' (Hughes, 1989) appears to be appropriate in the description of what has been going on in the automobile industry in the decade we have examined. A reverse salient, in fact, refers to the uneven growth of the TS components, some of which may lag behind the others and thus affect the growth dynamics of the overall network.

8. The chemical technological system

The macro analysis carried out in the first part of this book for the TS of the main OECD countries has shown that, no matter the country considered, the chemical sector always plays a pivotal role. On the one hand, its outdegree centrality is in general close to the maximum.[1] On the other hand, its indegree centrality is among the lowest, thus spurring one to investigate those few industrial sectors which can be included in the chemical techno-economic *filière*.

The system nature of the chemical sector is further confirmed by some 'stylised facts', which make its functional boundaries actually 'shifting' (Walsh, 1997, p. 117). At the outset, this is due to the fact that the upstream and downstream linkages of the firms involved in chemical processes naturally draw on an expanding spectrum of other activities, such as for example bio-technologies (Chapman and Edmond, 2000). As a result of this inherent pervasiveness, the chemical sector has come to embrace a wide array of production processes which were previously classified in other economic sectors. The most evident case is that of fertilisers, previously considered an outcome of the agricultural sector. To the cross-sectoral nature of the chemical processes we should add that, as we have seen in the previous chapters, intersectoral purchases of both intermediaries and sophisticated equipment represent for the chemical sector important means to get knowledge and innovation produced elsewhere. Finally, further intersectoral elements are introduced by the typical diversification strategies of the chemical companies, which resort to alliances, joint ventures and technological collaboration to a greater extent than to market and hierarchies. In the light of all these and other factors, a sectoral interpretation of this TS turns out to be extremely relevant in dealing with the functional boundaries of the chemical industry.

A similar argument applies to the geographical boundaries of the same industry. Indeed, the chemical sector is one of the few with respect to which the globalisation of the innovative process has been widely recognised with respect to the three dimensions along which it can be appreciated, that is: (i) innovation production, (ii) exploitation of innovative results and (iii) international innovation agreement (Archibugi and Michie, 1995). As far as the former two dimensions are concerned, it should be stressed once more that, over the last decade, chemical companies have largely resorted to diversification strategies. They have been largely implemented through the internationalisation of their business activities extensively, and through the decentralisation of their R&D to the relevant multinational subsidiaries (Walsh, 1997).

The transnational character of chemical activities is further reinforced by their intensity of 'corporate control' strategies, such as mergers, acquisitions, demergers, sell-offs and corporate swaps. Many of these have in fact been cross-border, both within and outside the EU (Chapman and Edmond, 2000). Finally, the chemical sector has undergone an important process of globalisation also with respect to a third dimension, that is, through collaborative research agreements and through the recruitment of overseas scientists and technologists (Hagedoorn, 1995).

As in the previous chapter, these features will be addressed at three different, but strongly interconnected, levels of analysis, pertaining to, respectively, the industrial side (Section 8.1), the innovative side (Section 8.2) and the international side (Section 8.3). Sticking to the methodology we have put forward for the sectoral analysis of the TS, these three 'sides' will be investigated by referring to, respectively, backward and forward linkages (industrial side), innovative proxies and network analysis (innovative side), revealed comparative advantages, merger and acquisitions, and foreign direct investments (international side). As all these analytical tools have already been discussed at length, in the following the results will be directly presented and commented upon straightforwardly.

8.1   THE INDUSTRY SIDE

8.1.1   General Outlook

In the last two decades the chemical industry has been one of the leading EU manufacturing sectors, both in terms of value-added and employment. In 1995, for example, the chemical sector sold in Western Europe, taken together, 495 billion US$, versus 372 billion US$ in the USA (European Commission, 1997, vol. 1).

In terms of total production, instead, with around 530 billion US$, the chemical sector accounted in 1998 for 15% of total manufacturing production in the EU, with a general upward trend for the main EU producers (Figure 8.1) (European Commission, 2000). Germany is by far the biggest EU producer, with around 28% of total production in 1998, while France comes second with a share of around 20%. Italy (around 15%) and Great Britain (around 10%) follow.

These data suggest that, as is widely recognised, Europe has in chemicals an important international competitive advantage with respect to the USA and Japan. Indeed, this is reflected by several indicators: (i) a sustained 'revealed technological advantage' (Patel and Pavitt, 1994), (ii) a positive balance of trade (European Commission, 1997, vol. 2, pp. 6-7), (iii) an outstanding position among the largest world chemical/pharmaceutical companies (Walsh, 1997, Table 5.12 and Table 5.13).[2]

A first very important aspect for our purposes is that the chemical sector is a capital-intensive, science-based sector, and this, coupled with the very important role that it plays with respect to the other sectors as a key supplier of intermediate goods, confirms the systemic nature of the chemical sector.

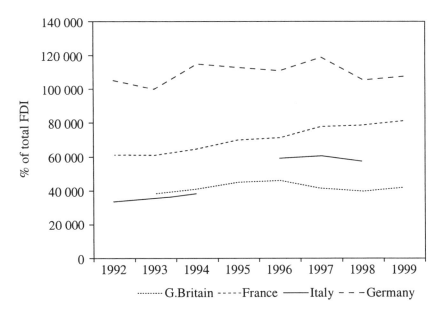

Figure 8.1   Total production in the chemical sector (1000 million US$)

A second system-relevant feature to be underlined is the segmentation of the chemical industry into a plethora of several sub-sectors. Indeed, unlike the motor vehicles sector (quite concentrated in the production of automobiles), the chemical sector comprehends many and heterogeneous sub-sectors, ranging from soap and detergents to fertilisers, from petrochemicals to pharmaceuticals, etc. In 1998, for example, the largest shares were those of pharmaceuticals (24%), plastics (15%) and petrochemicals (14%). The rest is quite fragmented.

This picture is reflected in each one of the four countries of the present application, although with some relevant differences, as is partially shown in Figures 8.2, 8.3, 8.4 and 8.5, where the various shares of the different sub-sectors (the reference is to sector 24 and 25 of the 'Classification of Economic Activities in the European Community' (Nace)) are depicted.

Quite interestingly, Germany and Italy, with respect to which the chemical sector represents, respectively, one of the most and one of the least competitive industries, show, respectively, the least and the most fragmented structures. A Schumpeterian interpretation of the virtuous role of variety, in line with our previous interpretation, could thus be put forward.

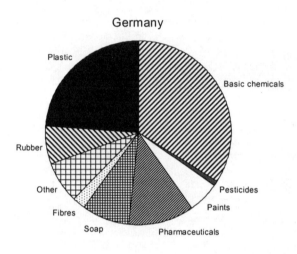

Figure 8.2   Production shares in the chemical sector in Germany (1998)

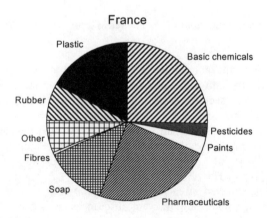

Figure 8.3   Production shares in the chemical sector in France (1998)

In spite of these relevant differences, an important degree of fragmentation characterises the sector in all the four countries considered. This fact confirms that standard kinds of industrial analysis might be misleading in the present case. On the other hand, a system analysis such as ours, aiming at capturing intersectoral linkages, turns out to be more adequate.

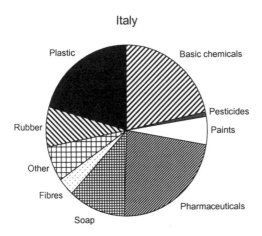

Figure 8.4   Production shares in the chemical sector in Italy (1998)

Figure 8.5   Production shares in the chemical sector in Great Britain (1998)

A final bit of evidence is about the international position of the European chemical sector. Indeed, and preliminarily to the analysis we will carry out in the following, it is worth remarking that the evidence about extra-EU imports and exports shows a consistent surplus. It grew from around 30 billion ECU, in 1995, to around 40 billion in 1998. Let us notice that the main European trading countries are the USA, Switzerland and Japan, both in terms of extra-EU exports and imports. A remarkable share is also exchanged with Central and Eastern European countries (Poland above all), which constitute the largest trading area after the three leading partners. Interestingly enough, the second most important area (after the USA) for extra-EU exports is represented by the countries of the Mediterranean Basin, followed by the Eastern and Central Europe countries.

After this very brief sketch, let us move to the different blocks of our system analysis, starting from the industrial one.

8.1.2   Backward and Forward Linkages

As we have argued in the previous chapter, standard industrial indicators are only partially useful in dealing with a 'shifting' economic sector, such as the chemical one. Backward and forward linkages, both direct and total, can instead be more helpful in complementing the sectoral analysis of an industry with a system kind of analysis. Accordingly, and for the sake of comparability, the relative indicators are worked out with respect to the same country set and sectoral disaggregation of the previous chapter (see Table 7.1 and Section 7.2.2). The results are presented in Table 8.1 and show the following evidence.

First of all, direct linkages are, partly because of the way they are obtained, more homogeneous than total ones, thus suggesting how analysis of subsequent production steps introduces important elements of differentiation with respect to the chemical industry. In looking at backward linkages, for example, it emerges that the British chemical sector draws *directly* on the underpinning production system more extensively than the other three countries (although with a notable recent decrease). However, once *indirect* effects are introduced, the German chemical sector stands as the most inductive for the production activities of the other sectors. From a reverse perspective, this suggests that the remarkable competitiveness of the German chemical sector also derives from a pervasive network of intermediate supply.

A second result concerns the higher homogeneity of forward linkages with respect to backward ones.[3] This result suggests that the chemical sector takes on an idiosyncratic role across the considered countries from a demand perspective, rather than from a supply one. Indeed, in terms of what the chemical sector provides to the others, the only remarkable differences concern the observed temporal trends. In particular, France emerges as the only country in which the recent 'explosion' of the chemical technological base (that is, in bio-technologies) has not translated into a recovery of forward linkages (as happened, instead, in Germany and Great Britain). The peculiar pattern of the French chemical sector also emerges by considering total forward linkages, this being the only case in which the production pervasiveness of the sector has decreased substantially (that is, below 2) in the late 1980s. In the light of the core role this sector plays in every TS, the results we have previously detected in comparing the French and the German TS here find an additional explanatory key.

Table 8.1   Chemical sector national backward and forward linkages (incl. drugs)

		Direct		Total		Total/Direct	
		Backward	Forward	Backward	Forward	Backward	Forward
France	1972	0.56	0.63	2.03	2.28	3.65	3.62
	1977	0.55	0.57	2.02	2.14	3.65	3.74
	1980	0.50	0.56	1.90	2.11	3.80	3.75
	1985	0.48	0.50	1.83	1.94	3.84	3.90
	1990	0.43	0.46	1.75	1.84	4.05	4.02
Germany	1978	0.59	0.60	2.18	2.25	3.67	3.75
	1986	0.54	0.55	2.01	2.09	3.75	3.80
	1988	0.53	0.54	2.00	2.05	3.77	3.81
	1990	0.54	0.58	2.03	2.17	3.75	3.74
Great Britain	1968	0.65	0.61	2.23	2.24	3.43	3.66
	1979	0.67	0.57	2.31	2.16	3.44	3.80
	1984	0.44	0.51	1.79	2.00	4.09	3.91
	1990	0.40	0.58	1.72	2.16	4.30	3.72
Italy	1985	0.53	0.64	1.95	2.27	3.67	3.54

In trying to appreciate the role of indirect production linkages, we can consider again the ratio between total and direct linkages, both backward and forward. To be sure, we should at first notice that the Total/Direct ratio is similar for backward and forward linkages, so that, unlike in other sectors (such as motor vehicles), the reference to subsequent production rounds does not introduce a substantial demand bias: the contribution of indirect supplies to the direct connectivity of the chemical TS is nearly the same as that of indirect requirements. On the other hand, let us also observe that the Total/Direct ratios increase over time, more for backward linkages than for forward linkages (apart from France), thus suggesting how the recent evolution of the chemical technologies has increased the weight of indirect relationships over direct ones. Finally, while the Total/Direct ratio for forward linkages is not very differentiating among the countries considered[4] that for backward linkages introduces further elements of heterogeneity. In particular, the latter shows a substantial increase over time for the British chemical sector. At the end of the considered period, the British chemical sector in fact comes to emerge as that in which final demand, and the indirect linkages it activates, exert the highest multiplicative effects on the connectivity of the TS. In other words, the British industrial system is actually more pervaded by chemical-based kinds of relationships than the relatively fewer direct linkages would suggest. Accordingly, a pure science and/or research-based analysis of the sector, which neglected this indirect relationships, would be more misleading here than in other cases.

8.2   THE INNOVATIVE SIDE

Turning our attention to the innovative activity performed by the chemical TS, as in the previous chapter, we will first look at the usual indicators of innovative effort (R&D expenditure and patenting activity). Then, we will evaluate the techno-economic interrelationships of the chemical TS by means of network analysis indicators.

8.2.1   R&D and Patents

As we have stressed on more than one occasion, R&D intensity is not a perfectly reliable indicator of innovative activity, mainly because it is an input proxy. On the other hand, these limitations get partially attenuated in a sector such as the chemical one, for which R&D is a nearly exclusive innovative input. Figure 8.6 shows the patterns of chemical R&D intensity for the four countries considered.

As expected, from the mid 1970s to the mid 1990s, R&D intensity has increased over time in all the countries, although with a cyclical pace. This result suggests that the effect exerted by the chemical 'business cycle' on the chemical R&D intensity has been greater than that of absolute expenditure, which has instead increased linearly. Once more, this fact confirms that the industrial kind of analysis performed in the previous section is more than opportune.

As far as the ranking of the countries is concerned, this appears quite stable over the observed period, with the sole exception of Great Britain. Indeed, while Germany and Italy constantly represent the 'ceiling' and the 'floor' of intensity values, with France in-between, starting from the early 1980s, the British chemical TS shows a progressive process of catching up, leading it to forge ahead in the early 1990s. The temporal span we are referring to, therefore, encompasses an important change in the European scenario of the most innovative chemical firms: from a German dominance in the 1980s, to a British one in the 1990s. This result has of course important implications for the interpretation of the evidence that follows.

Furthermore, the same kinds of results are also suggested by the analysis of patents.

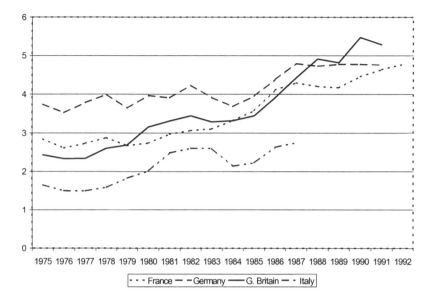

1975 1976 1977 1978 1979 1980 1981 1982 1983 1984 1985 1986 1987 1988 1989 1990 1991 1992

· · · France — — Germany ——— G. Britain — · Italy

Figure 8.6   R&D intensity in the chemical sector

On the one hand, being a proxy for innovative output, patents suffer the well-known limitations we have already addressed before. On the other hand, however, in the case of the chemical sector, patents also play other important roles in addition to rent appropriation. We refer to the opportunity of stabilising industrial cartels through entry barriers, and of organising technology licensing, thus allowing for the creation of a market for technology itself (Arora, 1997; Arora and Fosfuri, 2000). For these reasons, analysing the relative weight that chemical patents have in the total patenting activity of a certain country turns out to be extremely important.

In order to measure this latter kind of aspect, an indicator of Revealed Technological Advantages such as δ_{ic} (7.1) can be taken as a proxy of the chemical ($i = 7$ in Table 7.1) technological specialisation or despecialisation of a certain country c.[5]

In this last respect, Table 8.2 shows that, while in the early 1980s France and Germany reveal a technological specialisation in chemicals higher than Great Britain, from the mid 1980s onwards the British TS overcomes, in normalised terms, this specialisation lag. This is the result of quite different dynamics. On the one hand, France and Germany keep their international technological position unchanged over the decade, although after a substantial decrease in the mid 1980s. On the other hand, Great Britain shows a substantial increase in its technological advantage, especially from the first to the second period. Great Britain thus emerges as the country that has experienced the most consistent advancement in the technological development of the sector.

Table 8.2   Normalised revealed technological advantages for the chemical sector

	early 1980s	mid 1980s	early 1990s
France	0.105	0.092	0.105
Germany	0.155	0.092	0.155
Great Britain	0.108	0.155	0.152
Italy	–	0.188	–

Source: USPTO, OEIP/TAF Database, 1996.

This result somehow confirms our previous R&D findings. However, if indicators of innovative outputs are considered instead of input ones, the British forging-ahead is more limited: in the early 1990s, in fact, Germany still dominates the other countries in terms of patent specialisation. Another relevant mismatch between the R&D and the patent-based analysis is given by the Italian chemical sector. In spite of a relatively low R&D intensity, Italy in fact stands as the country with the highest technological specialisation in the sector (in the mid 1980s). The hypothesis of a remarkable international competitiveness obtained through an innovative capacity which is mainly informal and tacit rather than formal and explicit, can thus be at least suggested.

8.2.2   Innovative Pervasiveness and Dependency

As in the case of the automobile sector, so for the chemical one, a deeper analysis of the innovative side is carried out with respect to interactive kinds of aspects: the relative weight of innovative diffusions on innovative acquisitions (that is, pervasiveness/dependency) is the first of them.[6]

As expected, the chemical sector turns out to be highly pervasive (Table 8.3). Since the innovation flows we are considering are embodied, the role of the chemical sector as producer of innovations which are then channelled towards other sectors through intermediate acquisitions is emphasised by the 'material' nature of its technological base.

In spite of this general result, very different patterns emerge in the four countries, depending on the relative weight of the two sides, which interact in the embodied diffusion process: industrial interactions and innovative (R&D) efforts. In the case of France, the substantial decrease in the intensity of intersectoral linkages over time counteracts the steady increase in R&D intensity: accordingly, the pervasiveness of the sector is decreasing. For Great Britain, instead, the remarkable trend of R&D intensity weighs relatively more than that of industrial interactions, so that the chemical sector is increasingly more pervasive. The two effects apparently neutralise each other in the German case, whose pervasiveness thus emerges as quite structural.

Table 8.3 *Chemical innovative pervasiveness and dependency (incl. drugs)*

		Absolute	Normalised
France	1977	11.09	0.83
	1980	11.02	0.83
	1985	7.76	0.77
	1990	7.65	0.77
Germany	1978	16.68	0.89
	1986	13.38	0.86
	1988	12.77	0.85
	1990	17.05	0.89
Great Britain	1979	10.82	0.83
	1984	11.60	0.84
	1990	19.38	0.90
Italy	1985	17.91	0.89

In interpreting the results of the pervasiveness/dependency analysis, we should keep in mind that these are attributes that emerge by relating innovative diffusions and acquisitions in absolute terms. In order to investigate their centrality, as well as their sectoral direction, the network analysis of their dichotomised values turns out to be more useful. This is where we will now turn our attention.

8.2.3   Network Analysis

For the sake of comparability, network analysis will be carried out for the same cut-off values of the previous chapter, that is: $k = 0.001$, thus retaining almost all the flows (acquisitions larger than 0.1%), and $k = 0.005$, thus considering 'large' flows only (greater than 0.5%).

First of all, Table 8.4 shows how central the chemical industry is with respect to the same set of sectors as in the previous chapter (see Table 7.3).

Although the outdegree centrality of the sector is in general, and as expected, higher than the indegree centrality,[7] it is remarkable that the in-out gap increases substantially in moving from one cut-off value to the other. Cutting out small flows seems to amount to excluding a notable number of innovative acquisitions only, so that innovative diffusions appear also quantitatively more consistent, and not only more numerous.

Table 8.4   Chemical Freeman's degree centrality

Cut-off values		0.001		0.005	
		In	Out	In	Out
France	1980	7	18	4	17
	1985	9	18	4	17
	1990	9	18	3	17
Germany	1978	6	18	2	17
	1986	9	18	2	17
	1988	7	18	2	17
	1990	7	18	1	17
Great Britain	1979	12	18	2	17
	1984	10	18	2	18
	1990	8	18	1	18
Italy	1985	7	18	2	17

Indeed, in passing from 0.001 to 0.005 there is a very large decrease in the indegree centrality, while the outdegree centrality remains substantially unaltered. This is particularly true for the British chemical sector, quite idiosyncratic also in this last respect, as highly innervated by the other sectors but for small innovative flows only. Indeed, while it is connected to more than eight of the other sectors by 'tiny' innovative flows (higher than 0.1% of the total), it comes to receive substantial innovative acquisitions (that is, higher than 0.5% of the total) from no more than two other sectors (one in 1990).

At the other extreme, the chemical sector with the highest number of consistent acquisitions (4) is the French, although its initial (in the early 1980s) innovative dependency was lower than the British. Finally, let us observe that the Italian chemical sector appears to be weakly innervated by the other sectors even for small innovative flows, thus confirming the interpretation of a loosely connected TS. Apart from the mid 1980s, quite surprisingly, a similar result also holds with respect to Germany.

As far as the temporal analysis is concerned, the outdegree centrality of the sector is nearly constant, at its maximum values. As for the indegree centrality, instead, while consistent innovative acquisitions remain quite steady, small ones (with some relevant exceptions) count progressively more in France and Germany, and progressively less in Great Britain.

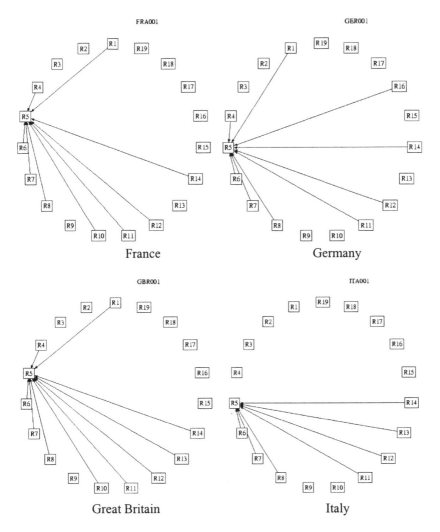

Figure 8.7   Oriented graphs, mid 1980s (k = 0.001)

Since so far our analysis has focused only on the number of innovative diffusions and acquisitions of the chemical TS, we now turn to the analysis of the oriented graphs, which is a more qualitative kind of analysis.

Sticking to the methodological choices of the previous chapter, Figures 8.7 and 8.8 report the nodes and the edges of such oriented graphs for the two cut-offs, with respect to the mid 1980s only (for which Italy is also observable). Furthermore, since the chemical sector is highly pervasive (the outdegree centrality is systematically at maximum or nearly maximum), for

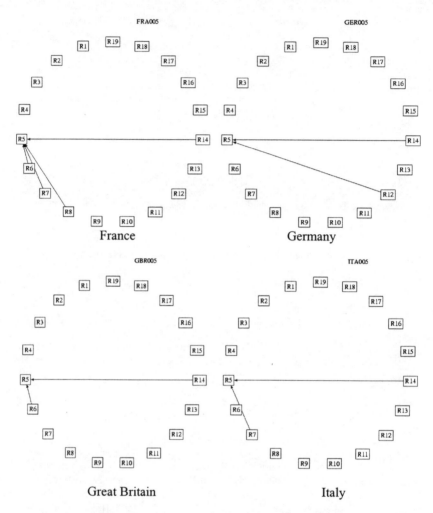

Figure 8.8   Oriented graphs, mid 1980s (k = 0.005)

the sake of convenience we have reported indegree arches only (outward flows are thus omitted from both figures).

When nearly all the relevant flows are considered ($k = 0.001$), the in-flow structure of the chemical sector (Sector 5) is quite similar for France, Germany and Great Britain, with edges both in the superior semi-circle, and in the inferior semi-circle of the oriented graphs. Quite apart from the previous TS we instead find Italy. Its relatively weaker systemic nature is thus confirmed by the absence of innovative acquisitions from the superior semi-circle, which contains the least innovative of the other sectors. As we have already said, in Italy the chemical sector seems to be set in an isolated core, made up of the other high-tech sectors, but with few interactions with the peripheral ones.

When only large innovative flows are considered ($k = 0.005$), electrical apparatus (Sector 14) is the only sector from which the chemical sector gets substantial innovative acquisitions in all four countries, while its energetic base, that is, petroleum and coal products (Sector 6), pervades it only in Great Britain and France. To be sure, France actually emerges as the country where the network of consistent innovative diffusions is the most pervasive, given that substantial acquisitions are exceptionally channelled also by rubber and plastics (Sector 7) and non-metallic mineral products (Sector 8). In Italy and Germany, instead, these come from, respectively, rubber and plastics (Sector 7) and non-electrical machinery (Sector 12), somehow reflecting the influence of the underpinning industrial structure of the two countries.

8.3   THE INTERNATIONAL SIDE

As for the automobile sector, the international analysis of the chemical sector will be twofold. Indeed, sticking to a system methodology also for the international side, the geographical boundaries of the chemical TS will be drawn by considering different means of internationalisation: in particular, trade and foreign direct investments. For each of them, suitable indicators will be applied, following the methodological considerations of Chapter 7.

8.3.1   Bilateral Revealed Comparative Advantages

As we have previously argued, by means of a bilateral version of the Balassa revealed comparative advantages indicator (that is, β_{ic}^{j} defined as in (7.5)), it is possible to investigate whether the chemical exports (that is, the i sector of the present case) of a certain country (c) perform better (if $\beta_{ic}^{j} > 1$) or worse (if $0 < \beta_{ic}^{j} < 1$) than the rest of its industrial sectors with respect to a specific area (j). In other words, such an indicator allows us to map geographically the relative patterns of specialisation (despecialisation) of a certain country. As far as the chemical sector is concerned, some regularities emerge (Table 8.5).[8]

First of all, the European market seems to offer strong comparative advantages only to the technological leaders of the sector (see the previous section): Germany and, first of all, Great Britain. The OECD area, as a whole, looks instead less 'selective' than the European one, allowing all the countries to increase their comparative advantages or even, as in the case of France, to turn a European disadvantage in an OECD revealed comparative advantage.[9] However, the same market extension does not help to fully 'revert' the structural despecialisations of the sector, namely that of Italy.

Indeed, apart from an appreciable, but temporary comparative advantage in China (mid 1970s and early-middle 1980s), and (as for the automobile sector) in the East European country of the group, the Italian chemical industry does not seem able to penetrate effectively any other international market, neither developed nor less developed. To be sure, we have to remark that Italy is the only country for which the values for the non-OECD area are greater than those for the OECD area, suggesting a particular bias of Italian chemical exports towards less developed countries.

Table 8.5   Bilateral revealed comparative advantages in the chemical sector (incl. drugs)

	EU	USA	Japan	Brazil	Czech Rep.	Singapore	China	OECD	Non-OECD
					1975				
France	0.36	2.05	1.42	1.13	1.02	1.80	0.18	1.10	0.90
Germany	1.07	1.39	1.82	0.77	1.13	1.44	0.74	1.17	1.10
Great Britain	1.14	1.28	0.96	0.97	1.40	1.70	0.63	1.15	1.02
Italy	0.65	0.99	0.73	0.54	0.92	0.99	2.27	0.72	0.91
					1980				
France	0.41	1.94	1.91	0.62	1.53	1.02	0.70	1.23	0.98
Germany	1.09	1.52	1.63	0.99	1.27	0.92	1.28	1.17	1.26
Great Britain	1.14	1.19	0.91	0.65	1.19	1.38	0.31	1.13	1.07
Italy	0.58	0.94	0.62	0.46	1.02	0.49	2.77	0.65	0.76
					1985				
France	0.37	2.73	1.72	0.88	1.57	1.16	0.98	1.45	1.08
Germany	1.07	1.48	1.55	1.26	0.99	1.43	1.08	1.22	1.31
Great Britain	1.28	1.70	1.34	1.07	1.44	1.80	0.71	1.39	1.23
Italy	0.62	1.02	0.70	0.60	1.06	0.77	1.73	0.72	1.01
					1990				
France	0.21	1.76	1.53	1.15	1.57	1.61	0.47	1.29	1.13
Germany	1.06	1.62	1.21	1.16	1.12	0.99	0.56	1.16	1.15
Great Britain	1.29	1.68	1.25	1.27	1.90	1.45	0.62	1.36	1.29
Italy	0.54	0.88	0.33	0.49	0.83	0.52	0.58	0.58	0.68
					1993				
France	0.24	1.55	1.44	1.35	1.92	1.70	0.82	1.29	1.34
Germany	1.01	1.64	1.26	0.96	1.00	1.06	0.53	1.12	1.09
Great Britain	1.29	2.04	1.48	1.43	1.73	1.25	1.12	1.41	1.42
Italy	0.59	0.94	0.51	0.54	0.74	0.51	0.42	0.66	0.66

As far as Germany and Great Britain are concerned (the most competitive countries of the sector), let us observe that their specialisation model appears quite geographically distributed, proving to be based on extensive, and not only intensive, technological capabilities. Out of the two, however, and confirming at the international level what we had detected at the innovative level, it is Great Britain whose relative market share increases more substantially. Indeed, although initially polarised, especially in the EU and the USA, the specialisation pattern of Great Britain has extended over time, becoming in the early 1990s the country with the highest comparative advantages in nearly all the considered geographical areas.

Some final considerations are due to the other representative countries of the selected geographical areas. The Brazilian market, for example, after having hosted, for some time in the 1980s, the supremacy of France and Germany, has recently turned into the area through which Great Britain has extended its international chemical advantage over the world. Quite interestingly, this kind of shift has been accompanied by another inverse one, such as the recent overtaking by France with respect to Great Britain in the emerging market of Singapore.

Other dynamics, in addition to those we have pointed out above, could be identified in principle, but only by further limiting the relevant temporal spans and the countries under comparison, and thus ending up with a more fragmented kind of evidence. To be sure, it seems to us that the lack of quite general geographical and temporal trends in the chemical specialisation patterns of the European countries, especially when compared with the regularities of the automobile ones, is itself an indicator of the dynamic nature of the sector. Over the last twenty years, both the most competitive countries and the most trade-inducing areas for chemicals have changed, often and remarkably, identifying a TS whose geographical boundaries are actually 'shifting'.

8.3.2 Mergers and Acquisitions

Given the high intensity of 'corporate control' operations, which characterises the chemical sector, a special bit of international analysis must be dedicated to the contribution of these operations to the actual degree of internationalisation of the sector.

As in the case of international trade, in this last respect also, the European area identifies a quite crucial portion of the world territory. Indeed, in terms of merger-acquisition events, the chemical industry has turned out to be, over the period 1986-1995, relatively more Euro-globalised than other sectors (Table 8.6). The percentage of such events which occurred at a cross-border level has in fact been very high (nearly 69%) relative to the corresponding figure for most other sectors:[10] of course, this also reflects, as we said, the dominance of multinational enterprises in the chemical industry.

Secondly, let us observe how the acquisitions of European-owned assets by firms based in non-EU countries (in Table 8.6 termed international) dominate EU transactions, thus reflecting the global attractiveness of the European technological base of this sector.

Table 8.6   *National and cross-border mergers/acquisitions in the EU chemical industry (1986-1995)*

	Mergers/acquisition events	
	Number	Percentage
National	994	31.2
Cross-border, of which EU[1]	879	27.6
International[2]	1308	41.1
Total	3181	100

Notes:
1. Including Austria, Finland and Sweden from 1995.
2. Including acquisitions within EU by companies based in Austria, Finland and Sweden from 1986 to 1994.
Source: Chapman and Edmond (2000, p. 761).

Focusing now on intra-EU mergers and acquisitions, we see that the acquirer versus target matrix relative to the considered countries suggests two notable considerations (Table 8.7). First of all, at an aggregate level (that is, looking at the totals by row and by column in Table 8.7), it emerges that Great Britain, Germany and France have been, in the same period, more interested in 'corporate control' operations than Italy and the other European countries as a whole: both in 'active' (acquirer) and in 'passive' (target) terms. Their leading position as chemical producers of the EU seems therefore to play a role also in determining the 'scale' of the firm-based transactions of the sector.

In this last respect, let us also observe that, out of the three leading countries, Great Britain concentrates a disproportionate share of the mergers/acquisitions of the period. This suggests that, in addition to the technological base, an important role in inducing this kind of operation is played by the nature of the market for corporate control. Indeed, it is quite well-known that, in the chemical but also in other sectors, the Anglo-Saxon model is more open, and less affected by technical and institutional barriers than the other countries considered.

A second order of considerations concerns the 'cross-border intensity' of the mergers/acquisitions of the sector (that is, the ratio between the on-the-diagonal and the out-of-diagonal elements of the Table 8.7 matrix). In this last respect, France and Italy represent two polar extremes, respectively, globalised and nation-based. Indeed, in France, only 50% of the total 'corporate' events of the period have occurred internally, versus the 68% of Italy. Furthermore, the distribution of the chemical 'corporate' events in the other countries has been highly polarised in Italy, while it has been quite diffused in France. If we also observe that, over the relevant temporal span, France has been the most important external target of the countries considered (while Great Britain has been that of all the other EU countries), we can conclude that the French chemical sector has actually been the most Euro-globalised.

Table 8.7   *Number of events involving acquirers and target companies by country base (1986–1995)*

Acquirer	Country of origin – Target					
	France	Germany	Great Britain	Italy	EU*	Total
France	188	43	30	45	67	373
	50.4%	11.5%	8.0%	12.1%	18.0%	100%
Germany	50	246	31	32	69	428
	11.7%	57.5%	7.2%	7.5%	16.1%	100%
Great Britain	50	51	372	27	73	573
	8.7%	8.9%	64.9%	4.7%	12.7%	100%
Italy	17	5	3	74	10	109
	15.6%	4.6%	2.8%	67.9%	9.2%	100%
EU*	34	38	65	27	131	295
	11.5%	12.9%	22.0%	9.2%	44.4%	100%
Total	339	383	501	205	350	1778

Note: * Austria, Finland and Sweden not included.

Source: Chapman and Edmond (2000, p. 762).

In concluding this analysis of the chemical 'corporate control' operations, let us observe how the same operations have contributed to a substantial reshaping of the European ownership structure of the sector (Table 8.8).

Quite significantly, the results are consistent with those we have obtained by looking at the other 'sides' of the TS. As a whole, in fact, there has been, over the 1980s, a systematic transfer of chemical ownership from the countries of Southern Europe to companies based in Northern Europe. The most significant net gainers in terms of merger/acquisition operations (that is, with a ratio higher than 1) are actually Great Britain and France, while the most significant net losers (that is, with a ratio lower than 1) are Italy and Spain. In tracing these results to the chemical dynamics previously identified, we should not forget that the same results are also affected by the dominant position of multinational enterprises in the former two countries, and by the massive sales of state-owned assets in chemicals in the latter two.

Table 8.8   Acquiring and target companies by country (percentages)

	Chemical industry (1986/90)			All sectors (1990/95)		
	Acquirer	Target	A/T	Acquirer	Target	A/T
France	22.6	17.9	1.26	18.5	13.8	1.64
Germany	21.6	16.7	1.29	14.4	25.5	0.56
Great Britain	2.4	15.8	1.52	26.5	17.5	1.51
Italy	4.4	15.8	0.28	4.3	6.9	0.62
EU*	100.0	100.0		100.0	100.0	

Note: *EUR 12 for chemical industry; EUR 15 for all sectors.
Source: Chapman and Edmond (2000, p. 763).

In conclusion, let us observe that, while the acquirer/target ratios in chemicals are generally aligned with that of all the other sectors, this is not the case for Germany: a net gainer of corporate control in chemicals, but a net loser across the broad spectrum of the other economic activities. Several explanations could be put forward in this last respect: the size of the German economy – which makes it an attractive target of corporate control operations – the substantial number of family-owned SMEs – with insufficient capital to position in the large 'chemical' market – and the sale of former East German companies, are the most relevant among them.

8.3.3   Foreign Direct Investments

Although a quite useful globalisation indicator, cross-border mergers and acquisitions represent only a limited sub-set of the international investments of a sector, that is, of its foreign direct investments. Indeed, chemical multinational corporations are engaged in a broader range of activities, which determine their actual volume of sales (Table 8.9). In this last respect, the global span of the European chemical sector appears, in the late 1980s, narrower than the motor vehicles sector. Although in all the four countries at least one chemical company is among the top 10 transnational corporations (TNC), in none of them it is among the top three, while this happens in the majority of the countries for motor vehicles. What is more, chemical companies are among the top 10 foreign affiliates only in two of the four countries, still with a relatively low ranking.

A closer look at the figures underpinning these rankings (Table 8.9) shows how, although in general not very high, the global profile of the chemical sector is differentiated between two groups of countries. Indeed, in France and Germany chemical companies represent relatively smaller TNC (in terms of sales) than those of other sectors. This is particularly true for France, while in Germany their low dimension is compensated by a higher number of TNC chemical companies.[11] In Italy and Great Britain, instead, chemical companies are closer to the leading TNC of the other sectors. Quite significantly, this higher sales global coverage seems to prevent chemical companies from placing themselves among the largest foreign affiliates in the same countries.

Table 8.9   *Ranking of chemical companies (excl. petroleum) among the 10 largest TNC and among the largest foreign affiliates by sales (1988)*

	Company	Rank	Home economy	Sales (million US$)
Largest transanational corporations abroad				
France	Rhône-Poulenc S.A.	9		109670.6
Germany	BASF AG	5		24173.7
	Hoechst AG	6		23328.0
	Bayer AG	7		23045.6
Great Britain	ICI	4		20816.7
Italy	Montedison S.p.a.	4		10848.8
Largest foreign affiliates in host economy				
France	ICI France	10	Great Britain	1213.4
Germany	Unileverhaus	8	GB/Netherl.	4313.2
Great Britain	–			
Italy	–			

Source: UNCTAD (1993).

As in the case of motor vehicles, in order to get rid of undesired scale effects, chemical foreign direct investments have been related to the total FDI stock of the corresponding country (Figure 8.9).

At the outset, the analysis of the outward ratios provides an important qualification to our previous results about the French chemical sector. Although it is the most Euro globalised in terms of mergers and acquisitions, the relative incidence of its outward FDIs does not reach, in the early 1980s, 4% of the total. This share is substantially inferior to that of the other countries, in particular Germany, where it nearly reaches one-fifth (18%).

Over the 1980s, the outward ratios for the chemical sector in general decrease, suggesting how the transnational process, over the same period, has extended to other sectors in addition to the most inherently globalised (such as the chemical one). Although the French chemical sector is the only one for

which this ratio actually increases, in the early 1990s the ranking of the
countries remains the same. In particular, Germany is still the only case
whose percentage is substantially higher than 10%, thus establishing itself as
the country with the most global outward-oriented chemical sector.

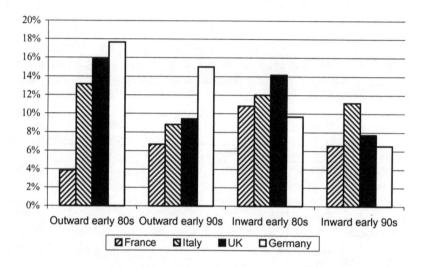

Figure 8.9   Stock of chemical FDI as a proportion of total FDI stock

As far as the inward ratios are concerned (Figure 8.4), in the early 1980s
Great Britain emerges as the country where the incidence of foreign chemical
FDI stocks is the highest. The 'robust' chemical technological base of the
country, which is also among the most outward-oriented ones, seems
therefore to play an important role as attractor of foreign companies, at least
initially.

Indeed, over the decade considered, the incidence of chemical FDI as a
proportion of inward total stocks also shows an overall decrease, still
suggesting a sectoral extension of the globalisation process. However, this
occurs to a definitively lower extent in Italy. Accordingly, in the early 1990s,
Italy overtakes Great Britain as the country where investments made by
chemical multinational enterprises count relatively more than elsewhere. The
well-known restructuring process in the Italian chemical sector over the
decade certainly had an important role in determining this result.

Before relating the previous chemical (outward) ratios to the total FDI
'involvement' share of the relative country, and thus determining what, in the
previous chapter, we have called a revealed transnational advantages

indicator (that is, γ_{ic} in (7.6)), let us briefly consider the FDI balance of the chemical sector of the four considered countries (Figure 8.10).

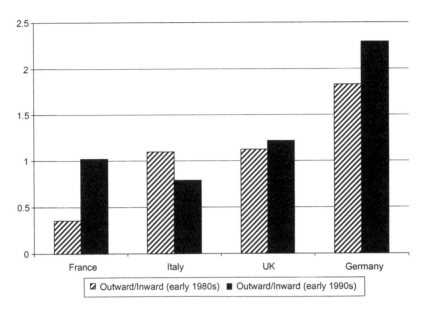

Figure 8.10   Outward/inward ratio for chemical FDI stocks

Quite significantly, in the early 1980s, France is the only country of the four with a negative FDI chemical balance (that is, a ratio lower than 1). Germany sits at the opposite extreme, as the country in which the chemical technological base is exploited (although it is not very attractive for foreign affiliates), or possibly enriched, through investments that multinational corporations perform abroad. Italy and Great Britain sit in the middle of the previous two extremes, but with a very modest positive balance.

Because of the relevant temporal trends we have observed above, the picture of the early 1990s is substantially different from the previous one. Indeed, France switches from a highly dependent position to a relatively balanced one. Conversely, Italy, where the incidence of inward chemical FDI decreases much less than that of the outward FDI, switches to a quite appreciable dependent position. Finally, Great Britain, and in particular Germany, strengthen their positive balance and emerge as countries where the chemical sector has a typical outward net orientation.

The results of the chemical outward FDI ratios can finally be used to work out the chemical (that is, i based) transnational specialisation of a certain country c, γ_{ic} (Table 8.10). As we expected, in both periods Germany is the most transnationally specialised country in the chemical sector. Although the transnational structure, and not only the transnational scale, of the operations of the sector is more accentuated than elsewhere, the German chemical specialisation decreases over the decade, reflecting both a catching up by the other countries and a progressive extension of the global activities of Germany itself.

Table 8.10   Chemical revealed transnational advantages

	early 1980s		early 1990s	
	absolute	normalised	absolute	normalised
France	0.42	-0.41	0.78	-0.13
Germany	1.94	0.32	1.74	0.27
Great Britain	1.74	0.27	1.09	0.04
Italy	1.44	0.18	1.02	0.01

Quite specialised, and still with a decreasing trend, are also Great Britain and Italy, although the reference to the symmetric version of the indicator (that is, γ_{ic}^{*} of (7.7)) suggests how the despecialisation process has been somewhat stronger in Great Britain than in Italy.

Consistently with the results of the previous bits of our transnational analysis, France shows a remarkably different pattern. Indeed, on the one hand, it is the only country which is structurally despecialised in the chemical sector, whose transnational efforts turn out to be more concentrated in other more competitive sectors (automobiles, among them). On the other hand, still unlike the other countries, the value of γ_{ic}^{*} for France increases substantially over the decade. The superior growth of the chemical FDI with respect to the total FDI stock of the country (that is, the numerator of (7.7) in the definition of γ_{ic}^{*}), in the presence of a transnational 'involvement' share which is substantially stable (that is, the denominator of (7.7)), is, along with an important recovery of corporate control, the main determinant of this significant temporal pattern.

8.4   CONCLUSIONS

In concluding, and before summing up the main results of this chapter, we should stress once more that a system kind of analysis is, with respect to the chemical sector, 'nearly unavoidable'. Indeed, as we have observed in the first section, the problems of boundaries, both functional and geographical, that we have identified in dealing with the automobile sector are even more relevant here because of their intrinsic 'shifting' nature. Indeed, the chemical sector over the last two decades has encompassed a wide variety of products and production processes previously pertaining to other economic sectors.

Although the results we have obtained in this chapter are somehow blurred and less univocal than in the case of the automobile sector, some regularities can however be traced, both across the countries considered and over time. First of all, the extent to which the chemical TS extends over the other sectors through the direct provision of intermediate commodities (direct forward linkages) does not differ significantly among the four countries considered. On the other hand, the same TS takes on an idiosyncratic role from a demand perspective, with respect to which Great Britain, at the beginning of the retained period, and Germany, at the end of it, show stronger backward linkages than the other countries. The reference to both direct and indirect productive relationships somehow attenuates the heterogeneity of backward linkages across the countries. However, their ratio increases over time everywhere, thus suggesting that the recent evolution of the chemical technologies has increased the weight of the different intermediate rounds of the chemical production processes.

The analysis of the innovative side yields both expected and unexpected results. First of all, the R&D intensity of the chemical sector has increased over the 1980s in all the countries considered, but moving from different initial profiles and with different speeds, so that the picture we observe at the beginning of the 1990s appears quite different too. The forging ahead of Great Britain with respect to France, initially, and Germany, afterwards, is the most remarkable example of this reshuffling.

Another important piece of evidence concerns the innovative diffusion process based on chemicals. Embodied chemical innovations spread over the other sectors extensively so that the relative TS is structurally pervasive. However, very different patterns emerge in the four countries, depending on the relative weight with which the two sides of the techno-economic relationships (that is, industrial interactions and innovative efforts) interact in the embodied diffusion process. For example, on the one hand, a decreasing intensity of production linkages makes the French pervasiveness of the sector decrease over the 1980s. However, on the other hand, a remarkable pattern of R&D intensity makes the British chemical pervasiveness increase over the same period.

Finally, once again, network analysis enables us to refine the investigation of the innovation side of the chemical sector, although only with respect to its in-flow structure (its outdegree centrality is in fact at maximum in all the countries). In particular, it is only in some countries (France and Germany) in which the chemical sector gets innovated both by (few) high-tech and low-tech industries, while in others (namely Italy) the innovative contribution of the other sectors is negligible even when we consider 'small' innovative flows.

Interesting results also emerge from the analysis of the international side. First of all, as far as the international trade of chemicals is concerned, we

observe that the European market offers strong comparative advantages only
to the technological leaders of the sector (that is, Germany and Great
Britain). Furthermore, our analysis adds to this result an important
qualification: the specialisation pattern of the leaders appears quite
distributed from a geographical point of view, proving to be based on
extensive, and not only intensive, technological capabilities.

As far as foreign direct investments are concerned, apparently, the
internationalisation process of the chemical sector has not been very
consistent over the 1980s: unlike what we have observed for the automobile
sector, for example, in none of the four countries considered did a chemical
company rank among the top three transnational corporations. On the other
hand, however, a deeper analysis of the relative international mergers and
acquisitions suggests that the chemical industry has actually turned out to be,
over the decade analysed (1986-1995), relatively more Euro-globalised than
other sectors. Moreover, the chemical 'corporate control' operations have
contributed to a substantial reshaping of the European ownership structure,
somehow confirming the results we have obtained by looking at the other
'sides' of the TS: a systematic transfer of chemical ownership from the
countries of Southern Europe to companies based in Northern Europe is in
fact aligned to a similar shift in the innovative performances of the sector.

A last remark is due with respect to the specialisation structure that the
analysis of foreign direct investments suggests. Indeed, from such an analysis
the geographic shift that we have observed in the sector appears less evident:
Germany, rather than Great Britain, emerges as the most transnationally
specialised country in the chemical sector over the whole retained period.
Conversely, France emerges as the only country which is structurally
despecialised in the chemical sector. Hence, it turns out to be one country
whose transnational efforts are more concentrated in other more competitive
sectors (as we have seen in the previous chapter, the automobile sector is one
of the most important among them).

NOTES

1.   Indeed, the innovative processes of the chemical sector also pervade several
     other industries, being in turn shaped by the corresponding techno-economic
     relationships.
2.   The same body of evidence also suggests that US and European firms have
     been more successful in facing competition from Japan and the newly
     industrialised countries in the chemical rather than in the electronic sector
     (Yoxen and Green, 1990).
3.   The variation coefficient of backward direct linkages is 2.5 times greater than
     the forward ones, while that of backward total linkages is 2 times greater than
     the corresponding forward ones.
4.   Let us remember that both the numerator and the denominator of this ratio are
     quite homogeneous.

5. Let us remember that a normalised version of δ_{ic} can be built up and interpreted following a transformation such as (7.2).
6. The relevant indicators in this last respect are those of (7.3) and (7.4).
7. Indegree and outdegree centrality indicators are defined as in (5.2).
8. The 'target' countries j are the same as in Chapter 7.
9. Quite significantly, France compensates for its European comparative disadvantages by focusing, more than the other three countries, on the USA and on Japan, but with a recent loss in these areas too.
10. The percentage of the cumulative 1986-95 total mergers and acquisitions for all sectors is only 30%.
11. Germany in fact stands out as the country where chemical transnational sales are the most distributed. On the other hand, and quite significantly, this diffused TNC chemical model leaves room for chemical affiliates from other countries, especially from Great Britain.

Conclusions

The material we have conveyed in this book is quite wide and heterogeneous. Although all the chapters implement a TS analysis based on (intersectoral) innovation flows, different specifications have been used at different points, both in terms of methodological choices and of empirical coverage. Accordingly, specific conclusions have been stated at the end of each chapter, and we do not need to recap them here. Hence, the conclusions of this book will rather stress some more general points we maintain as strongholds of our approach. We will thus try to convey, on the one side, the results upon which we feel confident to have reached a sufficient degree of robustness and, on the other hand, some hints about the research lines our system analysis might lead us to further develop.

A first set of results we want to draw the attention of the reader to is of a theoretical and methodological nature. Indeed, we think we have developed a sufficiently compact methodology (constituted by the set of relationships between the four building blocks of the TS) to be used as both a theoretical and an empirical tool.

From a theoretical perspective, it seems to us that the concept of TS could act as a catalyst for the several efforts, attempted so far, at unifying different system approaches to the analysis of innovation. The relevance of this result is the more appreciable, the more we think about the crucial trade-off between theoretical rigour and consistency, on the one hand, and empirical applicability and 'replicability', on the other hand, that seems to affect this field of research. Although the solution to this trade-off is often underscored by the pragmatic need to apply the relevant system concepts in comparative kinds of analysis, we think that such a need should not undermine the search for precision and compactness of the concepts to be used in the comparisons themselves. Indeed, it is on the basis of these tenets that we have developed an 'exportable' tool of analysis, one that can be easily applied in systems comparisons while maintaining unchanged its defining features. In this last respect, thus, we think we have at least partially remedied both a theoretical-methodological gap and an empirical-applied flaw.

Indeed, the relevance of the TS concept we have developed is also appreciable from an empirical point of view. Its degree of compactness seems to be very promising for comparative purposes. And the need we have pointed out during the course of the book for a close integration between our own and more traditional tools of analysis, seems to us a demonstration of complementarity and parallelism, thus calling for even more interrelatedness, rather than being a signal of incongruence and disagreement.

Related to the previous point is a second set of results, of a more methodological nature. Indeed, we have shown that the empirical-comparative analysis of the TS can be made extremely powerful through a pluralistic methodology based on a virtuous integration of two instruments of analysis that have so far been held separate: intersectoral analysis and network analysis of innovation flows. Each instrument in fact mutually benefits from the potentialities of the other. Although at the price of some limitations (mainly posed by the utilisation of input-output analysis), their integration has allowed us to develop a novel analysis of techno-economic linkages, which are crucial for a system perspective of technological change.

Coming now to the empirical results, a first general point has to do with the capacity of our comparative approach to detect institutional kinds of differences among TS, even between those with very similar techno-economic performances. Indeed, in investigating macro TS, the structural analysis of their internal and external relationships has allowed us to cluster them in groupings which do not significantly diverge from those obtainable by looking at their institutional set-up: for instance, of their underlying models of capitalism. Similar insights have emerged from the sectoral cases we have explored, concerning their degree of 'intersectoralisation' (both industrial and innovative) and of internationalisation (or transnationalisation).

The second point to be stressed concerns the structural nature of the empirical results we have obtained. As for the macro TS, the clusters we have identified are quite stable over time. Indeed, it seems that only countries with less systemic characteristics must force structural change to a certain degree, in order to keep up with the rest. The model of convergence we have observed, in fact, is a non-linear one. As far as the sectoral perspective is concerned, in this case also, the TS we have investigated reveal a certain degree of persistence in their aggregate industrial and innovative patterns, although in the face of relevant micro-turbulence and turmoil.

The third and last point we wish to offer as a general insight concerns the results obtained by the application of network analysis. Although the most standard results obtained by the relevant literature about the sectoral patterns of technological change are confirmed (such as those of the Pavitt taxonomy, in terms of innovative pervasiveness and/or dependence), original evidence emerges about some idiosyncrasies both in terms of sectoral channels of innovative diffusion, and about country and/or sector-specific innovative cores and terminals.

Indeed, along with significant cases of clustering (at the macro level) and structural similarities (at the sectoral level), important differences have also been detected among the TS investigated. Such differences, once related to apparently less dissimilar techno-economic performances, seem to confirm the view that the latter depend on a complex set of relationships. TS performances result from a historical and institutional co-evolution process, in which technology and economic structure are intertwined, and in which it is hard to trace just one or a few single relevant features. Thus, different TS, characterised by completely different types of interrelationships among their constituent units, or by different degrees of openness towards the outer environment, can work equally well in terms of certain performances. From this fact we infer that differences in techno-economic performance are neither a sort of 'measure' of relative backwardness, nor do they depend on any single element or on a few 'wrong' factors.

These and other general conclusions the reader might have found diluted at the end of each chapter seem to us convincing enough to justify pursuing further the research program we have endorsed over these last few years. Some points for the agenda have already been identified in the book: the need to refine the analysis of foreign and institutional sub-systems is just one of them. Some others have attracted our attention while the book was being written according to its original structure, and have therefore been left to future research by the authors and, possibly, by some other persuaded scholars: extending the comparative analysis to less developed or developing countries, enlarging the sectoral focus to cover innovation in services and, above all, updating the input-output tables framework which underpins the whole book are only a few of the natural, future research lines of this book.

Bibliography

Abernathy, W. and Utterback, J. (1975), 'A dynamic model of process and product innovation', *Omega*, **3**, 639-656.

Adams, J.D. (1990), 'Fundamental stocks of knowledge and productivity growth', *Journal of Political Economy*, **98**, 673-702.

Aghion, P. and Howitt P. (1998), *Endogenous Growth Theory*, Cambridge: MIT Press.

Albert, M. (1991), *Capitalisme contre capitalisme*, Paris: Editions du Seuil.

Amendola, G., Guerrieri, P. and Padoan, P.C. (1992), 'International patterns of technological accumulation and trade', *Journal of International and Comparative Economics*, **1**, 173-197.

Archibugi, D. (1988), 'Alla ricerca di una misurazione utile dell'innovazione tecnologica', *L'Industria*, **2**, 231-264.

Archibugi, D. and Michie, J. (1995), 'The globalisation of technology: a new taxonomy', *Cambridge Journal of Economics*, **19**, 121-140.

Archibugi, D. and Michie, J. (1998), 'Technical change, growth and trade: new departures in institutional economics', *Journal of Economic Surveys*, **12**, 313-320.

Arora, A. (1997), 'Patents, licensing, and market structure in the chemical industry', *Research Policy*, **26**, 391-403.

Arora, A. and Fosfuri, A. (2000), 'The market for technology in the chemical industry: causes and consequences', *Revue d'Économie Industrielle*, **92**, 317-334.

Arrow, K. (1962), 'Economic welfare and the allocation of resources for invention', in *The Rate and Direction of Inventive Activity*, Princeton: Princeton University Press.

Arthur, B. (1989), 'Competing technologies, increasing returns, and lock-in by historical events', *Economic Journal*, **99**, 116-131.

Arthur, B. (1994), 'Industry location patterns and the importance of history', in *Increasing Returns and Path Dependence in the Economy*, Ann Arbor: University of Michigan Press.

Bartley, W. (1987), 'Philosophy of biology versus philosophy of physics', in Radnitzky, G. and Bartley, W. (eds), *Evolutionary Epistemology, Theory of Rationality, and the Sociology of Knowledge*, La Salle, Illinois: Open Court.

Bergemann, D. and Hege, U. (2001), 'The financing of innovation: learning and stopping', *CEPR*, WP no. 2763.

Bertalanffy, L. von (1968), *General System Theory*, London: Allen Lane.

Bijker, W., Hughes, T. and Pinch, T. (1989), *The Social Construction of Technological Systems*, Harvard: MIT Press.

Breschi, S. and Malerba, F. (1997), 'Sectoral innovation systems: technological regimes, Schumpeterian dynamics, and spatial boundaries', in Edquist, C. (eds), *Systems of Innovation. Technologies, Institutions and Organisations*, London: Pinter.

Brown, C. (1980), 'Industrial policy and economic planning in Japan and France', *National Institute Economic Review*, **93**, 59-75.

Brown, M. and Conrad, A.M. (1967), 'The influence of research and education on CES production relations', in Brown, M. (ed), *The Theory and Empirical Analysis of Production*, New York: Columbia University Press.

Caldwell, B. (1991), 'Clarifying Popper', *Journal of Economic Literature*, **29**, 1-33.

Campbell, D. (1987a), 'Evolutionary epistemology', in Radnitzky, G. and Bartley, W. (eds), *Evolutionary Epistemology, Theory of Rationality, and the Sociology of Knowledge*, La Salle, Illinois: Open Court.

Campbell, D. (1987b), 'Blind variation and selective retention in creative thought as in other knowledge processes', in Radnitzky, G. and Bartley, W. (eds), *Evolutionary Epistemology, Theory of Rationality, and the Sociology of Knowledge*, La Salle, Illinois: Open Court.

Cantelon, P. (1995), 'The origin of microwave telephony – Wave of change', *Technology and Culture*, **36**, 560-582.

Cantwell, J. (1995), 'The globalisation of technology: what remains of the product cycle model?', *Cambridge Journal of Economics*, **19**, 155-174.

Carlsson, B. (ed.) (1995), *Technological Systems and Economic Performance: the Case of Factory Automation*, Dordrecht: Kluwer.

Carlsson, B. and Eliasson, G. (1994), 'The nature and importance of economic competence', *Industrial and Corporate Change*, **3**, 537-561.

Carlsson, B. and Stankievicz, R. (1991), 'On the nature, functions and composition of technological systems', *Journal of Evolutionary Economics*, **1**, 93-118.

Chapman, K. and Edmond, H. (2000), 'Mergers/acquisitions and restructuring in the EU chemical industry: patterns and implications', *Regional Studies*, **34**, 753-767.

Clark, N. and Juma, C. (1987), *Long Run Economics. An Evolutionary Approach to Economic Change*, London: Pinter.

Coe, D.T. and Helpman, E. (1995), 'International R&D spillovers', *European Economic Review*, **39**, 859-887.

Cohen, W. and Levinthal, D. (1989), 'Innovation and learning: the two faces of R&D', *Economic Journal*, **99**, 569-596.

Commons, J. (1931), 'Institutional economics', *American Economic Review*, **21**, 648-657.

Constant, E. (1980), *The Origins of the Turbojet Revolution*, Baltimore: Johns Hopkins University Press.

Cooke, P. (1996), 'Regional innovation systems: an evolutionary approach', in Baraczyk, H., Cooke, P. and Heidenreich, R. (eds), *Regional Innovation Systems*, London: University of London Press.

Cyert, R. and March, J. (1992), *A Behavioral Theory of the Firm*, Engelwood Cliffs: Prentice-Hall.

Dahmén, E. (1989), '"Development blocks" in industrial economics', in Carlsson, B. (ed), *Industrial Economics*, Boston: Kluwer.

Darwin, C. (1859), *The Origin of Species by Means of Natural Selection*, Harmondsworth: Penguin.

David, P. (1985), 'Clio and the economics of QWERTY', *American Economic Review, Papers and Proceedings*, **75**, 332-337.

Davis, A.L. (1988), *Technology Intensity of U.S. Canadian and Japanese Manufactures Output and Exports*, US Department of Commerce, International Trade Administration.

De Liso, N. and Metcalfe, S. (1996), 'On technological systems and technological paradigms', in Helmstädter, E. and Perlman, M. (eds), *Behavioral Norms, Technological Progress, and Economic Dynamics*, Ann Arbor: University of Michigan Press.

De Marchi, N. (ed.) (1988), *The Popperian Legacy in Economic*, Cambridge: Cambridge University Press.

DeBresson, C. (ed.) (1996), *Economic Interdependence and Innovative Activity*, Cheltenham, UK and Brookfield, US: Edward Elgar.

DeBresson, C., Sirilli, G., Hu, X. and Luk, F.K. (1994), 'Structure and location of innovative activity in the Italian economy: 1981-1985', *Economic System Research*, **6**, 135-158.

DeBresson, C., Sirilli, G., Lemay, J., Hu, X. and Luk, F.K. (1996), 'Innovative clusters in Italy (1981-1985)', in DeBresson, C. (ed.), *Economic Interdependence and Innovative Activity*, Cheltenham, UK and Brookfield, US: Edward Elgar.

Dore, R. (1992), *Japanese Capitalism, Anglo-Saxon Capitalism. How will the Darwinian Contest Turn Out?*, Occasional Paper no. 4, Centre for Economic Performance.

Dosi, G. (1982), 'Technological paradigms and technological trajectories: a suggested interpretation of the determinants and directions of technical change', *Research Policy*, **11**, 147-162.

Dosi, G. (1984), 'Technological paradigms and technological trajectories', in Freeman, C. (ed.), *Long Waves in the World Economy*, London: Pinter.

Dosi, G. (1988a), 'Sources, procedures, and microeconomic effects of innovation', *Journal of Economic Literature*, **26**, 1120-1171.

Dosi, G. (1988b), 'The nature of the innovative process', in Dosi, G., Freeman, C., Nelson, R., Silverberg, G. and Soete, L. (eds), *Technical Change and Economic Theory*, London: Pinter.

Dosi, G. (1999), 'Some notes on national systems of innovation and production, and their implications for economic analysis', in Archibugi, D., Howells, J. and Michie, J. (eds), *Innovation Policy in a Global Economy*, Cambridge: Cambridge University Press.

Dosi, G. and Egidi, M. (1987), *Substantive and Procedural Uncertainty: An Exploration of Economic Behaviours in Complex and Changing Environments*, DCR Discussion Papers, SPRU, Brighton, University of Sussex.

Dosi, G. and Nelson, R. (1994), 'An introduction to evolutionary theories in economics', *Journal of Evolutionary Economics*, **4**, 153-172.

Dosi, G., Freeman, C., Nelson, R., Silverberg, G. and Soete, L. (eds) (1988), *Technical Change and Economic Theory*, London: Pinter.

Dosi, G., Pavitt, K. and Soete, L. (1990), *The Economics of Technical Change and International Trade*, New York: Harvester Wheatsheaf.

Eaton, J., Gutierrez, E. and Kortum, S. (1998), *European Technology Policy*, WP no. 6827, NBER, Cambridge.

Edquist, C. (1997a), 'Systems of innovation approaches – their emergence and characteristics', in Edquist, C. (ed.), *Systems of Innovation. Technologies, Institutions and Organisations*, London: Pinter.

Edquist, C. (ed.) (1997b), *Systems of Innovation. Technologies, Institutions and Organization*, London: Pinter.

Edquist, C. and Johnson, B. (1997), 'Institutions and organisations in systems of innovation', in Edquist, C. (ed.), *Systems of Innovation. Technologies, Institutions and Organisations*, London: Pinter.

Edquist, C. and Lundvall, B. (1993), 'Comparing the Danish and Swedish systems of innovation', in Nelson, R. (ed.), *National Innovation Systems. A Comparative Analysis*, New York: Oxford University Press.

Edquist, C. and McKelvey, M. (2000), *Systems of Innovation: Growth, Competitiveness and Employment*, Cheltenham, UK and Northampton, US: Edward Elgar.

Ergas, H. (1987), 'The importance of technology policy', in Dasgupta, P. and Stoneman, P. (eds), *Economic Policy and Technological Performance*, Cambridge: Cambridge University Press.

European Commission (1997), *Panorama of EU Industry*, Brussels: Official Publication of the European Communities.

European Commission (2000), *Panorama of EU Industry*, Brussels: Official Publication of the European Communities.

Evenson, R. and Putnam, J. (1988), *The Yale-Canada Patent Flow Concordance*, Economic Growth Centre Working Paper, Yale University.

Faust, C. and Wasserman, S. (1995), *Social Network Analysis*, Cambridge: Cambridge University Press.

Feenberg, A. (1991), *Critical Theory of Technology*, New York: Oxford University Press.

Foss, N. (1993), 'Theories of the firm: contractual and competence perspectives', *Journal of Evolutionary Economics*, **3**, 127-149.

Foss, N. (1994), 'Realism and evolutionary economics', *Journal of Social and Evolutionary Systems*, **17**, 21-40.

Foss, N. (1996), 'Capabilities and the theory of the firm', *Revue d'Économie Industrielle*, **77**, 7-28.

Fransman, M. (1995), 'Is national technology policy obsolete in a globalised world? The Japanese response', *Cambridge Journal of Economics*, **19**, 95-119.

Freeman, C. (1979), 'The determinants of innovation', *Futures*, **11**, 206-215.

Freeman, C. (1982), *The Economics of Industrial Innovation*, London: Pinter.

Freeman, C. (1988), 'Japan: a new national system of innovation?', in Dosi, G., Freeman, C., Nelson, R., Silverberg, G. and Soete, L. (eds), *Technical Change and Economic Theory*, London: Pinter.

Freeman, C. (1992), 'Innovation, changes of techno-economic paradigm and biological analogies in economics', in *The Economics of Hope*, London: Pinter.

Freeman, C. (1994), 'The economics of technical change', *Cambridge Journal of Economics*, **18**, 463-514.

Freeman, C. (1995), 'The "National System of Innovation" in historical perspective', *Cambridge Journal of Economics*, **19**, 5-24.

Freeman, C. and Lundvall, B. (eds) (1988), *Small Countries Facing the Technological Revolution*, London: Pinter.

Freeman, C. and Perez, C. (1986), *The Diffusion of Technical Innovations and Changes of Techno-economic Paradigm*, paper presented at the Conference on Innovation Diffusion, March, Venice.

Freeman, L.C. (1979), 'Centrality in social networks: conceptual clarification', *Social Network*, **1**.

Georgescu-Roegen, N. (1976), *Energy and Economic Myths. Institutional and Analytical Economic Essays*, New York: Pergamon Press.

Georghiou, L., Metcalfe, S., Gibbons, M., Ray, T. and Evans, J. (1986), *Post Innovation Performance. Technological Development and Competition*, London: Macmillan.

Gibbons, M. and Metcalfe, S. (1986), *Technological Variety and the Process of Competition*, Discussion Papers in Economics, no. 53, University of Manchester.

Gille, B. (1986), *The History of Techniques, Vol. 1*, New York: Gordon and Breach.

Goto, A. and Suzuki, K. (1989), 'R&D capital, rate of return on R&D investment and spillover of R&D in Japanese manufacturing industries', *Review of Economics and Statistics*, **71**, 555-564.

Gregory, R. (1993), 'The Australian innovation system', in Nelson, R. (ed), *National Innovation Systems. A Comparative Analysis*, New York: Oxford University Press.

Griliches, Z. (1979), 'Issues in assessing the contribution of research and development to productivity growth', *The Bell Journal of Economics*, **10**, 92-116.

Griliches, Z. (1990), 'Patents statistics as economic indicators: a survey', *Journal of Economic Literature*, **28**, pp. 1661-1707.

Griliches, Z. (1992), 'The search for R&D spillovers', *Scandinavian Journal of Economics*, **94**, S29-S47.

Hagedoorn, J. (1995), 'The economics of cooperation among high-tech firms', paper presented at the conference of the economics of High Technology Competition and Cooperation in Global Markets, Hamburg, 2-3 February.

Hagedoorn, J. and Schakenraad, J. (1993), 'Strategic technology partnering and international corporate strategies', in Hughes, K. (ed.), *European Competitiveness*, Cambridge: Cambridge University Press.

Hahlweg, K. (1991), 'On the notion of evolutionary progress', *Philosophy of Science*, **58**, 436-451.

Harary, F. (1969), *Graph Theory*, London: Addison-Wesley.

Hirshleifer, J. (1977), 'Economics from a biological viewpoint', *Journal of Law & Economics*, **20**, 1-52

Hodgson, G. (1988), *Economics and Institutions. A Manifesto for a Modern Institutional Economics*, Cambridge: Polity Press.

Hodgson, G. (1993a), 'Institutional economics: surveying the "old" and the "new"', *Metroeconomica*, **44**, 1-28.

Hodgson, G. (1993b), *Economics and Evolution*, Cambridge: Polity Press.

Hodgson, G. (1997), 'The evolutionary and non-Darwinian economics of Joseph Schumpeter', *Journal of Evolutionary Economics*, **7**, 131-145.

Hodgson, G. (1998), 'The approach of institutional economics', *Journal of Economic Literature*, **36**, 166-192.

Hodgson, G., Samuels, W. and Tool, M. (1994), *Institutional and Evolutionary Economics*, Aldershot, UK and Brookfield, US: Edward Elgar.

Howells, J. (1999), 'Regional systems of innovation?', in Archibugi, D., Howells, J. and Michie, J. (eds), *Innovation Policy in a Global Economy*, Cambridge: Cambridge University Press.

Hughes, T. (1989), 'The evolution of large technological systems', in Bijker, W., Hughes, T. and Pinch, T. (eds), *The Social Construction of Technological Systems*, Harvard: MIT Press.

Jaffe, A.B. (1986), 'Technology opportunity and spillovers of R&D', *American Economic Review*, **76**, 984-1001.

Jaffe, A.B. (1988), 'Demand and supply influences in R&D intensity and productivity growth', *Review of Economics and Statistics*, **70**, 431-437.

Jaffe, A.B. (1989), 'Real effects of academic research', *American Economic Review*, **79**, 957-970.

Johnson, B. (1992), 'Institutional learning', in Lundvall, B. (ed.), *National Systems of Innovation. Towards a Theory of Innovation and Interactive Learning*, London: Pinter.

Kaldor, N. (1985), *Economics without Equilibrium*, Cardiff: University College Cardiff Press.

Kamien, M. and Schwartz, A. (1982), *Market Structure and Innovation*, Cambridge: Cambridge University Press.

Kelm, M. (1997), 'Schumpeter's theory of economic evolution: a Darwinian interpretation', *Journal of Evolutionary Economics*, **7**, 97-130.

Khalil, E. (1992), 'Economics and biology: eight areas of research', *Methodus*, **4**, 29-45.

Khalil, E. (1993), 'Neo-classical economics and neo-Darwinism: clearing the way for historical thinking', in Blackwell, R., Chatra, J. and Nell, E. (eds), *Economics as Worldly Philosophy*, London: Macmillan.

Knoke, D. and Kuklinski, J. (1982), *Network Analysis*, Beverly Hills: Sage.

Knudsen, T. (1998), *Whither Natural Selection?*, WP no. 18 July, Odense University.

Kuhn, T. (1962), 'Comment', in NBER, *The Rate and Direction of Inventive Activity: Economic and Social Factors*, Princeton: Princeton University Press.

Kuhn, T. (1970a), *The Structure of Scientific Revolution*, Chicago: University of Chicago Press.

Kuhn, T. (1970b), 'Logic of discovery or psychology of research?', in Lakatos, I. and Musgrave, A. (eds), *Criticism and the Growth of Knowledge*, Cambridge: Cambridge University Press.

Lakatos, I. (1978), 'Falsification and the methodology of scientific research programmes', in *The Methodology of Scientific Research Programmes. Philosophical Papers 1*, Cambridge: Cambridge University Press.

Lazlo, E. (1972), *Introduction to Systems Philosophy. Toward a New Paradigm of Contemporary Thought*, New York: Gordon and Breach.

Leoncini, R. (1997), 'A model of science and technology relationships', *Science and Public Policy*, **24**, 337-346.

Leoncini, R. (1998), 'The nature of long-run technological change: innovation, evolution and technological systems', *Research Policy*, **27**, 75-93.

Leoncini, R. and Montresor, S. (2001), 'Struttura produttiva e processo innovativo: un'analisi intersettoriale del sistema tecnologico italiano', *Rivista Italiana degli Economisti*, **6**, 169-206.

Leoncini, R., Maggioni, M. and Montresor, S. (1996), 'Intersectoral innovation flows and national technological systems: network analysis for comparing Italy and Germany', *Research Policy*, **25**, 415-430.

Loasby, B. (1989), *The Mind and Method of the Economist*, Aldershot, UK and Brookfield, US: Edward Elgar.

Loasby, B. (1991), *Equilibrium and Evolution*, Manchester: Manchester University Press.

Los, B. (1997), 'The empirical performance of a new interindustry technology spillover measure', paper presented to the EAEPE Conference, Athens.

Los, B. and Verspagen, B. (1996), *R&D Spillovers and Productivity: Evidence from US Manufacturing Microdata*, MERIT Research Memorandum 96-007, Limburg University, Maastricht.

Luhmann, N. (1990), 'The autopoiesis of social systems', in *Essays on Self-Reference*, New York: Columbia University Press.

Lundvall, B. (1988), 'Innovation as an interactive process: from user-producer interaction to the national system of innovation', in Dosi, G., Freeman, C., Nelson, R., Silverberg, G. and Soete, L. (eds), *Technical Change and Economic Theory*, London: Pinter.

Lundvall, B. (ed.) (1992a), *National Systems of Innovation. Towards a Theory of Innovation and Interactive Learning*, London: Pinter.

Lundvall, B. (1992b), 'User-producer relationships, national systems of innovation and internationalisation', in Lundvall, B. (ed.), *National Systems of Innovation. Towards a Theory of Innovation and Interactive Learning*, London: Pinter.

Lundvall, B. (1996), 'National systems of innovation and input-output analysis', in DeBresson, C. (ed.), *Economic Interdependence and Innovative Activity*, Cheltenham, UK and Brookfield, US: Edward Elgar.

MacKenzie, D. and Wajcman, J. (eds) (1985), *The Social Shaping of Technology*, Milton Keynes: Open University Press.

Magnusson, L. (ed.) (1994), *Evolutionary and Neo-Schumpeterian Approaches to Economics*, Boston: Kluwer.

Malerba, F. (1992), 'Learning by firms and incremental technical change', *Economic Journal*, **102**, 845-859.

Malerba, F. (1993), 'The national system of innovation: Italy', in Nelson, R. (ed.), *National Innovation Systems. A Comparative Analysis*, Oxford: Oxford University Press.
Malerba, F. and Orsenigo, L. (1995), 'Schumpeterian patterns of innovation', *Cambridge Journal of Economics*, **19**, 47-65.
Marengo, L. and Sterlacchini, A. (1990), 'Intersectoral technology flows. Methodological aspects and empirical applications', *Metroeconomica*, **41**, 19-39.
Masterman, M. (1970), 'The nature of a paradigm', in Lakatos, I. and Musgrave, A. (eds), *Criticism and the Growth of Knowledge*, Cambridge: Cambridge University Press.
Mattessich, R. (1978), *Instrumental Reasoning and Systems Methodology*, Dordrecht: Holland.
Matthews, R.C.O. (1984), 'Darwinism and economic change', *Oxford Economic Papers*, **36**, Supplement, 91-117.
McFetridge, D. (1993), 'The Canadian system of industrial innovation', in Nelson, R. (ed.), *National Innovation Systems. A Comparative Analysis*, New York: Oxford University Press.
McGuire, S. (1999), 'Sectoral innovation patterns and the rise of new competitors: the case of civil aerospace in Asia', *Industry and Innovation*, **6**, 153-70.
McKelvey, M. (1991), 'How do national systems of innovation differ? A critical analysis of Porter, Freeman, Lundvall and Nelson', in Hodgson, M. and Screpanti, E. (eds), *Rethinking Economics*, Aldershot, UK and Brookfield, US: Edward Elgar.
McNulty, P. (1968), 'Economic theory and the meaning of competition', *Quarterly Journal of Economics*, **82**, 639-656.
Metcalfe, S. (1989), 'Evolution and economic change', in Silberston A. (ed.), *Technology and Economic Progress*, London: Macmillan.
Metcalfe, S. (1995), 'The economic foundations of technology policy: equilibrium and evolutionary perspectives', in Stoneman, P. (ed.), *Handbook of the Economics of Innovation and Technological Change*, Oxford: Blackwell.
Metcalfe, S. (1998a), *Evolutionary Economics and Creative Destruction*, London: Routledge.
Metcalfe, S. (1998b), 'Innovation as a European problem: new perspectives and old on the division of labour in the innovation process', paper presented at the Conference on Rethinking Technological Innovation: New Paradigms, New Policies, October, Fondazione Agnelli, Turin.
Metcalfe, S. and Boden, M. (1991), 'Innovation strategy and the epistemic connection: an essay on the growth of technological knowledge', *Journal of Scientific and Industrial Research*, **50**, 707-717.

Metcalfe, S. and Georghiou, L. (1998), 'Equilibrium and evolutionary foundations of technology policy', *STI Review*, **22**, 75-100.

Metcalfe, S. and Gibbons, M. (1987), 'On the economics of structural change and the evolution of technology', in Pasinetti, L.L. and Lloyd, P. (eds), *Structural Change, Economic Interdependence and World Development*, London: Macmillan.

Metcalfe, S. and Gibbons, M. (1989), 'Technology, variety and organization: a systematic perspective on the competitive process', in Burgelman, R. and Rosembloom, S. (eds), *Research on Technological Innovation, Management and Policy*, London: JAI Press.

Miller, R. and Blair, P. (1985), *Input-Output Analysis: Foundations and Extensions*, Englewood Cliffs: Prentice-Hall.

Mitchell, J. (1969), 'The concept and use of social networks', in Mitchell, J., *Social Networks in Urban Situations*, Manchester: Manchester University Press.

Mokyr, J. (1990a), *The Lever of Riches. Technological Creativity and Economic Progress*, New York: Oxford University Press.

Mokyr, J. (1990b), 'Punctuated equilibria and technological progress', *American Economic Review, Papers and Proceedings*, **80**, 350-354.

Momigliano, F. and Siniscalco, D. (1982), 'The growth of service employment: a reappraisal', *BNL Quarterly Review*, **142**, 296-306.

Montresor, S. (1996), 'Flussi innovativi e flussi produttivi intersettoriali: i sistemi nazionali di innovazione in un'ottica input-output', *Economia Politica*, **2**, 171-208.

Montresor, S. (1998), 'Un'analisi intersettoriale dei sistemi tecnologici: evidenze empiriche su alcuni paesi dell'area OCSE nel decennio 1980-1990', unpublished PhD dissertation, University of Bologna.

Mowery, D. and Oxley, J. (1995), 'Inward technology transfer and competitiveness: the role of national innovation systems', *Cambridge Journal of Economics*, **19**, 67-93.

Mowery, D. and Rosenberg, N. (1979), 'The influence of market demand upon innovation: a critical review of some recent empirical studies', in Rosenberg, N. (1982), *Inside The Black Box: Technology and Economics*, Cambridge: Cambridge University Press.

Mumford, L. (1964), 'Authoritarian and democratic technics', *Technology and Culture*, **5**, 1-8.

Nelson, R. (ed.) (1993a), *National Innovation Systems. A Comparative Analysis*, New York: Oxford University Press.

Nelson, R. (1993b), 'What has been the matter with neoclassical growth theory?', in Silverberg, G. and Soete, L. (eds), *The Economics of Growth and Technical Change*, Cheltenham, UK and Brookfield, US: Edward Elgar.

Nelson, R. (1995), 'Recent evolutionary theorizing about economic change', *Journal of Economic Literature*, **33**, 48-90.

Nelson, R. and Rosenberg, N. (1993), 'Technical innovation and national systems', in Nelson, R. (ed.), *National Innovation Systems. A Comparative Analysis*, New York: Oxford University Press.

Nelson, R. and Winter, S. (1974), 'Neoclassical v. evolutionary theories of economic growth: critique and prospectus', *Economic Journal*, **84**, 886-905.

Nelson, R. and Winter, S. (1977), 'In search of a useful theory of innovation', *Research Policy*, **6**, 36-75.

Nelson, R. and Winter, S. (1982), *An Evolutionary Theory of Economic Change*, Cambridge, MA: Harvard University Press.

Niosi, J. and Bellon, B. (1996), 'The globalisation of national innovation systems', in de la Mothe, J. and Paquet, G. (eds), *Evolutionary Economics and the New International Political Economy*, London: Pinter.

Nitecki, M. (ed.) (1988), *Evolutionary Progress*, Chicago: The University of Chicago Press.

North, D. (1990), *Institutions, Institutional Change and Economic Performance*, Cambridge: Cambridge University Press.

North, D. (1991), 'Institutions', *Journal of Economic Perspectives*, **5**, 97-123.

Odagiri, H. and Goto, A. (1993), 'The Japanese system of innovation: past, present, and future', in Nelson, R. (ed.), *National Innovation Systems. A Comparative Analysis*, New York: Oxford University Press.

OECD (1992), *Technology and the Economy. The Key Relationships*, Paris: OECD.

OECD (1994a), *The Input-Output Database*, Paris: OECD.

OECD (1994b), *The Anberd Dataset*, Paris: OECD.

OECD (1999), *Managing National Innovation Systems*, Paris: OECD.

OECD (various years), *Main Science and Technology Indicators*, Paris: OECD.

Papaconstantinou, G., Sakurai, N. and Wyckoff, A. (1996), 'Embodied technological diffusion: an empirical analysis for 10 OECD countries', *STI Working Papers* 1996/1.

Paquet, G. (1996), *Technonationalism and Meso Innovation Systems*, http://iir1.uwaterloo.ca/MOTW96/summer96/GillesPaquet.html

Park, W.G. (1995), 'International R&D spillovers and OECD economic growth', *Economic Inquiry*, **33**, 571-591.

Pasinetti, L.L. (1973), 'The notion of vertical integration in economic analysis', *Metroeconomica*, **25**, 1-29.

Patel, P. (1995), 'Localised production of technology for global markets', *Cambridge Journal of Economics*, **19**, 141-153.

212   *Bibliography*

Patel, P. and Pavitt, K. (1991), 'Europe's technological performance', in
Freeman, C., Sharp, M. and Walker, W. (eds), *Technology and the Future
of Europe*, London: Pinter.

Patel, P. and Pavitt, K. (1994), 'The nature and economic importance of
national innovation systems', *STI Review*, **14**, 9-32.

Patel, P. and Pavitt, K. (1995), 'Patterns of technological activity: their
measurement and interpretation', in Stoneman, P. (ed.), *Handbook of the
Economics of Innovation and Technological Change*, Oxford: Blackwell.

Pavitt, K. (1984), 'Sectoral patterns of technical change: towards taxonomy
and a theory', *Research Policy*, **13**, 343-373.

Pelikan, P. (1988), 'Can the imperfect innovation systems of capitalism be
outperformed?', in Dosi, G., Freeman, C., Nelson, R., Silverberg, G. and
Soete, L. (eds), *Technical Change and Economic Theory*, London: Pinter.

Pinch, T. and Bijker, W. (1984), 'The social construction of facts and
artefacts: or how the sociology of science and the sociology of technology
might benefit each other', *Social Studies of Science*, **14**, 399-441.

Porter, M. (1990), *The Competitive Advantage of Nations*, London:
Macmillan.

Prigogine, I. (1976), 'Order through fluctuation: self-organization and social
system', in Jantsch, E. and Waddington, C. (eds), *Evolution and
Consciousness: Human Systems in Transition*, Reading: Addison-Wesley.

Putnam, J. and Evenson, R. (1994), 'Inter-sectoral technology flows:
estimates from a patent concordance with an application to Italy', mimeo,
Yale University.

Quadrio Curzio, A. and Scazzieri, R. (1983), *Sui momenti costitutivi
dell'economia politica*, Bologna: Il Mulino.

Robson, M., Townsend, J. and Pavitt, K. (1988), 'Sectoral patterns of
production and use of innovations', *Research Policy*, **17**, 1-14.

Romer, P. (1986), 'Increasing returns and long-run growth', *Journal of
Political Economy*, **94**, 1002-1037.

Romer, P. (1990), 'Endogenous technological change', *Journal of Political
Economy*, **98**, 71-102.

Rosenberg, N. (1976a), *Perspectives on Technology*, Cambridge: Cambridge
University Press.

Rosenberg, N. (1976b), 'On technological expectations', in (1982), *Inside
The Black Box: Technology and Economics*, Cambridge: Cambridge
University Press.

Rosenberg, N, (1982), *Inside the Black Box: Technology and Economics*,
Cambridge: Cambridge University Press.

Rosenberg, N. (1994), *Exploring the Black Box: Technology, Economics and
History*, Cambridge: Cambridge University Press.

Ruttan, V. (1959), 'Usher and Schumpeter on invention, innovation, and technological change', *Quarterly Journal of Economics*, **73**, 596-606.

Sahal, D. (1981a), *Patterns of Technological Innovation*, Reading: Addison-Wesley.

Sahal, D. (1981b), 'Alternative conception of technology', *Research Policy*, **10**, 2-24.

Sahal, D. (1985), 'Technology guide-posts and innovation avenues', *Research Policy*, **14**, 61-82.

Samuels, W. (ed.) (1989), *Institutional Economics*, Cheltenham, UK and Brookfield, US: Edward Elgar.

Sankar, J. (1998), 'Technological diffusion: alternative theories and historical evidence', *Journal of Economic Surveys*, **12**, 131-176.

Saviotti, P. (1986), 'Systems theory and technological change', *Futures*, **18**, 773-786.

Saviotti, P. (1988), 'Information, variety and entropy in technoeconomic development', *Research Policy*, **17**, 89-103.

Saviotti, P. (1996), *Technological Evolution, Variety and the Economy*, Cheltenham, UK and Brookfield, US: Edward Elgar.

Saviotti, P. (1997), 'Innovation systems and evolutionary theories', in Edquist, C. (ed.), *Systems of Innovation. Technologies, Institutions and Organization*, London: Pinter.

Saviotti, P. and Metcalfe, S. (eds) (1991), *Evolutionary Theories of Economic and Technological Change*, Chur: Harwood Academic Publishers.

Saxenian, A. (1994), *Regional Advantage. Culture and Competition in Silicon Valley and Route 128*, Cambridge, MA: Harvard University Press.

Scherer, F.M. (1982), 'Inter-industry technology flows and productivity measurement', *Review of Economics and Statistics*, **64**, 627-634.

Scherer, F.M. (1984), 'Using linked patent and R&D data to measure interindustry technology flows', in Griliches, Z. (ed.), *R&D, Patents and Productivity*, Chicago: Chicago University Press.

Schmookler, J. (1966), *Invention and Economic Growth*, Cambridge, MA: Harvard University Press.

Schnabl, H. (1995), 'The subsystem-MFA: a qualitative method for analysing national innovation systems – The case of Germany', *Economic Systems Research*, **7**, 383-396.

Schumpeter, J. (1934), *The Theory of Economic Development*, Cambridge, MA: Harvard University Press.

Schumpeter, J. (1939), *Business Cycles: A Theoretical, Historical and Statistical Analysis of the Capitalist Process*, New York: McGraw-Hill.

Schumpeter, J. (1943), *Capitalism, Socialism and Democracy*, New York: Harper & Row.

Bibliography

Schumpeter, J. (1947), 'The creative response in economic history', *Journal of Economic History*, **7**, 149-159.

Schumpeter, J. (1965), 'Economic theory and entrepreneurial history', in Aitken, H. (ed.), *Exploration in Enterprise*, Cambridge, MA: Harvard University Press.

Scott, J. (1991), *Social Network Analysis. A Handbook*, Cambridge, MA: MIT Press.

Silverberg, G., Dosi, G. and Orsenigo, L. (1988), 'Innovation, diversity and diffusion: a self-organisation model', *Economic Journal*, **98**, 1032-1054.

Simon, H. (1982), *Models of Bounded Rationality. Behavioral Economics and Business Organization*, Cambridge, MA: MIT Press.

Soete, L. (1988), 'Technical change and international implications for small countries', in Freeman, C. and Lundvall, B. (eds), *Small Countries Facing the Technological Revolution*, London: Pinter.

Stephan P. (1996), 'The economics of science', *Journal of Economic Literature*, **34**, 1199-1235.

Stigler, G. (1957), 'Perfect competition, historically contemplated', *Journal of Political Economy*, **65**, 1-17.

Teece, D. (1988), 'Technological change and the nature of the firm', in Dosi, G., Freeman, C., Nelson, R., Silverberg, G. and Soete, L. (eds), *Technical Change and Economic Theory*, London: Pinter.

Terleckyj, N. (1974), *Effects of R&D on the Productivity Growth of Industries: An Exploratory Study*, Washington: National Planning Association.

Tuomi, J. (1992), 'Evolutionary synthesis: a search for the strategy', *Philosophy of Science*, **59**, 429-438.

UN (various years), *International Trade Statistical Yearbook*, New York: United Nations.

UNCTAD (1993), *World Investment Directory*, New York: United Nations.

UNDP (1994), *Human Development Report*, New York: UNDP.

van Meijl, H. (1994), 'Endogenous technological change: the case of information technology', unpublished PhD dissertation, Limburg University, Maastricht.

Verspagen, B. (1995), *Measuring Inter-Sectoral Technology Spillovers: Estimates from the European and US Patent Office Databases*, Merit Research Memorandum 2/95-007, Maastricht.

Verspagen, B. (1997) *Estimating International Technology Spillovers Using Technology Flow Matrices*, MERIT Research Memorandum 1/97-004, Maastricht.

Verspagen, B. and De Loo, I. (1998), *Technology Spillovers Between Sectors and Over Time*, paper presented to the Twelfth Input-Output Conference, New York.

Verspagen, B., van Moergastel, T. and Slabbers, M. (1994), *MERIT Concordance Table: IPC-ISIC (rev.2)*, MERIT Research Memorandum 2/94-004, Maastricht.

Vincenti, W. (1984), 'Technological knowledge without science: the innovation of flush riveting in American airplanes, ca.1930-ca.1950', *Technology and Culture*, **25**, 540-576.

Virtaharju, M. and Akerblom, M. (1993), *Technology Intensity of Finnish Manufacturing*, Statistics Finland.

Walker, W. (1993), 'National innovation systems: Britain', in Nelson, R. (ed.), *National Innovation Systems. A Comparative Analysis*, New York: Oxford University Press.

Walsh, V. (1997), 'Globalization of innovative capacity in the chemical and related products industry', in Howells, J. and Michie, J. (eds), *Technology, Innovation and Competitiveness*, Cheltenham: Edward Elgar.

Winner, L. (1985), 'Do artifacts have politics?', in MacKenzie, D. and Wajcman, J. (eds), *The Social Shaping of Technology*, Milton Keynes: Open University Press.

WIPO (1989), *International Patent Classification. Fifth Edition (1989). Volume 9 Guide, Survey of Classes and Summary of Main Groups*, München: WIPO.

Wise, G. (1985), 'Science and technology', *Osiris*, **1**, 229-246.

Witt, U. (ed.) (1993), *Evolution in Markets and Institutions*, Heidelberg: Phisica-Verlag.

Young, R. (1993), 'Darwin's metaphor and the philosophy of science', *Science as Culture*, **3**, 375-403.

Yoxen, E. and Green, K. (1990), *Scenarios for Biotechnology in Europe: A Research Agenda*, Brussels: Official Publication of the European Communities.

Author index

Author index

Gibbons, M. 7, 8
Gille, B. 25
Goto, A. 57
Green, K. 194
Gregory, R. 83, 100
Griliches, Z. 60, 67

Hagedoorn, J. 170
Hahlweg, K. 29
Harary, F. 109
Hege, U. 113
Helpman, E. 68
Hodgson, G. xxiv, 20, 21, 29, 30
Howells, J. 26
Howitt, P. 29
Hughes, T. xvii, 16, 19, 26, 27,
    31, 42, 46, 167

Jaffe, A.B. 57, 69
Johnson, B. xvi, 21, 22, 30
Juma, C. 9

Kaldor, N. 29
Kamien, M. 28
Kelm, M. 29
Khalil, E. 29, 30
Knoke, D. 108
Knudsen, T. 30
Kuhn, T. 10, 11, 12, 30
Kuklinski, J. 108

Lakatos, I. 40
Leoncini, R. xx, 42, 80, 88, 112
Levinthal, D. 52
Loasby, B. 29
Los, B. 68
Luhmann, N. 35, 46
Lundvall, B. xxi, 22, 25, 26, 50,
    51, 67, 75, 78, 82, 83, 100

MacKenzie, D. 31
Magnusson, L. 29

Malerba, F. 23, 118, 131
March, J. 23
Marengo, L. 59, 65, 68, 69, 150
Masterman, M. 30
Mattessich, R. 36
Matthews, R.C.O. 7
McFetridge, D. 83, 84, 88
McGuire, S. 132
McKelvey, M. xvi, 31
McNulty, P. 29
Metcalfe, S. 7, 8, 10, 26, 31, 38
Michie, J. xxiv, 169
Miller, R. 51, 64
Mitchell, J. 109
Mokyr, J. 8
Momigliano, F. 56, 62
Montresor, S. xx, 50, 67, 69, 70,
    150
Mowery, D. 83
Mumford, L. 31

Nelson, R. xxi, xxiv, 6, 8, 9, 22,
    23, 25, 26, 29, 78, 80, 88, 97
Niosi, J. 83
Nitecki, M. 29
North, D. 21, 22, 30

Odagiri, H. 79, 126
Oxley, J. 83

Papaconstantinou, G. 53, 60, 65,
    67, 69
Paquet, G. 83
Park, W. G. 69
Pasinetti, L. 56
Patel, P. 26, 28, 60, 79, 81, 83,
    88, 97, 170
Pavitt, K. 24, 26, 28, 60, 67, 79,
    83, 96, 97, 145, 170
Pelikan, P. 31
Perez, C. 9
Pinch, T. 31

Subject index